East Asia
and the Pacific

East Asia and the Pacific

Challenges for U.S. Policy

Robert G. Sutter

with a contribution by
Larry Niksch

LONDON AND NEW YORK

First published 1992 by Westview Press

Published 2018 by Routledge
52 Vanderbilt Avenue, New York, NY 10017
2 Park Square, Milton Park, Abingdon, Oxon OX14 4RN

Routledge is an imprint of the Taylor & Francis Group, an informa business

Copyright © 1992 by Taylor & Francis

All rights reserved. No part of this book may be reprinted or reproduced or utilised in any form or by any electronic, mechanical, or other means, now known or hereafter invented, including photocopying and recording, or in any information storage or retrieval system, without p ermission in writing fromthe publishers.

Notice:
Product or corporate names may be trademarks or registered trademarks, and are used only for identification and explanation without intent to infringe.

Library of Congress Cataloging-in-Publication Data
Sutter, Robert G.
  East Asia and the Pacific : challenges for U.S. policy / Robert G. Sutter with a contribution by Larry Niksch.
    p. cm.
  Includes bibliographical references (p.   ) and index.
  ISBN 0-8133-1370-8
  1. East Asia—Relations—United States. 2. United States—Relations—East Asia. 3. Asia, Southeastern—Relations—United States. 4. United States—Relations—Asia, Southeastern. 5. Pacific Area—Relations—United States. 6. United States—Relations—Pacific Area. I. Title.
DS518.8.S88 1992
327. 7305—dc20
                                                                92-15868
                                                                    CIP

ISBN 13: 978-0-367-00441-5 (hbk)
ISBN 13: 978-0-367-15428-8 (pbk)

Contents

1 Introduction and Overview   1

Lessons for Today, 8
Current Issues in Asia and the Pacific, 9
The U.S. Role, 10
Notes, 13

2 The Evolution of U.S. Policy in Asia and the Pacific   15

Roots of American Foreign Policy in Asia, 15
Policy During the Carter and Reagan
    Administrations, 21
Notes, 28

3 Japan: Partner or Competitor?   29

U.S.-Japanese Relations at a Crossroads? 29
Economic Factors, 30
Political-Military Changes, 31
Domestic Factors, 31
Growing Strains in Relations, 32
Economic Issues, 33
Technology Policy Issues, 36
Security Issues, 37
Political Issues, 40
Environmental Issues, 43
U.S. Policy Approaches, 43
Notes, 46

4 U.S.-Chinese Relations in Adversity   49

New Challenges for Chinese Policy, 51
Shifts in Global Politics, 52
U.S.-Soviet Collaboration in Asia, 53
Beijing's Response, 53
Chinese Policy, 55

U.S. Policy, 57
Notes, 69

5 U.S. Policy Concerning Taiwan, Hong Kong — 71

The Changing U.S. Interest in Taiwan, 71
U.S.-PRC-Taiwan Relations, 1979–1991, 73
Current Problems, 75
Economic Prospects, 78
Internal Politics, 79
Competing U.S. Policy Choices, 82
Hong Kong's Transition to PRC Rule: U.S.
   Policy Concerns, 85
Notes, 89

6 Korean-U.S. Relations — 91

U.S. Interests in South Korea, 93
Economic Issues, 94
Security Issues, 96
Political Issues, 100
U.S. Policy Approaches, 101
Notes, 103

7 Policy Concerns in Indochina: A Peace Settlement in Cambodia and Possible Normalization with Vietnam — 105

A Settlement in Cambodia: U.S. Interests, Options,
   and Policy Debate, 108
Possible U.S.-Vietnamese Normalization, 114
U.S.-Vietnamese Relations Since 1975, 114
U.S. Interests and Policy Objectives, 118
Vietnam's Predicament, 119
U.S. Policy Options, 121
Notes, 123

8 Relations with ASEAN in 1990: The Issue of the Philippine Bases — 125

Philippine Base Negotiations, 126
Background on the Philippine Bases, 128
The Bases in U.S. Policy, 129
Filipino Attitudes Toward the Bases, 132
Issues in the Negotiations and the Agreement, 134

Contents

    Impact of U.S. Military Withdrawal, 136
    Impact of an Extension of Base Rights, 139
    Notes, 140

9   **Australia, New Zealand, and the Pacific Islands**   141

    U.S. Interests in Oceania, 141
    Opposition to Nuclear Weapons: Impact on the
      ANZUS Alliance, 142
    Soviet Influence, 147
    U.S. Association with France, 148
    U.S. Tuna Fishing; U.S. Farm Export Policy, 149
    Political, Economic, and Environmental Issues
      Affecting Pacific Island Nations, 150
    Options for U.S. Policy, 150
    U.S. Political Attention, Foreign Assistance,
      Diplomatic Presence, 152
    Notes, 153

10 **Conclusion: A Framework for Assessing Overall Trends in U.S. Policy Toward East Asia and the Pacific**   155

    Notes, 159

Suggested Readings   161
Index   167

1

Introduction and Overview

It was commonplace in late 1991 to state that America's role in East Asia and the Pacific was in transition. Indeed, it is widely known that the underpinnings of past U.S. policy in Asia and the Pacific, as in other parts of the world, are subject to significant change. The strangely reassuring bipolarity of the Cold War world has given way increasingly to a much less well structured new world order, where sometimes conflicting trends of economic competition, military instability, and political turmoil intersect and complicate U.S. foreign policymaking.

Few argue anymore that the United States can pull away from Asia and the Pacific. Our economies have become increasingly intertwined; U.S. economic well-being is increasingly dependent on foreign economic interchange. Asia has half of the top ten U.S. trading partners. In 1990, Japan had $65 billion in direct investment in the United States, and the United States had more than $17 billion invested in Japan. Some $100 billion in U.S. government securities held by Japanese helped to finance a substantial portion of the U.S. budget deficit.[1]

Much has been made of U.S. leadership in the multinational alliance opposed to Iraq's invasion of Kuwait; but U.S. leaders are among the first to acknowledge the importance of Japan's financial contribution in this effort. China also was important in the Gulf crisis because it held crucial veto power in the U.N. Security Council. Both Asian states have significant roles to play in the postwar situation in the Gulf, as the United States labors to help restore order, rebuild destroyed economies, and establish arms limitation and technology transfer regimes designed to foster regional peace and stability.

Meanwhile, the steady increase of Asian-American personal, cultural, and other interaction has grown to a level that affects all major aspects of American society. Large-scale Asian immigration to the United States since the 1960s has made Asian-American communities important social, economic, and political forces in most American states and in national affairs. Students from Asian countries represent the largest group of foreign students seeking advanced training and greater intellectual opportunity in the United States. Travel to Asia for business, education, and tourism has been a steadily growing feature of American life.

In the wake of World War II, it was clear that the United States played the dominant role in Asia and the Pacific. It shouldered the leading security role, nurtured the economies of allied and associated states, and fostered, to some degree, greater political pluralism. For several decades, the United States relied on its dominant military and economic power in order to achieve U.S. goals and to secure U.S. interests in the region. By late 1991, that situation had changed, posing new challenges for U.S. policy. This change is the result of several factors, including the following:

- The East Asian countries are increasingly powerful economically, exert greater political influence in Asian and world affairs, and to some extent register greater importance in world military affairs.
- The decline in the Soviet threat due to the collapse of the Soviet Union and the elimination of the related threat of communist infiltration/insurgency means that many East Asian countries that had looked to the United States as a security guarantor have less obvious incentive to seek U.S. support.
- The U.S. government has less economic power at its disposal for Asia and the Pacific. Budget constraints sharply limit the U.S. military presence and foreign assistance levels. There are competing U.S. budget priorities coming especially from the instability in the Middle East and in Eastern Europe and the Soviet republics. U.S. leaders also are concerned to focus resources on domestic needs in order to remain a leader in what is seen as a highly competitive international economic environment.
- The U.S. private sector also has limited resources. It must focus on domestic priorities as well as seek foreign opportunities in an increasingly economically competitive and interdependent world.

Thus, at present, the United States can no longer play the dominant role in the East Asia–Pacific region as it did in the past. Indeed, playing such a dominant role had sometimes led to costly mistakes, notably the protracted U.S. conflict in Indochina. The United States can't afford costly policy mistakes, and yet the United States needs to remain involved in order to preserve important interests. In this context, American leaders would appear to need to use U.S. resources—political, economic, military, and cultural—as effectively as possible. American policymakers, backed by informed public opinion, will need to have the knowledge and the ability to decide when and how to accommodate, confront, or otherwise deal with East Asian–Pacific countries and trends that affect important

U.S. interests and policy goals. To assist the formation of effective U.S. policy, American leaders and the general public need to think about the answers to such questions as: What are U.S. interests in the current East Asian-Pacific environment? In what direction does the United States want to encourage development in the region and what are its goals? and What strategies can the U.S. government use to achieve those goals?

When looking at broad trends in U.S. interaction with Asia, analysts see three overarching goals.[2] First, the United States has remained concerned with maintaining a balance of power in the region that is favorable to American interests. This concern implies that U.S. policy continues to oppose efforts at domination of the region by a power or group of powers hostile to the United States. Second, the United States has endeavored to advance its economic interests in the region through involvement in economic development and expanded U.S. trade and investment. A third major goal, centered on American culture and values, has involved efforts to foster democracy, human rights, and other trends deemed culturally progressive by Americans.

The degree of emphasis placed on these goals by U.S. leaders has varied over time, as has the ability of U.S. leaders to set priorities and organize objectives as part of a coherent national approach serving the interests of the United States. Historians remind us that the roots of American policy in Asia go well back in time. In the next chapter, a review of the highlights of U.S. policy toward the region shows deeply rooted but often poorly defined policy interests.[3] During much of the nineteenth century, informal economic and cultural activities (e.g., trade, tourism, and missionary endeavors) were the main elements of U.S. relations with East Asia and the Pacific. There were few formal geopolitical arrangements. The Spanish-American War, U.S. naval expansion, and the acquisition of Pacific possessions changed this situation. American economic and military power grew; the United States became a major world actor by the time of World War I. The American experience in Asia at that time was as much military and economic as it was cultural. But there still was little sense of order among the various aspects of American-Asian relations. The United States supported the balance of power in the region and promoted trade and political reform movements, but failed to establish precedence for one set of goals over another or to show how these respective goals reinforced each other.

One of President Woodrow Wilson's strengths was his ability to conceptualize a vision for the United States. In foreign affairs, Wilson strove to provide a comprehensive view of international affairs in which military, economic, and cultural aspects were jointly considered in order to establish a better world order. A world system of collective security would stabilize international order and peace; economic interdependence, economic contacts, and the promotion of cultural change would lead to greater democracy and human rights. As a rising world power, the United States would be willing to work with other powers in playing a military role for the cause of world peace. American economic power would be of advantage to others; U.S. markets, financial resources, technology, and business abilities would assist both developed and developing countries. Wilson was perhaps best known for the emphasis he placed on American values and for his efforts to spread reformist ideals in the interest of promoting national and individual progress and dignity.

In the 1920s, in many respects, there was considerable progress toward fulfilling Wilson's goals in Asia, but in the 1930s there was a stark reversal. Japan moved toward an autarkic military-backed development strategy for Asia, challenging basic U.S. development and cultural ideals and threatening American security and economic interests. Japan's search for autarky was related to the Great Depression and the resulting world economic crisis that undermined the Wilsonian system of global interdependence.

At first, Americans seemed to respond to the challenge of Japan, Nazi Germany, and others to the Wilsonian world order by reverting to a traditional isolationist posture. Over time, however, President Franklin D. Roosevelt formulated what some viewed as a "new Wilsonianism." His approach recalled Wilson's commitment to an integrated world order—militarily, economically, and culturally. It noted that the United States would be more willing to become militarily involved to preserve world order and balance. The U.S. government would play a more direct economic role with an emphasis on the open door and interdependence. Roosevelt's "four freedoms" speech of January 1941 contained Wilsonian cultural principles such as human rights and self-determination. Significantly, it added newly prominent values such as social justice and racial equality. The complications of the post–World War II international situation and the start of the Cold War severely undermined Roosevelt's vision. Principles of economic interdependence, human rights, and democratization remained American goals. But now these were subordinated to an overall strategic concept in which military confrontation between the United States and the Soviet Union became the overriding framework for American policy. Asia became part of a global anti-Soviet coalition. American troops and bases were maintained in Japan, Korea, the Philippines, and eventually in Taiwan. Japan was encouraged to rearm. Defense alliances were established with these countries and with Australia and New Zealand. The People's Republic of China (PRC) was "contained," denied recognition and trade.

Military-strategic considerations of the Cold War provided the key to Asian international affairs and American–East Asian relations for at least two decades, the 1950s and 1960s. As the richest country on earth, accounting for 50 percent of the world's income and industrial production at the end of World War II, the United States spent billions of dollars and tens of thousands of lives to uphold the arrangement. America's Cold War strategy assisted the economic growth of Japan and later other newly industrializing countries (NICs) in Asia. An economically healthy Japan was seen to be insurance against the danger of its falling under Soviet or Chinese influence. Washington helped Japan's reentry into the international economic arena by supporting its membership in organizations such as the General Agreement on Tariffs and Trade (GATT) and the International Monetary Fund (IMF). And the United States tolerated trade between Japan and the PRC. It was comparatively easy for the United States to bear the main security burden and to promote economic development in Asia at this time because the 1950s and 1960s were periods of high U.S. economic growth. Until at least the late 1960s, the U.S. government seemed to judge that the United States could afford to engage in a costly military containment in Asia and elsewhere and to remain calm even as Japan and the West European nations expanded their trade and industrial production and came to challenge American economic supremacy.

The U.S. withdrawal from Indochina, the U.S.-China rapprochement, the U.S.-Soviet détente in nuclear arms, and the oil shocks of the 1970s shook the foundation of the Cold War system in Asia. The United States incorporated mainland China into the Asian security system and turned to the Asian countries to contribute more to their own defense. It expected Japan as well as the West European countries to do more to help stabilize international economic conditions. As the world entered a period of zero or negative growth combined with double-digit inflation, the United States could no longer function as the commanding promoter of international economic transactions. Instead, it became much more concerned with safeguarding its own, more narrow interests. Gaps developed between the security and the economic aspects of U.S. relations with its allies, especially Japan. Increasingly, some in the United States began questioning the relationship with Japan, charging that Japan was taking advantage of American protection to get a "free ride" on its defense. They judged that Japan should contribute more to regional security. Japan in the mid-1970s maintained a low posture on defense issues. In this context, some American officials began considering China as a more reliable potential ally.

The 1980s generally saw the United States successfully adjust to changing geopolitical circumstances and promote a favorable political-military balance in Asia and the Pacific. American interests in democracy and human rights also made surprising gains; and the United States developed increasingly important economic relations with the dynamic East Asian economies. But the national indebtedness and a perceived decline in U.S. economic competitiveness relative to the dramatic growth of Japan and other East Asian economies posed a host of economic policy problems for

U.S. leaders as they sought to adjust U.S. relations with countries in the region.

Militarily, the success of the U.S. armed forces buildup begun by President Jimmy Carter and accelerated by President Ronald Reagan was of major importance. Taken together with the development of a closely collaborative U.S.-Japanese security relationship during the tenure of Prime Minister Yasuhiro Nakasone (1982–1987), the buildup allowed U.S. officials greater leeway and assurance in dealing with security issues. In particular, the United States established a policy consensus that lowered past U.S. dependence on China in the strategic calculus, and thereby reduced the U.S. incentive to make concessions on Taiwan and other issues for the sake of keeping China supportive of U.S. interests vis-à-vis the USSR.

The stability of the balance of power in Asia was reinforced by the more moderate Soviet foreign policy in the region following the coming to power of Mikhail Gorbachev in 1985. At a minimum, Moscow seemed sincerely interested in easing tensions around its periphery, thereby gaining at least a temporary "breathing space" in which to revive the ailing Soviet economy.

Economically, the 1980s were truly remarkable for Asian countries. They started the decade with barely 10 percent of the world's output; by the late 1980s the Asian nations—including Japan, China, the "four dragons" or NICs (i.e., South Korea, Taiwan, Hong Kong, and Singapore), and the other countries of the Association of Southeast Asian Nations (ASEAN)[4]—had doubled their economic share. Their combined export trade expanded rapidly, increasing from 15 percent of the world's total to 25 percent by 1988, and they recorded huge surpluses with the United States ($27 billion in 1981, $105 billion in 1987). American trade with these countries far surpassed trade with the Europeans. The Asian economies grew more rapidly than those of other parts of the world, and their funds began to pour into the United States to finance part of its deficits. America and Asia, in other words, were economically more interdependent than ever.[5]

But this economic interdependence was seen by many as exacerbating a perceived decline in U.S. relative power in the world—a source of concern to many Americans. During the Cold War, America's ability to counter Soviet power and promote economic growth and political stability abroad was based heavily upon U.S. economic strength and its willingness to make economic "sacrifices" to achieve military and political goals. A large if fluctuating military budget, a substantial foreign aid program, and a willingness to allow the exports of other countries steadily greater access to the U.S. market were regarded as prices that could be paid without undue sacrifice by most Americans. U.S. economic predominance eroded somewhat in the 1970s, and in the 1980s America's economic position was seen by some to be so seriously weakened that its long-term ability to sustain its role in the world was cast into doubt.

These adverse economic trends occurred for many reasons. Economic progress abroad, especially in East Asia, intensified competitive pressures to a level America had not experienced since before World War II, when foreign trade had a much smaller impact on the U.S. economy. But many of the causes were homegrown. Educational standards had not kept pace with international competitive demands. Neither had product quality; businesses gave increasing priority to short-term profits and financial mergers. Investment levels were inadequate for a more competitive international environment and America's already low levels of savings declined, especially as a result of the rising federal budget deficits. The dollar soared, and with it the U.S. trade deficit, greatly increasing the pressures for protectionism.

The rapid economic growth of Asia provided a basis for ever-increasing cultural and other informal U.S.-East Asian interchange. Many in Asia were impressed by the overall stability and human progress associated with the representative, pluralistic political decisionmaking process used in the West. They pressed for similar political reforms in several heretofore authoritarian Asian states. The widely perceived failure of communism to bring substantial material gains added to the anti-authoritarian trends in several countries. Major political liberalization took place in the 1980s in the Philippines, Korea, Taiwan, and Mongolia. Upsurges of demands for democratic reform also swept China and Burma, but were suppressed by force.

The collapse of communism in Eastern Europe and subsequently in the Soviet Union, the thaw in U.S.-Soviet relations, and the progress toward democracy and political reform in several East Asian and other states reinforced American interest in pursuing closer interaction with reforming Asian countries. It made cultural elements a more important consideration in the making of American foreign policy.

The U.S. reaction to the Chinese government's crackdown on the Tiananmen Square demonstrations in June 1989, is a case in point. Determined to remain constructively engaged with the Chinese leaders despite his condemnation of their crackdown, President George Bush attempted to hold policy in his own hands and resorted to secret diplomacy, special treatment, and other exceptions from a more normal pluralistic U.S. decisionmaking process.

In contrast, the American people, media, interest groups, and, to a considerable degree, U.S. legislators traditionally placed a strong emphasis on morality or values as well as realpolitik or "national interest" in American foreign policy. The Tiananmen massacre sharply changed American views about China. Instead of pursuing policies of political and economic reform, the leaders in Beijing were now widely seen as following policies antithetical to American values and therefore as unworthy of American support. Rapidly changing U.S.-Soviet relations also meant that there was no longer a realpolitik or national security rationale of sufficient weight to offset the new revulsion with Beijing's leaders and their repressive policies.

Other parts of the world, meanwhile, saw political, economic, and security changes that attracted wide and generally positive attention from American people, media, interest groups, and legislators. Eastern Europe and the Soviet Union were increasingly following policies of reform in their government structures and economies that seemed to be based on values of individual freedom, political democracy, and economic free enterprise that were well regarded in the United States. As a result, these American groups tended at times to push U.S. government decisionmakers to be more forthcoming in negotiations and interaction with their East European and Soviet counterparts involving arms control, trade, foreign assistance, and other matters.

The importance of this shift in domestic U.S. opinion regarding China and the former Soviet bloc countries appeared to be of greater significance than it might have been in the past in determining the course of U.S. foreign policy. Since the start of the Cold War, the executive branch had been able to argue, on many occasions quite persuasively, that such domestic U.S. concerns with common values should not be permitted to override or seriously complicate realpolitik U.S. interests in the protracted struggle and rivalry with the USSR. Now that it was widely seen that the Cold War was ending and the threat from the USSR was greatly reduced, the ability of the executive branch to control the course of U.S. foreign policy appeared somewhat weakened. The administration could no longer argue that the dangers of Cold War contention and confrontation required a tightly controlled foreign policy.

Lessons for Today

There is little on the horizon in late 1991 to suggest the recent series of changes affecting American policy toward Asia and the Pacific will halt soon. In particular, the movement away from a Cold War framework, in which security interests held pride of place, will likely continue. Considerations of economic competitiveness and U.S. political values and culture will have more importance in U.S. policy.

What is unclear, however, is how these different U.S. goals and objectives will affect U.S. policy at any given moment. Sometimes, U.S. policy will appear to give great emphasis to ideology—as it did during the off-again, on-again debate over sanctions and trade restrictions against China from 1989 to the present. But the same U.S. policymakers can appear quite pragmatic in the face of a perceived need to protect U.S. security interests in a dangerous situation. Thus, there was little outcry about resumed high-level U.S.-Chinese contacts in fall 1990, as observers recognized the U.S. need to remain on reasonably good terms with China in order to secure PRC support for U.N. Security Council resolutions against Iraq's invasion of Kuwait.

It also appears likely that U.S. policymakers will have a difficult time formulating a new vision of Asian policy similar to those of Wilson and Roosevelt. U.S. priorities will change depending on a number of key variables, including the status of reform and cohesion in the former Soviet Union; Japan's willingness to contribute to international efforts to promote stability and development; China's leadership and political crisis; and U.S. ability to come up with effective ways to prosper and develop in the increasingly competitive international economic environment. A prudent course at present would be to review American assets and potential trouble spots in policy toward the region, recognizing where U.S. policies are consistent or not consistent with longstanding U.S. security, economic, and cultural goals. In this way, U.S. leaders and the general public would appear better prepared to make decisions that effectively marshall their limited power to deal with future issues.

Current Issues in Asia and the Pacific

- Soviet intentions. Events in 1991—including the August 1991 coup attempt—had a sobering effect on those in the West who portrayed a bright future for a reforming Soviet Union. The path taken by reform has become a zigzag pattern and its end point is unclear. The basic cohesion of what was called the Soviet Union is ended. The power of its parts, notably Russia, has declined markedly and will probably continue to do so for the near future. Thus, Russian ability to create dangers for U.S. security interests in Asia and the Pacific will probably continue to decline. Moscow also appears interested in working more closely with the United States and allied and associated states in easing tensions and promoting economic development. U.S. interests in pursuing this opening will depend in part on how American leaders and the public view the regime in Moscow; they will likely be less collaborative with a regime that is internally repressive and ideologically regressive or weak and unable to bring about meaningful reform.
- A different set of U.S. concerns would be posed were the breakup of the Soviet Union to lead to serious instability in Central and Eastern

Soviet Asia. This would have a likely negative effect on Mongolia, China, and perhaps other neighboring countries.
- Regional trouble spots include Cambodia, Korea, Burma, the Philippines, and Hong Kong. Most are being handled in a way that reduces rather than increases the likelihood of great-power confrontation involving the United States. There are serious territorial disputes affecting Asian stability; and the arms races in South Asia, on the Korean peninsula, in the Taiwan Strait and in Southeast Asia pose several potentially difficult issues for U.S. policy. But the reduction of great-power confrontation concerning most of these territorial and arms-buildup issues has helped to ease U.S. concerns over these problems.
- Political instability is often related to uncertain leadership succession and thus raises questions for U.S. policy in dealing with China and North Korea in particular. Political prospects are also uncertain in Vietnam, the Philippines, Papua New Guinea, Fiji, and Vanuatu. The thrust of U.S. policy in these cases has been increasingly to support greater reform and political liberalism, although U.S. security and economic interests will doubtless continue to cause U.S. policy to moderate the ardor of such backing in some cases.
- Economic rivalry in Asia and the Pacific will focus on such issues as disputes over access to regional and world markets, especially the U.S. market, and disagreement over access to resources, notably oil, in disputed territorial areas (e.g., the conflicting claims for the rights of off-shore drilling). It is hard to know how deeply felt ambivalent attitudes toward Japan by other Asian countries will translate into action. Most Asian states appear to be too dependent on Japanese investment, aid, and trade to risk an open break with this critical Asian economic giant.[6]
- Defining new relationships. Among the many challenges facing U.S. policymakers in the fluid situation in Asia and the Pacific will be a need to define specific U.S. interests in relations with important regional actors. Topping the list is the need to define the U.S.-Japan "global partnership" in the current changing world environment.

The U.S. Role

There are several features likely to characterize the U.S. role in dealing with these issues in the period ahead:

- American foreign policy probably will not be focused on East Asia—Pacific—it will be more likely to focus on the Middle East, the former Soviet Union, and Eastern Europe. Also American policy attention in

Introduction and Overview

general may become diverted to deal with pressing U.S. domestic issues.
- American policy toward the region may remain complicated by the need to achieve agreement within a politically divided government where one party controls the executive branch and the other controls the Congress.
- American government and private sector interaction with the region face strong resource constraints.
- Security interests are likely to continue to compete with U.S. economic and political interests for pride of place in U.S. policy toward the region.
- Because of past practice and intraregional suspicions, there is unlikely to emerge one coherent structure for U.S. policy in Asia. Rather, U.S. leaders will need to seek their goals through global mechanisms (e.g., the U.N., IMF, World Bank, Organization for Economic Cooperation and Development (OECD), GATT); regional means (Asian-Pacific economic groups, ASEAN, South Pacific Forum); and bilateral arrangements (U.S. security treaties, foreign aid, market-access accords, political contacts).

As to specific recommendations, U.S. interests in Asia argue for a cautious policy based on American ties with traditional friends and allies in the region. It seems foolish and inconsistent with U.S. goals not to preserve the longstanding good relations with Japan and with friends and allies along the periphery of Asia and in Oceania. Their security policies and political-cultural orientations are generally in accord with U.S. interests. Opinion surveys claim that the American public and some U.S. leaders see Japan as an economic competitive "threat" to U.S. well-being, surpassing the military threat posed to the United States in the recent past by the Soviet Union. But few polls of U.S. public opinion or U.S. leaders support the argument that it is now in America's interest to focus its energies on the need to confront the Japanese economic threat in a way that confrontation with the Soviet Union came to dominate U.S. policy during the Cold War.[7]

This is not to minimize the difficulties U.S. leaders will face in coming up with an appropriately balanced policy toward Japan. The failure in U.S.-Japanese relations during the crisis caused by Iraq's invasion of Kuwait in August 1990 seemed to have important lessons for U.S. policy. Some saw Japan's reaction to the Gulf crisis as proof that the Japanese political system is incapable of actions other than those narrowly designed to ensure Japan's economic dominance in world affairs. But others saw a more complicated picture where American leaders held unrealistic expectations of Japan. They judged that future U.S.-Japanese burden-sharing arrangements over international issues could work to America's advantage, provided the United States works closely and incrementally with the Japanese government.

Caution is in order in anticipating future U.S. relations with other major regional actors—Russia, China, and India. All three are preoccupied with internal political-development crises. None appears to be seeking to foment tensions or major instability in the region. All seek better ties and closer economic relations with the West and with the advancing economies of the region. U.S. policy would appear well advised to work closely with these governments wherever there is possible common ground on security, economic, or political issues.

For a time in the 1970s, it appeared that U.S. policymakers had allowed U.S. preoccupation with the Soviet threat to lead to formulation of an Asian policy that relied heavily on close collaboration with China. And in the late 1980s, close U.S.-Soviet relations, especially between Secretary of State James Baker and Soviet Foreign Minister Eduard Shevardnadze, took on new salience in determining U.S. policy toward the region. In the 1990s, the political and economic uncertainties surrounding both regimes make it imprudent for U.S. policy to rely heavily on either Beijing or Moscow. A cautious modus vivendi and exploitation of mutually advantageous common ground seems to provide the best U.S. policy in dealing with both regimes in Asia in the period ahead. Meanwhile, the uncertainties surrounding the political future of the Indian government and the traditionally low level of U.S. interest in the subcontinent argue for a low-key American posture in this area as well. In other areas, U.S. officials would be well advised to try to capitalize on the greater international interest in arms control and other measures to ease tension following the Persian Gulf war. This could lead to more effective measures to deal with sensitive arms proliferation issues, in South Asia and Korea in particular.

In considering U.S. assets available to influence trends in the region, U.S. leaders would probably be wise to go slow in reducing U.S. military presence in the region. The economic savings of such a cutback would be small; the political costs could be high, inasmuch as most countries in Asia have been encouraging the United States to remain actively involved in the region to offset the growing power of Japan or the potential ambitions of China or others. Perhaps an appropriate middle course would involve a trimmed down U.S. presence that would continue to preserve regional stability and would receive political and economic support from countries in the region.

Finally, a largely unseen but very important asset of the United States has to do with American values and culture, which enjoy great influence in the region. Increased U.S.-Asian interchange through economic, educational, political, immigration, or other channels has greatly increased

Introduction and Overview

mutual understanding on both sides of the Pacific. This interaction has positioned the United States well to influence trends among the newly powerful developed countries in Asia in order to move their policies in ways advantageous for U.S. interests. U.S. government officials have an opportunity to lead in this effort through effective government communication, education, and other programs—low-cost public diplomacy efforts that have potential big payoffs for U.S. power and influence in the region.

* * *

A few words are in order regarding how to use this book. It is designed to bring readers with an interest in U.S. policy issues in Asia and the Pacific up-to-date, as of September 1991, regarding specific policy areas. Thus, the first two chapters provide respectively an overview of U.S. policy and review its history up to recent years. The next seven chapters focus on issues in U.S. policy concerning specific Asian-Pacific policy areas, namely Japan, China, Taiwan and Hong Kong, Korea, Cambodia and Vietnam, the Philippine bases, and Australia, New Zealand, and the Pacific islands. Obviously, not all areas of U.S. policy interest are included, but an effort has been made to be comprehensive in assessing the implications for U.S. policy in these highly important areas. The chapters are designed to stand alone, without necessary reference to other chapters. A brief conclusion links developments in the region with the broad trends in the ongoing debate on U.S. foreign policy after the Cold War. The last part of the book lists readings that may prove useful to readers in further exploration about contemporary U.S. policy concerns.

Notes

1. These figures were used by U.S. State Department officials in explaining the interdependence of the United States and Japan. For background information, see Robert Worden and Ronald Dolan, eds., *Japan: A Country Study* (Washington, DC: U.S. Government Printing Office).

2. See the suggested readings at the end of this book.

3. The framework for this analysis was influenced strongly by the work of Akira Iriye, especially a presentation he made on September 26, 1990, at the Woodrow Wilson Center for Scholars, Washington, DC, on the issue of U.S.–East Asian relations.

4. In addition to Singapore, ASEAN members are Brunei, Indonesia, Malaysia, the Philippines, and Thailand.

5. See, among others, U.S. Department of State, "U.S. Policy in East Asia and the Pacific" Bureau of Public Affairs Selected Document No. 30, August 1988.

6. See, among others, Richard Cronin, *Japan, the United States and the Prospects for the "Asia-Pacific Century"* (Singapore: Institute for Southeast Asian Studies, 1991).

7. See, among others, William Watts et al., *America and Japan: How We See Each Other* (Commission on U.S.-Japan Relations for the Twenty-First Century, Washington, DC: May 2, 1990)

2

The Evolution of U.S. Policy in Asia and the Pacific

Looked at broadly, current U.S. policy represents the culmination of a longstanding pursuit of three sets of objectives in policy toward Asia and the Pacific. First, the United States remains concerned with maintaining a balance of power in Asia favorable to American interests and opposed to efforts at domination of the region by hostile powers. Second, U.S. economic interests in the region grow through involvement in economic development and expanded U.S. trade and investment. Third, U.S. culture and values prompt efforts to foster democracy, human rights, and other culturally progressive trends in Asia, along with other parts of the world. The priority given to each of these goals has changed over time. U.S. leaders have varied in their ability to set priorities and organize U.S. objectives as part of a well-integrated national approach to Asia.

Roots of American Foreign Policy in Asia

The roots of American foreign policy in Asia extend to the formative experiences of the eighteenth and nineteenth centuries.[1] At that time, the United States endeavoring to be seen as a nation interested in peaceful and friendly dealings with the world, focused primarily on commercial and cultural affairs. American–East Asian relations, like U.S. relations with other parts of the world, were characterized by informal activities such as trade, tourism, and missionary endeavors. Military and related diplomatic considerations played only a minor role and were almost always subordinate to commerce and shipping. Economic activities, in turn, were secondary to cultural relations. American trade with Asia never amounted to more than a few percent of total U.S. trade, whereas thousands of Americans went to Asia as missionaries and in other capacities to bring American civilization to Asia. The U.S. initiatives in this regard were timely in that Japan, China, and Korea were in the midst of the process of modernization—a process that benefited from the presence of American educators, scientists, engineers, travelers, and missionaries who offered Asian elites and others needed advice and information. Thus, in the first phase in their encounter, which ended with the nineteenth century, America and Asia met at three levels—strategic, economic, and cultural—but the cultural dimension was clearly the most significant.[2]

The situation changed markedly as the United States fought a war in the Philippines, started a naval expansion program, and acquired Pacific possessions. The United States developed as a major power in the Pacific and, by extension, in Asia as well. Simultaneously, American trade and investment in Asia grew. The United States exported industrial products and invested capital in railways and mines in East Asia, as well as elsewhere. The period between the Spanish-American War and World War I was a time of transformation in U.S. policy. By 1914, the United States had one of the largest navies in the world and naval bases in the Caribbean and the Pacific; the Panama Canal had just been opened. As the world's leading industrial producer, the United States had become a major exporter of manufactured goods, especially to Asia and Latin America.

The American experience in Asia had become as much military and economic as cultural. Thousands of American soldiers and sailors experienced warfare in the Philippines. Many thousands served during the Boxer uprising in China at the turn of the century. Hundreds of marines were stationed in China to safeguard Peking's access to the sea. The American military began considering the possibility of war with Japan, which, too, was developing as a military power in the Asian-Pacific region. The United States did not contemplate a war with Japan in the immediate future, but it became concerned with maintaining some sort of balance of power in the region, a task which it could not leave to the other powers alone. Economically, too, there was strong competition between American and Japanese cotton textiles imported into Manchuria. The United States affirmed its interest in the economic open door as official policy in part in order to prevent Japan from establishing its dominance over the China market. At the same time, economic ties between the United States and Japan grew. Japan shipped 30 percent of its exports to America. Japan obtained hundreds of millions of dollars of U.S. loans as it fought a war against Russia and managed its expanding empire on the Asian continent.[3]

The cultural dimension of U.S. policy also remained strong. The Progressive movement reinforced the American sense of mission. The reformist impulse found an outlet in Asia, particularly China, which was trying to transform itself into a modern state. Many reformers in China were open to the Progressive emphasis on education; they were coming to the view that educational reform must precede other changes. In their efforts to chart a new political order for China following the collapse of the Manchu dynasty, some Chinese reformers also eagerly turned to the U.S. constitution for a model. Japanese reformers, on their part, drew inspiration from American capitalism, and Japanese radicals from American socialism. Thus, the sense of cultural connections grew. But missing was a sense of order among the various aspects of American-Asian relations. Balance-of-power politics, trade, and reform movements continued without a clear sense of priority or interrelationships.

More coherence for U.S. foreign policy was provided by President Woodrow Wilson. He set out a comprehensive definition of international affairs in which military, economic, and cultural aspects were integrated in order to establish more progressive world order. International peace would be maintained by a system of collective security, economic interdependence, and cultural change in order to promote democracy and human rights everywhere. To carry out such a foreign policy, the United States would play a military role in cooperation with other nations. U.S. resources would be available to open up markets of the world, to help other countries through loans, investment, and technology transfer, and to collaborate with other advanced nations in the development of dependent areas. U.S. universalistic values and reformist ideals would be used to transform world conditions. Of course, Wilson's conception was not just an agenda of selfless ideals; it meshed international and national affairs in ways that promoted U.S. interests.

For East Asia, Wilson's approach called for an end to the naval race with Japan and to the latter's attempted domination of China, and sought a new security arrangement on the basis of cooperation with Japan, Great Britain, and other powers. U.S. policy challenged Japan's and other nations' monopolistic economic enclaves in China and called for outside powers to accept anew the doctrine of the open door. America promoted democratization in Asia, as well as elsewhere, and supported reformist movements in China and Japan.

For a time, the Wilsonian agenda put an end to the wartime antagonism between the United States and Japan. There was a "collective security" in the Pacific on the basis of naval disarmament agreements and other accords, such as those at the Washington Conference of 1921–1922; American goods, capital, and technology flowed into China and Japan. Japan shifted its China policy away from military to economic interests. During, the decade the Americanization of Japan and China was promoted through the spread of American movies, consumer goods, and, even more important, political, economic, and social ideas.

In contrast, the 1930s was a time of the coming to power of leaders in Japan who were oriented toward military strength. Military expenditures grew much faster than the economy. To justify such increases the military undertook aggressive acts in China and prepared for war against the Soviet Union, the United States, and Britain. In order to pay for such expenditures, Japan sought to establish control over the resources and markets of the Asian continent and the European colonies in Southeast Asia.

Japan undertook these ultimately destructive policies as part of a misguided effort to establish an autarkic region, an area of economic self-sufficiency in Asia that would, it was thought, enrich the country as well as contribute to financing the military force. The Great Depression and world economic crisis added impetus to Japan's effort and helped to undermine the Wilsonian system of global interdependence. Rather than relying on close economic relations with the United States and an open door in China, the Japanese decided to reduce their dependence on the West and monopolize the markets and resources of Asia. The Japanese never quite gave up their fascination with, and even dependence on, America's material and popular culture, but Japanese leaders during the 1930s were determined to reduce the influence of the ideals of democracy, individualism, and human rights. To counter these influences, Japanese leaders focused on the absence of racial equality seen in the practice of U.S. policy at home and abroad. The Japanese military in the 1930s repeatedly asserted that their determination to get Westerners out of their region was Asia's answer to American (and Western) racial injustice.

The Americans' initial isolationist reaction to Japanese militarism and Nazi Germany gave way over time to a new vision authored by President Franklin D. Roosevelt. He formulated what some refer to as a new Wilsonianism to bring the world out of the turmoil and chaos of the 1930s.[4] Roosevelt's vision shared with the original Wilsonianism a commitment to an integrated world order—militarily, economically, and culturally. The United States would be more willing to augment its armed forces and to be involved in different parts of the world to maintain a balance of power. It also would cooperate more closely with a few other powers to police world order. This was still selective security, but with a greater readiness to use force. The past stress on the open door and interdependence remained, but the government, not just the private sector, would be ready to help other countries undertake economic change. At the same time, worldwide bodies, such as the International Monetary Fund (IMF) and the World Bank, would be established to monitor and, to some extent, control trade and monetary transactions among nations to ensure a more open international economic system. Roosevelt's "four freedoms" speech of January 1941 contained principles that were Wilsonian—such as human rights and self-determination—but it also mentioned new values such as social justice and racial equality, values of particular importance to Asians.

Roosevelt's vision defined a new phase of American-Asian relations. After defeating Japan, the United States and its allies (including China and other Asian countries and people resisting Japanese aggression) would reestablish regional order on the basis of this definition. As codified at the Cairo, Yalta, and Potsdam conferences, as well as through various other meetings, the new regional arrangement would be based on close cooperation among victorious nations particularly America, China, Great Britain, and the Soviet Union. Japan would be disarmed and democratized. Korea would be unified and eventually become independent, and the European colonies in Southeast Asia would be ultimately granted independence, but in the meantime placed under a trusteeship scheme under the aegis of the United Nations. Economic liaisons would be fostered throughout the Asian-Pacific region.

The complications of the postwar situation in Asia and the start of the Cold War severely undermined this scheme. Principles of economic interdependence, human rights, and democratization remained. But these were now subordinated to an overall strategic conception in which military confrontation between the United States and the Soviet Union became the overriding framework of American policy. Asia became part of a global anti-Soviet coalition. American troops and bases were maintained in Japan, Korea, the Philippines, and eventually in Taiwan and elsewhere. Japan was encouraged to rearm; defense alliances were established with these countries, Australia, and New Zealand. The communist People's Republic of China was ostracized, denied recognition and trade.

The military-strategic consideration of the Cold War provided the key to Asian international affairs and American–East Asian relations for at least two decades, the 1950s and 1960s. Accounting for more than half of the world's income and industrial production at the end of the war, the United States put forth billions of dollars and tens of thousands of lives to uphold the arrangement. It fought two wars for the same purpose. It is clear to most observers that the origins and consequences of the Korean and the Vietnam wars were part of the same picture, the primacy of strategic considerations in America's approach to Asia. What is subject to more debate is the notion that had the vision of Franklin Roosevelt retained a stronger influence in postwar American policy, there might have been a greater readiness to come to grips with the profound social and cultural changes taking place in China, Korea, Vietnam, and elsewhere, and to deal with them in an integrated fashion, not simply in the framework of the global balance of power.

One consequence of America's Cold War strategy in Asia was Japanese economic growth. American officials thought an economically healthy Japan would be the best guarantee against its falling under Soviet or Chinese influence. Washington helped Japan's reentry into the international economic arena through membership in organizations such as the GATT and IMF. And the United States even tolerated trade between Japan and the PRC, which, if small in comparison with Japanese trade with the United States or Southeast Asia, steadily grew in importance for China because of the latter's increasing alienation from the Soviet Union. In retrospect, its seems remarkable that America was supportive of Japanese economic interests; Japan appeared to give little in return. In part, this was because the 1950s and 1960s were periods of high growth, and until at least the late 1960s, the United States could afford to engage in a costly war in Southeast Asia and to remain calm even as Japan and the European nations expanded their trade and industrial production and came to challenge American economic supremacy.

The U.S.-PRC rapprochement, the U.S.-Soviet détente in nuclear arms, and the oil shocks of the 1970s shook the foundation of the Cold War system in Asia. The United States incorporated mainland China into the Asian security system and turned to the Asian countries to contribute much more to their own defense. U.S. leaders expected Japan as well as the European countries to do more to help stabilize international economic conditions. Given a period of negative growth and double-digit inflation, the United States was no longer the dominant international economic leader. It was more concerned with safeguarding more narrow national interests. With Japan and other allies, significant gaps developed between the security and economic aspects of U.S. relations. Trade disputes grew, U.S. voices criticized Japan for taking advantage of American military protection, and U.S. officials asked whether Japan should contribute more to regional security. Japanese leaders remained unwilling to devote more than one percent of the GNP on defense. Japan's 1976 "general guidelines for defense policy" reiterated the nation's commitment to a small-scale military force for purely defensive purposes. To some American officials, China began to be seen as a more promising potential ally.

Following the collapse of U.S.-backed regimes in South Vietnam and Cambodia in 1975, U.S. policy in Asia was in considerable disarray. Indeed, authority was challenged from several quarters in the United States. The Watergate scandal and the ensuing resignation of President Richard Nixon in 1974, followed by Hanoi's takeover of South Vietnam the following year, left American credibility badly damaged and its policies (especially toward Asia) uncertain in the eyes of both friends and adversaries. There was particular concern in the U.S. government just after the fall of Saigon that North Korea might think the time was opportune to strike militarily against South Korea.

Within the United States there was a rising concern over issues of morality regarding both the ends and means of foreign policy. America had become involved in a policy of détente—the idea that there were good

The Evolution of U.S. Policy

as well as bad communists confused many people. Higher standards were demanded and additional constraints imposed upon the presidency. The War Powers Resolution imposed new restraints on the president's freedom to use military force. Congress passed laws requiring countries that received U.S. economic or military assistance to meet certain minimum (if vague) human rights standards domestically, and later the administration was required to publish an annual report on human rights conditions in all countries. Congress enacted numerous "legislative vetoes," requiring the president to provide it with notice of proposed arms deliveries and allowing it to veto such actions.

Policy During the Carter and Reagan Administrations[5]

President Carter came to office holding many of the beliefs of the critics of the Vietnam War and of the Nixon-Kissinger emphasis on political realism and balance-of-power policies. The president seemed determined to shift the emphasis of U.S. policy from power toward morality, and to give less attention to seeking specific short-term advantages over the Soviet Union. He had several genuine accomplishments: the Panama Canal treaty, the Camp David accords, and the establishment of full diplomatic relations with China. Yet the Carter administration was ultimately overwhelmed by a combination of events over which it had little control, combined with its own divisions and vacillation. Among the key events were the Iranian revolution and the ensuing hostage crisis, the second oil shock, and growing Soviet strategic military power. The Soviets became more assertive in several parts of the world. Notably, Moscow intervened militarily in Afghanistan at the end of 1979 to shore up the communist regime, which had seized power in a coup in 1978, but was threatened by internal conflicts and the growing strength of anticommunist tribesmen. The different approaches of Secretary of State Cyrus Vance and National Security Adviser Zbigniew Brzezinski in dealing with the Soviets were never clearly resolved by Carter until Soviet aggressiveness and Vance's resignation in the wake of a failed hostage rescue attempt in 1980 made the issue moot. Carter's public vacillation on such issues as the neutron bomb and his startling statement that he had learned more about the USSR as a result of its invasion of Afghanistan than he had ever known previously convinced many Americans he was naive, inept, and indecisive. Despite his emphasis in the late 1970s on rebuilding U.S. military power, there was a widespread American (and foreign) view that the U.S. position vis-à-vis the Soviet Union was deteriorating.

Carter initially benefited from the lack of serious challenges faced by the United States after the fall of South Vietnam. Nonetheless, his administration from the outset faced a problem in Asia because of his 1975 public statement that the United States should withdraw its ground troops from South Korea over the next several years. Carter had been critical of the Republic of Korea (ROK) for its suppression of human rights, and the "Koreagate" scandal involving alleged Korean gifts of money to U.S. members of Congress in an attempt to secure continued U.S. support of South Korea's military security had generated widespread criticism of Seoul. While President Carter insisted that U.S. air force units would remain in Korea and the U.S.-ROK Security Treaty would still be valid, South Koreans of all political persuasions were fearful that withdrawing U.S. troops would remove a key factor deterring North Korea. The Japanese government as well as most friendly Asian nations was also worried about what it saw as a further American retreat from Asia and as another example of American unilateralism on an issue of vital interest to many Asian countries. (The administration's efforts to normalize diplomatic relations with Vietnam, although ultimately unsuccessful, increased the concern of congressional critics over Carter's initial approach to Asian issues.) Even China, though publicly calling for the removal of U.S. troops from Korea, was widely reported to have told U.S. officials that it understood the need for its presence.

Two factors led President Carter to reverse his position and agree early in 1979 to keep U.S. ground troops in South Korea. First, there were few domestic political pressures pushing him to follow through on his promise. Second, opponents of the move pressed for a major intelligence study of the North Korean military forces, which in 1978 concluded that North Korean forces were much larger, better equipped, and more offensively oriented than previously thought, providing the justification Carter needed to shift his position.

The Carter administration devoted considerable effort to complete the formal structure of U.S.-Chinese reconciliation, begun during the Nixon administration, by establishing full diplomatic relations with the PRC. The problem facing the administration was how to recognize the PRC and break diplomatic relations with the Republic of China (ROC) in Taiwan—which Beijing insisted upon—without either undermining that island's possibility of determining its own future or creating a political backlash within the United States. On December 15, 1978, the U.S. and PRC governments announced their agreement to establish full diplomatic relations on January 1, 1979. The announcement indicated a measure of flexibility on the part of Beijing. The U.S.-ROC Security Treaty would end, but only a year after the United States notified the ROC of its intent to terminate the treaty, which followed the procedure specified in the treaty. Second, Beijing insisted that U.S. arms sales to Taiwan were unacceptable, but the United States said they would continue. Nonetheless, the two countries established diplomatic relations despite disagreement on this key issue.

The agreement was supported by U.S. allies in Asia, although with varying degrees of enthusiasm. Even though the agreement won broad support within the United States, particular aspects were subjected to considerable criticism by certain groups. Members of Congress were upset over the administration's failure to consult with Congress before shifting recognition from the ROC to the PRC, as called for in a nonbinding amendment to the International Security Assistance Act of 1978. The administration had known it would have to absorb such attacks, but had felt that widespread consultation would have resulted in leaks that could have upset the delicate negotiations with Beijing. More serious were the charges raised by moderates, some liberals, conservatives, and by many Democrats as well as most Republicans, that the communiqué issued by Washington and Beijing and the draft law on relations with Taiwan submitted by the administration were much too vague, and that U.S. concern about Taiwan's security and its right to purchase arms needed to be written into law.

President Carter's Asia policy played a significant role in the 1980 presidential campaign. Ronald Reagan attacked Carter's emphasis on human rights, which he argued was applied more strongly against U.S. allies than was appropriate. He castigated Carter's admission that the Soviet invasion of Afghanistan had taught him much about Soviet behavior as an indication of Carter's naivete. And Reagan also attacked Carter's policy toward Taiwan, saying that the U.S. should reestablish "official" relations with Taiwan as a loyal and dependable ally.

After the 1980 election, continued rancor between President Reagan, who took a hard-line foreign policy stance, and the Congress, which was divided between a democratically controlled House and a Republican Senate, appeared likely. In fact, there emerged a growing spirit of bipartisanship in U.S. Asia policy during the 1980s. In part this had to do with the fact that the administration's actions were seldom as strong as its rhetoric might have suggested. Democrats also came to see a need for a stronger U.S. defense and foreign policy in the face of continued Soviet expansion. And the administration and Democratic leaders were willing to consult and compromise on key issues.

Shortly after he took office, President Reagan invited South Korean president Chun Doo Hwan to the United States and gave him strong public backing. There apparently was at least an implicit agreement that President Chun would release opposition leader Kim Dae Jung and allow him to leave the country, which he did. President Reagan could thus point to an early success for quiet diplomacy, and Seoul felt it had a firm friend in the White House.

The administration also formulated its strategy and tactics toward Japan in a calm manner. Instead of publicly criticizing Japan for not spending enough on defense in relation to GNP, the focus was placed upon the appropriate roles and missions Japanese forces should undertake in conjunction with U.S. forces. Tokyo, in 1981, accepted the primary responsibility for it own air defense and agreed to develop the capability to help defend the sea lanes to 1,000 miles to the east and south. Japan's steady though small increases in defense spending were regarded by the U.S. administration with satisfaction. Congressional criticism continued but had no major affect on U.S. policy.

The president also sought to moderate past strong support for Taiwan while resisting continuing PRC demands for a cutback in U.S. arms sales to Taiwan and other issues. The U.S. military buildup and the close U.S.-Japanese security relationship reduced China's strategic importance to the United States. The administration established a consensus among U.S. policymakers by the mid-1980s. There was general agreement that the role of the PRC in the U.S. policy calculus was less important. U.S. officials felt less compelled to make additional sacrifices regarding Taiwan for the sake of ensuring close relations with the PRC.

The stability of the balance of power in Asia in the 1980s was underscored by the more moderate Soviet foreign policy in the region following the coming to power of Mikhail Gorbachev in 1985. At a minimum, Moscow seemed interested in the latter 1980s in easing tensions around its periphery, thereby gaining at least a temporary "breathing space" in which to revive the ailing Soviet economy. At the same time, Gorbachev highlighted political and economic initiatives designed to increase Soviet influence abroad. Gorbachev had more difficulty in expanding Soviet influence in Asia than in Europe, and he appeared to view an opening to China as a key link in efforts to improve Soviet influence in the region. Soviet leaders followed through on their repeated pledges to ease military tensions with China by addressing substantive Chinese security concerns. Beijing had summarized these concerns as the so-called "three obstacles" to improved Sino-Soviet relations posed by Soviet military occupation of Afghanistan, Soviet military presence along China's northern border, and Soviet support for Vietnam's military occupation of Cambodia.

The more stable security situation for U.S. interests in Asia in the 1980s offset the rise in U.S. economic disputes, especially with Japan. Asian countries advanced rapidly in economic development in the 1980s. They doubled their percentage of world output—from 10 to 20 percent—in ten years. Their combined export trade expanded similarly, leading to huge surpluses vis-à-vis the United States ($27 billion in 1981, $105 billion in 1987). The decade saw American trade with these countries surpass that with the Europeans. As the Asian economies grew, Asian investment began to enter the United States to finance part of its deficits. America and Asia, became economically more interdependent than ever. Many Americans were concerned that this economic interdependence exacerbated a perceived decline in U.S. relative power in the world. During the Cold War, America's ability to counter Soviet power and promote economic growth and political stability abroad depended heavily upon U.S. economic strength and its willingness to make economic "sacrifices" to achieve military and political goals. Such U.S. costs included a large, military budget, substantial foreign aid programs, and the free flow of exports of other countries to the U.S. market. By the 1980s, America's economic position was seen by some to be so seriously weakened that its long-term ability to sustain its role in the world was cast into doubt.

Among the many reasons of the perceived U.S. economic decline were economic progress abroad, especially in East Asia. This added to competitive pressures to a level America had not experienced since before World War II, when foreign trade had a much smaller impact on the U.S. economy. At home, U.S. educational standards had declined, as had product quality, and businesses gave increasing priority to short-term profits and financial mergers. Investment levels were inadequate for a more competitive international environment as were low U.S. savings levels. The federal budget deficits rose, as did the dollar, and with it the U.S. trade deficit, greatly increasing the pressures for protectionism.

The danger of protectionism grew for two main reasons. The first was economic. In 1971, the United States had its first trade deficit since World War II. Trade deficits continued, increasing in size through most of the 1970s and early 1980s, and averaged roughly $25 billion annually in 1979-1981. But a surplus in services meant that the United States had a current account surplus and was earning and paying its way in the world, except briefly in 1977 and 1978.

From 1980 there was a dramatic rise in the trade account deficit, which in 1986 amounted to $153 billion. This was due mainly to a sharp rise in imports from $245 billion in 1981 to $370 billion in 1986, while exports declined from $234 billion in 1981 to $217 billion in 1986. The deficit in the trade balance with Asia increased from $21.8 billion in 1981 to $95.7 billion in 1987. The total deficit for 1987 rose further to $159 billion, despite the fall in the dollar, with exports rising to $253 billion but imports continuing to increase to $412 billion. These trade deficits made the United States a debtor nation for the first time since World War I. It soon became the world's largest debtor nation.

Second, the Reagan administration was not following policies designed to ease trade tension with Asia. There were several factors behind the sharp rise of the U.S. trade deficit. The Latin American debt crisis, which forced many U.S. trading partners to curtail their imports, and slower growth in Europe—especially in 1983 and early 1984—played a part. Yet the greatest single cause was the high dollar, which increased in value by over 50 percent between 1980 and early 1985 in relation to the currencies of the ten largest industrial countries. This was caused mainly by the rising federal budget deficits (especially serious when personal savings were falling), which forced the United States to hold real interest rates higher than would otherwise have been necessary in order to attract capital from abroad. Administration leaders long denied that there was a problem with the high dollar, which they saw as a sign of strength. The administration's foreign trade and monetary policies were simply to leave things to the market.

By mid-1985 key figures in the administration were convinced that unless it changed its hands-off policy regarding the trade deficit, Congress would be swept along on a tide of protectionism and pass legislation along those lines. Thus in September 1985 the administration dramatically reversed its position of noninterference in the foreign exchange markets and worked out an agreement with the finance ministers and central bankers of the other four key industrial powers (Japan, Germany, Britain, and France) in the Group of Five to intervene in order to bring down the value of the dollar. It also undertook a number of specific initiatives to protect U.S. industries or to open foreign markets. But by that time the surge toward protectionism was steadily gathering strength, a trend that continued in 1986 and 1987 because the declining dollar initially increased rather than reduced the trade deficit. Moreover, some important trade partners, such as South Korea and, initially, Taiwan, resisted letting their currencies appreciate much relative to the dollar, and many corporations in Japan and Europe chose to hold price increases to a minimum in order to maintain market share even at the cost of greatly reduced profits.

Omnibus trade legislation passed both houses of Congress in 1987, although with many quite different provisions. Both bills had a mixture of trade-enhancing provisions (authority for a new round of multilateral trade negotiations, worker retraining provisions, and so on) and a variety of protectionist features. The dramatic upheavals in world financial markets in October 1987 induced some caution about any "protectionist" legislation.

The compromise bill approved by the House-Senate conference eliminated most of the strongest protectionist features in each bill but was still vetoed by President Reagan over a nontrade provision involving plant closing notification to workers. A bill was passed in late 1988 without this provision and became law, and its broad support suggested that the movement toward a more protectionist trade policy was unlikely to disappear from the political scene.

The decline in U.S. economic power relative to Japan and other up-and-coming world economic actors lay at the heart of the growing argument of those who saw the United States entering a period of decline. If Asian-Pacific geopolitics appeared more stable, economic vitality appeared to be the main source of political legitimacy in the 1990s. One does not have to agree with those who see the decline in U.S. power to note that the U.S. influence in the Asian-Pacific region in the 1990s was relatively but considerably less than it was before the 1970s. One must be careful, however, not to allow the change in U.S. military-economic influence to translate into a view of U.S. cultural influence. For in this arena, there seemed to have been no decline in U.S. influence. Indeed, the democratization movements in China, South Korea, the Philippines, Burma, and elsewhere were all inspired at least in some part by the American example. The 1989 student uprising in Beijing would not have been as massive or, at least initially, as successful without the knowledge that Americans were watching the event on television. The revolutionary innovations in information and communications technology, much of them products of American engineering, were weaving countries of the world closer together into a global network, and the sense of instantaneous communication was nowhere more pronounced than in the hitherto closed societies of Asia. Even in a more open society like Japan, there were forces tending further to Americanize people's life-styles. The two governments' attempt to discuss structural impediments in Japan that obstructed a freer flow of American goods and capital into the country were clearly an effort to alter Japanese cultural habits.

At the same time that American influence was transforming Asian societies, American society, too, was coming under increasing Asian influence. The immigration act of 1965, combined with various measures to resettle refugees, brought about an influx of Asians to the United States who came to account for 2.4 percent of the total population. In a state the size of California, the ratio was much higher, and there was an expectation that before long Asians might constitute one-third of the inhabitants. Immigrants from Vietnam, Thailand, Korea, Singapore, Taiwan, mainland China, and elsewhere were now much more visible in American society than earlier, and the American people became accustomed to Asian food, clothing, and religious practices. There were also hundreds of thousands of temporary visitors from Asia as tourists and students. In 1988 close to three million Japanese tourists came to America, and over 200,000 additional Japanese citizens resided in the United States studying and working. The number of Korean and Chinese students seem to have been even larger than that of Japanese students, and it was particularly significant that at the time of the Tiananmen crackdown in June 1989, as many as 40,000 Chinese students were scattered all over the United States.

Notes

1. Among the interesting interpretive work on this subject, see Akira Iriye, *Across the Pacific: An Inner History of American-East Asian Relations* (New York: Harcourt, Brace and World, 1967); James C. Thomson, Jr., et al., *Sentimental Imperialists: The American Experience in East Asia* (New York: Harper and Row, 1981); Earnest R. May and James Thompson, eds., *American-East Asian Relations, A Survey* (Cambridge, MA: Harvard University Press, 1972); Tyler Dennett, *Americans in East Asia, A Critical Study in United States Policy in the Far East in the 19th Century* (New York: Barnes and Noble, 1963); Akira Iriye, *The Cold War in Asia. A Historical Introduction* (Englewood Cliffs, NJ: Prentice Hall, 1974); Tang Tsou, *America's Failure in China* (Chicago: University of Chicago Press, 1963); Warren Cohen, ed., *New Frontiers in American-East Asian Relations* (New York: Columbia University Press, 1983).

2. This analysis is based heavily on that presented by Akira Iriye at the Woodrow Wilson Center for Scholars, September 26, 1990.

3. Whitney Griswold's, *The Far Eastern Policy of the United States* (New York: Harcourt, Brace, 1938) provides a useful overview for this period.

4. Based on Akira Iriye's review, September 26, 1990.

5. This summary is based particularly on the thoughtful assessment of William Barnds, "Trends in U.S. Politics and Their Implications for America's Asian Policy," in Robert Scalapino et al., eds., *Asia and the Major Powers: Domestic Politics and Foreign Policy* (Berkeley: University of California, 1988). For additional reading, see the suggested readings at the end of this book.

3

Japan: Partner or Competitor?

Japanese-U.S. relations are more uncertain today than at any time since World War II. As longstanding military allies and increasingly interdependent economic partners, Japan and the United States have worked closely together to build a strong, multifaceted relationship based on democratic values and interests in world stability and development. But strains have grown markedly in recent years as Japan's economic and technological power has developed enormously relative to that of the United States. Japan today is America's foremost economic and technological competitor. The thaw in the Cold War since 1989 and discord in U.S.-Japanese relations over the Iraq-Kuwait crisis of 1990–1991 raise new questions about the strategic rationale in the U.S.-Japanese alliance.

U.S.-Japanese Relations at a Crossroads?

U.S.-Japanese relations have grown enormously, especially over the past two decades, as the two societies and economies have become increasingly intertwined and interdependent.[1] The U.S.-Japanese combined gross national product now totals about one-third of the world's GNP. Japan receives about 11 percent of U.S. exports—a larger share than any other country except Canada, and the United States buys roughly one-third of Japan's exports, making it Japan's largest export market. In 1990, Japan had $65 billion invested in the United States, and the United States had more than $17 billion invested in Japan. Some $100 billion in U.S. government securities held by people in Japan helped to finance a substantial portion of the U.S. budget deficit. Economic exchanges reinforce a wide variety of scientific, technical, tourist, and other exchanges. Both societies continue to see each other as their main security ally in Asia and the Pacific. Recent changes have led to some decline in public opinion, though surveys show a historically high level of mutual friendship and respect. Nevertheless, substantial majorities of Americans and Japanese agree that the bilateral relationship is vital to both countries.

Growing interdependence has been accompanied by markedly changing circumstances at home and abroad that are widely seen to have created a crisis in U.S.-Japanese relations. Bush administration officials continue to emphasize the positive aspects of the relationship but warn that there is a need for "a new conceptual framework" for U.S.-Japanese relations.[2] Press reports document how the relationship has changed in recent years and how there is considerable debate in the United States and Japan over whether a closely cooperative U.S.-Japanese relationship is possible or appropriate for the 1990s.[3] An authoritative review of popular and media opinion warned of a "new orthodoxy" of "suspicion, criticism and considerable self-justification" which, it said, was endangering the fabric of U.S.-Japanese relations.[4]

Changes in three sets of factors stand out as most important in explaining the challenges currently facing U.S.-Japanese relations in the 1990s.

Economic Factors

There has been sweeping change in the relative power of the United States and Japan, especially in the last decade. This change goes well beyond the implications of the bilateral U.S. trade deficit with Japan, which remained at about $50 billion annually for the last several years and dropped to $41 billion in 1990. The persisting U.S. trade and budget deficits of the early 1980s led to a series of decisions in the middle of the decade that called for a major realignment of the value of U.S. and Japanese currencies, which strengthened Japan's ability to purchase U.S. goods and to invest in the United States. By the end of the decade, the United States had reversed its previous position as the world's largest creditor and had become the world's largest debtor. Japan, with its stronger currency, was the largest international creditor.

Japan's growing investment in the United States led to complaints from some American constituencies. Moreover, Japanese industry seemed well positioned to use its economic power to invest in the range of high-technology products where U.S. manufacturers still had the lead. U.S. ability to compete under these circumstances was seen as hampered by heavy personal, government, and business debt, a low savings rate, and other factors.

Based on its economic power and performance, Japan was able steadily to expand its role in the World Bank, the IMF, and other international financial institutions. Investment and trade flows made Japan by far the dominant economic actor in Asia. Japanese aid and investment became widely sought after in other parts of the world, and it appeared to many observers to be only a matter of time before such economic power would translate into political influence.

Political-Military Changes

The collapse of the Soviet empire in Eastern Europe and the growing preoccupation of Soviet leaders with massive internal political and economic difficulties prompted the U.S. and Japanese governments to reassess their longstanding alliance relationship and focus on the increasingly weakened Soviet threat. Officials on both sides of the alliance had tended to characterize the security alliance as the linchpin and the foundation of the relationship that should get pride of place over disputes concerning economic issues or other areas.[5] Some U.S. and Japanese officials and commentators emphasized the common dangers to U.S.-Japanese interests posed by the continued strong Russian military presence in Asia. They stressed that until Moscow follows its moderation in Europe with major demobilization and reduction of forces in the Pacific, Washington and Tokyo need to remain militarily prepared and vigilant.[6]

Increasingly, however, this line of argument is supplemented by those who emphasize other perceived benefits in close U.S.-Japanese security ties. Thus, the alliance is seen to deter other potential disruptive forces in East Asia, notably North Korea. Ironically, some U.S. officials have noted that the alliance relationship helps to keep Japan's potential military power in check and under the supervision of the United States.[7]

The post–Cold War environment has acted to strengthen the importance of economic prowess rather than military power as the major source of world influence in the 1990s. Under these circumstances, a military superpower, the USSR, was often depicted as a large Third World country trying desperately to stave off economic disaster and anxiously seeking aid, trade, and technical benefits from the developed countries. U.S. power is also seen as less than in the past, at least by some observers. They note that because of its debtor status and weakened economic standing relative to other countries, notably Japan, the United States must increasingly look to Japan and others to shoulder the financial burden entailed in the transformation of former communist economies in Eastern Europe and other urgent international requirements.

Domestic Factors

The declining Soviet/Russian threat, the rising power of the Japanese economy, increasingly close U.S. interaction (and related disputes) with Japan, and other factors have led to a decided shift in American opinion about Japan, and less marked but nonetheless notable shifts in Japanese opinion. In the United States, this shift is portrayed by answers to the question of which is more serious: the military threat from the Soviets or the economic "threat" or "challenge" from Japan. In a series of opinion polls since 1989, the majority answer to this question is Japan. Similarly, poll data from early 1990 show that a majority of Japanese said that negative American attitudes toward Japan were a reflection of U.S. anger at "America's slipping economic position." Meanwhile, Japanese opinion is showing greater confidence in Japan's ability to handle its own affairs without constant reference—as in the past—to the United States. Japanese belief in U.S. reliability as a world leader is also less than in the past.[8]

Opinion in both countries involves those who promote new or "revisionist" views of the U.S.-Japanese relationship. In the United States, prominent commentators warn of a Japanese economic juggernaut, out of control of the Japanese government, which must be "contained" by the United States. In Japan, commentators include those who argue that the United States is weak, dependent on Japan, and unable to come to terms with the economic competition of the world. They urge the Japanese government and people to strike out on an increasingly independent course in world affairs.[9]

At the same time, however, it is easy to overstate the degree of change in opinion in the United States and Japan. Thus, the vast majority of Americans still view Japan positively, have high levels of respect for Japanese accomplishments, and support the U.S. defense commitment to Japan. On the whole, the Japanese still consider the United States positively as their closest friend, the principal guardian of their external security, their most important economic partner and market, and the exemplar of a life-style that has much to offer—and envy.[10]

One reason for the shift in popular attitudes toward the negative over the past few years has been the media coverage that has accompanied U.S.-Japanese disputes and those involved in the disputes. Thus, U.S. members of Congress who criticize Japan's economic practices are given widespread and often sensationalized coverage in Japan even when the issue in dispute may be relatively minor in the overall relationship. In the United States, the furor and controversy that accompanied media treatment of the Japanese monograph, "The Japan That Can Say 'No'," seemed to mirror the Japanese media's sensational emphasis on the negative in U.S.-Japanese relations.

Growing Strains in Relations

Despite close consultations and repeated negotiations over trade, defense, and other issues, strains in bilateral relations have grown markedly in the last twenty years. In the mid-1960s, Japanese industry posed its first challenge to the American economy. Initially, U.S. manufacturers of textiles and light electronic goods complained about Japanese imports. Later, American manufacturers of automobiles, steel, and sophisticated electronic goods saw Japanese products take an increasing share of markets formerly held by them. Today, Japan has become America's foremost economic and technological competitor.

American ability to compete with Japan also has been called into question recently as a result of the persistent U.S. trade deficit with Japan and other countries, the rise in U.S. national indebtedness, and constraints on U.S. government spending. American policymakers have taken a series of steps in response to this situation. In the case of U.S. relations with Japan, many policymakers in the Congress and elsewhere have taken the lead in pressing for a firmer U.S. stance in opposition to perceived unfair economic practices by Japan. The Congress and the administration in recent years also have pressed Japan to use its growing economic resources in support of allied security goals, in Asia and elsewhere, that are more difficult for the United States to sustain in a period of budget restraint. Much attention focused in 1990-1991 on Japan's slow response to U.S. calls for Japan to shoulder more of the burden in support of the allied effort against Iraq's invasion of Kuwait and the Persian Gulf war.

The ability of U.S. and Japanese leaders to deal effectively with strains in relations has been affected by often conflicting attitudes and political pressures in Japan and the United States over economic, defense, and other issues; and by a recent leadership crisis in the Japanese government.

Economic Issues

Japan's Economic Practices

The U.S. trade deficit with Japan is a highly visible source of friction in U.S.-Japanese relations. (It ran at a level of $50 billion for several years until 1990, when it declined to $41 billion.) There are several perceived causes of the persisting large U.S. trade deficit with Japan and other countries: the results of recent macroeconomic policies of the United States and other major economic powers, Third World debt, a perceived decline in U.S. ability to compete with its trading partners, and unfair trading and economic practices of U.S. trading partners. Congress pressed in the Omnibus Trade Act of 1988 (P.L. 100-418) and other measures for a more active U.S. effort to promote change in the perceived unfair trading and other economic policies of foreign competitors.

In the case of Japan, the United States has focused in recent years on better access to the Japanese market as a means to remedy its trade deficit. Under pressure from the United States and others, Japan has gradually reduced formal barriers—tariffs and quotas—to imports. But a series of informal trade barriers—product standards and regulations, government procurement practices, and official administrative guidance and informal arrangements among Japanese retailers and suppliers—have prevented U.S. producers from acquiring appreciable shares of the Japanese market in sectors where the United States is competitive. The Bush administration on May 25, 1989, identified Japan as one of three priority countries for negotiations to achieve trade liberalization under the "Super 301" provisions of the 1988 Trade Act. Three priority practices were identified for investigation under the act: exclusionary procurement practices in the satellite and supercomputer sectors, and technical barriers to trade in forest products. By April 1990, progress had been noted in U.S.-Japanese talks concerning all three areas. In late April 1990, the Bush administration announced that Japan would not be identified as one of the priority countries under the "Super 301" provisions. The action was criticized by some members of Congress.[11]

On September 4, 1989, U.S. and Japanese subcabinet-level negotiations began in Tokyo on the so-called Structural Impediments Initiative (SII). These talks were designed to remedy trade-impeding problems in both countries. U.S. negotiators were interested in changing Japan's distribution and price mechanisms, exclusionary business practices, and incentives that lead to a high rate of Japanese domestic savings and investments. Japanese negotiators focused on U.S. low savings rates, budget deficits, and alleged shortsighted U.S. business strategies. The negotiators were slated to present an interim report in spring 1990 and a final report to the heads of government within a year. On April 5, 1990, the negotiators from Japan and the United States released an interim report on the SII talks in which the two sides agreed to take measures to address the structural impediments in their respective economies. On June 28, 1990, they released the final report in which they presented more details on their proposed remedies for the structural impediments. U.S. policymakers were concerned that Japan would follow up its proposals with implementation.

There was considerable skepticism in the United States that the SII talks would result in any significant benefit for U.S. producers. The talks were seen as a largely political exercise designed to manage the deep frustration felt by Americans over the continuing large trade deficit with Japan. In Japan, too, there was strong underlying dissatisfaction with persistent U.S. demands. Both Japanese and American critics were not optimistic that the substantial differences between the economic systems and priorities in Japan and the United States could be reconciled through such negotiations and arguments.

The United States also maintained tariff sanctions on selected electronic products from Japan because the U.S. share of the semiconductor market in Japan had not increased as was stipulated under a 1987 bilateral agreement. The expiration of that agreement in July 1991 was the subject

Japan: Partner or Competitor?

of hearings and other congressional interest in early 1991. A new agreement was reached in mid-1991 and the U.S. tariff sanctions were dropped. The United States protested Japan's restrictions on rice and other agricultural imports; U.S. officials criticized Japan's stance on rice as partly responsible for the impasse in 1990-1991 over agricultural trade issues in the Uruguay round of multilateral trade talks. Japan's construction industry was widely seen as partly closed to U.S. companies; this prompted the Bush administration to press Japan in May 1991 for greater opportunity for U.S. companies. Japan's patent system is also coming under close scrutiny in the Congress and elsewhere as a market access barrier.

Japanese Investment in the United States

Like the U.S. presence in Europe twenty years ago, Japan's overseas investments and manufacturing operations are generating fear and concern among some elements of the American public, although many Americans welcome Japanese investment. With investments of $300 billion, Japan is the second largest foreign investor in the United States, behind the first place British. Japanese investors have been surprised by the negative response to their U.S. investments in real estate and small technology-intensive companies. In a number of cases, Japanese investors have demonstrated their willingness to finance projects that many U.S. commercial banks have been unwilling to finance.[12]

Foreign investment is challenging some Americans' notions of U.S. economic independence and is confronting U.S. officials with difficult policy issues. Some U.S. companies resent capital inflows from Japan and the rising presence of Japanese companies in the economy, and these U.S. companies may try to persuade the government to protect them from foreign investors. In contrast, many in the United States actively seek Japanese investment. In 1989, thirty-three states and four port authorities had offices in Tokyo, largely for the purpose of attracting Japanese investments. State and local governments sometimes compete fiercely against one another for these investments.

As part of the Omnibus Trade Act of 1988, the Congress passed a provision granting the president the authority to suspend or prohibit any acquisition, merger, or takeover of a U.S. enterprise if the president determines that the foreign direct investment will threaten or impair the national security. Under this provision, a Japanese company was blocked in its attempt in early 1989 from acquiring a U.S. company involved in a contract concerning critical nuclear weapons technology. In October 1990, Congress passed a bill (S. 2516) to increase public access to and to better coordinate information on foreign investors.

Technology Policy Issues

As economic competition between the United States and Japan has moved increasingly into areas of high-technology, relations between the two on technology policy issues have become more important and often more contentious. Japan's level of technology has advanced rapidly and now equals or surpasses that of the United States in many key areas. With strong industrial research and an emphasis on efficient manufacturing technology, rapid product improvement in response to market needs, and high quality, Japan has been a successful competitor in many technologies and now dominates several important markets. Much of the trade deficit is due to U.S. purchases of products that U.S. companies no longer produce or are behind in product or process technology. Japan's progress in technology raises concerns about potential Japanese domination of areas of high-technology that are deemed critical for U.S. economic and military strength.

In addition to counteracting Japan's trade practices in high-technology industries, U.S. interest in Congress and elsewhere has focused on actions to catch up with or keep ahead of Japan in key technologies and to correct the imbalance in the flow of technology between Japan and the United States. Some initiatives have resulted from concern that the United States will lose key defense industries. In 1987, Congress established SEMATECH, a Defense Advanced Research Projects Agency (DARPA), and industry-supported research consortia to improve semiconductor manufacturing technology. Other initiatives intended to correct imbalances in the flow of technology between the United States and Japan have included the Japanese Technical Literature Act of 1986 (P.L. 99-382), which gave the Department of Commerce the authority to collect, translate, and disseminate Japanese language scientific information, and parts of the 1988 Trade Act that required international cooperative research and development (R&D) agreements to be negotiated so that they are reciprocal, equitable, and protect U.S. intellectual property. The U.S.-Japan science and technology agreement signed by President Reagan and Prime Minister Noboru Takeshita in June 1988 was negotiated along these lines. The FSX debate (described below) also reflects concerns over asymmetries in the flow of technology.

Several initiatives were passed in the 101st Congress addressing technology transfer between the United States and Japan. The FY1991 defense appropriations bill (P.L. 101-510) set aside $10 million for the Department of Defense (DOD) to enter into cooperative research agreements with Japan that concentrate on technological components and subsystems. The bill also directed the DARPA to open a "technology office" in Tokyo by the end of 1991. Other examples of programs started in part to respond to issues of competitiveness with Japan—such as funding for SEMATECH and federal support for research in High Definition Television—continued to receive congressional support.

At issue more recently is whether the initiatives to date are sufficient. Many feel that the United States needs a more comprehensive and coordinated science and technology policy focused on issues of international competitiveness. Others oppose further subsidies and a stronger government involvement in what they see as the proper domain of the private sector.

Security Issues

Japan's economic growth and trade surplus have contributed to the increased scrutiny that many in the United States have given to the U.S.-Japanese security relationship. U.S. concern over the perceived inequality in U.S.-Japanese security ties has grown as Japanese industries have prospered in American markets and the commitment of American military resources to protecting countries and sea lanes of vital importance to Japan seems more burdensome, given the severity of U.S. budget constraints. (The latter concern was especially important in 1987 and 1988, as a large number of U.S. warships protected sea lanes in the Persian Gulf that provided oil for Japanese industry and popular use; and in 1990 and 1991, as U.S. forces deployed to and engaged in combat in the Persian Gulf region following Iraq's invasion of Kuwait.)

American planners recognize that the U.S. military presence in Japan (50,000 personnel at a cost of over $7.6 billion per year) sustains U.S. interests in relations with the most important country in Northeast Asia.[13] It also supports American regional interests (e.g., provides reinforcements for South Korea, if needed, and helps in the defense of Alaska) and global interests, especially vis-à-vis the Soviet Union and China. The planners also acknowledge that the Japanese government helps to defray the cost of U.S. forces in Japan with a contribution of about $3 billion per year. On December 20, 1990, the Japanese government announced that it would increase its contribution by $600 million over the course of five years. This would increase Japan's contribution for American forces in Japan from 40 to 50 percent.

Although Japan's constitution and government policy preclude an assertive military role in international relations, Japan has undertaken to defend its sea lanes within 1,000 nautical miles of Japan, providing a credible deterrent to military aggressors and, thus, allowing greater flexibility in deploying U.S. forces throughout Asia and other regions. Japan's defense budget, based on a NATO formula that includes veterans costs, is over $30 billion a year, the third largest in the world after those of Russia and the United States.

Nevertheless, American officials have urged Japan to do more in its own defense and in support of allied interests. Some have been especially critical of the small percentage of Japan's GNP that goes for defense (about one percent, as opposed to about 5 percent for the United States) and the limited capabilities of the Japan Self-Defense Forces. Provisions of the FY1990–1991 DOD authorization bill (H.R. 2461), which was reported on November 6, 1989, called for U.S. negotiations with Japan on compensating the United States for the costs of U.S. forces in Japan and set several other goals for Japanese defense and foreign assistance efforts. On October 27, 1989, Congress passed the FY1990 military construction appropriations bill, which deleted 70 percent of all funding for new U.S. military construction in Japan. On November 19, 1989, Congress passed the FY1990 defense appropriations bill (H.R. 3072), which contained a provision calling on President Bush to negotiate with Japan to offset expenses for keeping U.S. forces in Japan.[14] On February 24, 1990, Defense Secretary Richard Cheney left Japan after five days of talks in which he reportedly told Japanese leaders of a proposed 10 percent reduction of U.S. forces in Japan over the next three years and received Japanese pledges of greater financial support for the costs of U.S. forces in Japan. The FY1991 defense appropriations bill (H.R. 5803) passed Congress in October 1990 with a provision that limited U.S. forces in Japan to 50,000 and reduced that limit by 5,000 annually unless Japan paid all direct costs of U.S. deployments in Japan. The president could waive the provision if he deemed it in the national interest. The FY1991 military construction appropriations bill (H.R. 5313) eliminated requested projects for Japan. The FY1992–FY1993 defense authorization bill (H.R. 2100) passed the House in May 1991 with several burdensharing provisions aimed at Japan and with praise for Japan's action in 1990 in bearing a greater share of the costs of stationing U.S. forces in Japan.

The Japanese argue that they are compensating for their relatively limited defense efforts by increasing support for allied security interests by other means. In particular, Japanese spokespersons have pointed to Japan's economic aid to South Korea, China, the Philippines, Thailand, Pakistan, and Turkey as providing assistance to countries of strategic importance to the United States. Indeed, Japan is now the largest donor of development assistance in Asia and became the largest aid donor in the world by 1990, surpassing global aid flows of the United States. The Bush administration and officials in Congress have been looking to Japan to bear major responsibility for the U.S.-backed multilateral aid initiative in the Philippines, and to play an important role in assisting the new reformist governments emerging in Eastern Europe. Critics charge, however, that Japanese aid efforts are clearly tied to infrastructure and development projects that will require large purchases of Japanese goods and services and otherwise assist the growth of Japanese industry, developments that could erode U.S. ability to compete in Third World markets.

Iraq-Kuwait Crisis, 1990-1991

Although Japan contributed nearly $13 billion to the allied cause in the Persian Gulf, Japan's response to the crisis created serious tensions between the U.S. and Japanese governments and their respective publics, with implications for future relations.[15]

Throughout the crisis, the Japanese public demonstrated a reluctance to be involved. Japanese officials and political leaders perceived the crisis mainly in terms of its effects on relations with the United States. This produced a hesitancy to act until the United States sent clear messages on what it wanted.

Japan was not able to meet U.S. proposals that it send military forces to the Gulf. Factors involved included Japan's peace constitution that played a decisive part in maintaining public sentiment against military involvement. The opposition political parties stressed defense of the constitution and blocked government proposals for military involvement. Prime Minister Toshiki Kaifu's performance reinforced the view that the Japanese government was reluctant and indecisive in its response. Warnings by a number of East Asian governments further complicated Japan's ability to play a military role. Press reports, leadership comments, and statements by U.S. and Japanese officials in interviews portrayed Japan's response to the crisis, and the U.S.-Japanese interaction, as a failure. The Japanese government appeared ill-prepared to deal with the crisis, slow to recognize its broader implications, and politically maladroit in dealing with U.S. requests for assistance. On the other hand, the Bush administration misjudged Japan's likely military role and underestimated the importance of public pacifist sentiment. Once it was clear what the Bush administration wanted in terms of financial contributions, the Japanese government was able to respond more effectively.

Broader implications for U.S.-Japanese relations at this time appeared to be more negative than positive. The episode embarrassed officials in the United States and Japan who had touted the benefits of a close U.S.-Japan "global partnership"; and strengthened those who argued that U.S. and Japanese policies and values are not compatible and provide little basis for reducing growing strains caused by U.S.-Japanese economic competition. Optimists hoped that the experience would give the Japanese government the ability to manage more effectively future international crises. A more common view stressed that institutional, political, legal, and traditional constraints on Japan's freedom of action are unlikely to be modified by Japan's current political leadership. As a result, greater attention may be devoted to economic disputes and the difficulties that arise in attempts to solve them.

The FSX Question

U.S. concerns over economic, technological, and defense relations with Japan notably came to a head earlier, in 1989, over the issue of the FSX fighter support program. After more than a year of negotiations, the U.S. and Japanese governments in late 1988 reached an agreement on a proposal that Japan would codevelop a modified F-16 (the so-called FSX) for its next generation of jet fighter aircraft. In early 1989, opponents of the deal in Congress and the administration urged reconsideration, pending a six-month review of the pact's long-term implications. They argued that it involved the sale of advanced U.S. technology at a low price to a potential major international competitor in the aircraft/arms sales market. Supporters of the deal pointed out that such a delay would complicate Japanese defense planning and ran the risk of undermining an agreement that in their view was in the U.S. interest.

The Bush administration reviewed and modified the deal before submitting it to Congress. On May 16, 1989, the Senate narrowly voted against blocking the sale and then adopted a modified resolution (S.J.Res. 113) that mandated requirements for how the deal would be carried out.[16] On June 7, 1989, the House considered and passed the Senate's version of S.J.Res. 113. President Bush vetoed the measure on July 31, 1989. On September 13, 1989, the Senate failed by one vote to override the veto. A possible source of new controversy emerged in late 1990 when Japanese officials were reported to be so concerned about the rising costs of the new plane that they were considering scaling back the program.

The importance of the FSX debate for the United States and Japan included a heightened awareness on both sides that concerns over economic and technological competitiveness would interfere with some planned security arrangements. While remaining close military allies, both governments would examine more closely defense technological cooperation with an eye toward its implications for each side's respective position in the highly competitive world economy.

Political Issues

Conflicting Attitudes and Other Political Pressures

Japanese and U.S. leaders have been unable to reconcile differences over economic, technology, or defense issues without addressing the conflicting attitudes and other political pressures that affect them as they deal with questions in U.S.-Japanese relations.

Japanese Views

Japanese opinion is far from uniform on important issues in Japanese-U.S. relations. Nevertheless, on trade issues, Japanese public opinion has generally opposed making concessions demanded by American critics.[17] Japan has generally seen its success in competition with U.S. manufacturers as well deserved. Japanese products are viewed as superior in quality to competing products from the United States. U.S. inability to penetrate the Japanese market is said to result less from formal or informal trade barriers than from a lack of U.S. diligence in developing markets in Japan and poorer quality and lower technical standards of American products.

The Japanese also have viewed American complaints on trade issues as inconsistent. At the start of the Reagan administration, the Japanese saw the United States move away from its focus on the trade deficit and toward concentration on agricultural quotas and nontariff barriers impeding U.S. trade and investment in Japan. But the growth of the trade deficit soon prompted some U.S. officials to complain again about the deficit as a major issue in U.S.-Japanese relations.

On defense, the Japanese constitution prohibits Japan from waging war, specifying that "land and sea forces, as well as other war potential, will never be maintained" by Japan. The constitution enjoys wide support in Japan; any attempt to amend its antiwar provisions would be sure to prompt great controversy. Moreover, the Japanese hold that many Asian countries would react with alarm to a rapid increase in Japan's defense efforts—a view shared by many Americans.

The Japanese government also had been reluctant to increase defense spending rapidly, in part because Japan had been running large budget deficits. Fiscal prudence requires that government spending be brought into line with available revenue. Japanese leaders could increase taxes or cut other programs, but such an approach has not fared well politically in the past. Prime Minister Nakasone failed to push a sales tax increase through the Diet in April 1987. Prime Minister Takeshita later succeeded, but it contributed to his political downfall in 1989.

Political considerations also underlie the Japanese government's resistance to U.S. agricultural imports. Japan's ruling party has antagonized its strong rural constituency by allowing more imports of lower-priced American farm products. Export-oriented businesses in Japan also wield considerable political influence through financial support of candidates in the ruling party. Japanese politicians are frequently wary of adopting policies on trade that would have a negative impact on these important political supporters.[18]

Japan's Leadership Difficulties

An impediment to effective Japanese-U.S. efforts to handle strains in their relations concerns the leadership crisis in Japan. Because of a widespread financial scandal involving the prime minister and other senior members of the ruling Liberal Democratic Party (LDP), Prime Minister Takeshita announced his resignation in April 1989. He was succeeded by Prime Minister Sosuke Uno, who was plagued by a sex-for-hire scandal. Uno led the LDP into national elections in July 1989 for the largely ceremonial upper house. The vote was an unprecedented defeat for the ruling LDP and victory for the Japanese Socialist Party. Uno resigned. On August 9, Toshiki Kaifu was elected prime minister and filled his cabinet with younger ministers and, in a rare break with tradition, two women.[19]

Kaifu led the LDP to victory in the February 18, 1990, elections for the more powerful lower house of the Diet. The LDP won 275 seats (versus 300 seats in the last election in 1986). Thus, the LDP held on to its majority control in the 512-seat lower house. Kaifu's stature within the LDP grew in 1990 but his ability to lead the party and Japan remained uncertain, especially after his failure to push through legislation in late 1990 allowing for Japan to send a small group of self-defense forces to the Persian Gulf. In late 1991, Kaifu was dropped in favor of a new prime minister, Kiichi Miyazawa.

Whatever the outcome of Japan's leadership difficulties, it was apparent that the Japanese government would have difficulty formulating policies or taking initiatives to deal with challenges posed by growing strains in U.S.-Japanese relations. Several analysts speculated that the LDP may find itself with a weaker leadership, reduced strength in the Diet, and eroding public support. In negotiations with the United States over trade, technology, and security issues, the LDP thus may be more susceptible to pressure from key constituent groups (for example, farmers and small retailers who oppose concessions to the United States on agricultural imports and on opening up the distribution system) and less willing to adopt policies favored by the United States.

An alternative view judges that the current political difficulties merely serve to exacerbate a chronic condition of weak political leadership in Japan. Proponents say that even under strong LDP majority rule, Japan's political leaders are subjected to various domestic pressures that make them unwilling to adopt policies favored by the United States. Similar pressures would presumably affect policies of a possible future opposition party government.

Environmental Issues

Some Americans have been critical of Japanese practices that are seen as detrimental to the world environment.[20] For many years, U.S. groups pressed for increasing restrictions on Japanese whaling practices. More recently, attention has focused on Japan's consumption of ivory, the use of "drift-net" fishing by some Japanese fleets in the Pacific Ocean, Japan's use of the shells of endangered sea turtles, and the logging practices of some Japanese enterprises in tropical rainforests in Asia and elsewhere. In the face of heavy criticism, the Japanese government often has urged Japanese enterprises to modify and reduce practices found to be detrimental to the world environment. But critics charge that Tokyo is usually reluctant to take meaningful action unless pressed by important foreign countries or international organizations.

U.S. Policy Approaches

There is broad support in the United States for a more assertive and forceful U.S. policy toward Japan, but there is a wide range of opinion on how strongly and in what ways the United States should press for change.

Important segments of American opinion favor employing protectionist measures to safeguard U.S. industries that are losing out to Japanese competitors. Some representatives of the U.S. auto and steel industries have been most outspoken in this regard. However, many other Americans are skeptical that protectionist measures will increase the efficiency of American industry, or they favor foreign competition as a means to keep product quality high and prices low, thereby slowing the growth of inflation in the United States. These observers frequently judge improved corporate performance and better-balanced macroeconomic policy as the best ways for the United States to cope with Japanese competition over the long haul.[21]

Many Americans also judge that Japan should do more in defense of the Japanese islands and the Northwest Pacific. Other Americans stress that the military balance in Northeast Asia does not require Japan to increase markedly its defense spending. Japan can better help the United States by using its great economic power—through aid grants and trade opportunities—to stabilize relations with important Asian and other states. Still other Americans say that a rapid increase in Japanese defense capabilities could alarm its neighbors and lead to regional instability detrimental to U.S. interests, and increased Japanese aid and trade could threaten U.S. access and influence in Asia as Japan rapidly becomes the dominant economic-political leader in the region.

At present, differing U.S. policy approaches toward Japan can be generally described as follows:

On one side are U.S. policymakers who argue that greater pressure is needed to push the Japanese out of past practices that are seen as detrimental to U.S. interest. The style of decision making in Japan is said to require strong outside pressure to effect change. And the changes sought are said to be of sufficient value to U.S. economic, technological, or security interests as to warrant the use of pressure, despite possible adverse nationalistic Japanese reactions. Moreover, pressure on Japan regarding these issues is also thought to have a useful demonstrative effect on other U.S. allies and trading partners.

Specific U.S. pressure tactics include: private pressure applied in negotiations, such as those associated with the "Super 301" process or the so-called Structural Impediments Initiative talks that began in September 1989; public criticism of Japan's economic, security, technology, or other policies; efforts to restrict the Japanese access to the U.S. market—current examples are "voluntary" restraints affecting Japanese automobile and steel imports; efforts to allow the value of the U.S. dollar to fall relative to that of the Japanese yen; and cutbacks in U.S. defense spending and/or military presence in Japan. Advocates judge that such measures would move Japan more toward meeting U.S. interests, although they acknowledge possible disadvantages for the United States.

Thus, a further decline in the value of the U.S. dollar relative to the yen would make Japanese products more expensive relative to U.S. products on the world market and would press the Japanese government to open its market more to foreign goods or face further upward push on the yen relative to the dollar. However, such changes are disruptive to U.S. relations with a broad range of trading partners and greatly increase the economic-political power and influence of Japan relative to that of the United States in Asia and in international financial institutions. Thus far, the changes have not led to a substantial dollar decline in the U.S. trade deficit with Japan. A cutback in the U.S. military presence in Japan could increase Japan's sense of vulnerability, which might prompt the Japanese to do more to protect Japan or otherwise share more of the allied defense burden. But, a U.S. pullback from Japan could reduce U.S. political influence in dealing with other powers in the region, undercut Japan's faith in the U.S. defense commitment, and prompt a reorientation in Japanese foreign policy contrary to American interests.

On the other side are those who judge that escalating U.S. pressure on Japan will not, by itself, appreciably meet U.S. needs in relations with Japan. Some Americans oppose stronger U.S. pressure on Japan on grounds that individual issues in U.S.-Japanese relations should not be allowed to seriously disrupt the bilateral relationship, which is seen as critically important for the United States. They judge that the benefits resulting from greater U.S. public pressure on Japan regarding specific economic, technology, or defense issues probably are not worth the disruption such pressure would cause in U.S.-Japanese ties; if pressure must be applied, it should be done discreetly, through private channels if possible, to avoid a counterproductive nationalistic Japanese reaction to this foreign pressure. They are particularly concerned that heavy U.S. pressure at present could further undermine the standing of the LDP, which emerged in 1990 from a series of leadership crises over the past year.

Other observers who play down the utility of U.S. pressure tactics on Japan say that the United States can help remedy strains in U.S.-Japanese relations apart from pressing Japanese leaders for economic, security, or other changes. Some stress that the U.S. trade deficit with Japan would improve markedly following serious efforts to cut the U.S. government's spending deficit and to promote policies that effectively encourage greater savings, technological development, productivity, and educational competence in the United States. They also warn that, given the rise of Japan's role as the dominant economic power in Asia and a major force in international financial and political institutions, the days are past when the United States could "lead" Japan in these areas. Rather, U.S. policy interests would be better served, in their view, by U.S. policy initiatives designed to build a new collaborative sharing of international power and influence in these areas by the United States and Japan. (Secretary of State Baker appeared to be suggesting such a relationship as part of a U.S./Japan-led, Pacific regionwide economic system in an policy speech in late June 1989.)[22]

A variant of this view says that as part of a more "realistic" U.S. posture that takes account of Japan's growing strength relative to the United States, the United States must recognize that Japan has different goals than the United States in economic, defense, and other policy areas, even though U.S.-Japanese mutual interests remain strong; and that because of its growing power, Japan is less likely than in the past to change these goals in the face of U.S. pressure tactics. This view holds, for example, that the Japanese economic-political system is oriented in support of investment and the Japanese "producer" rather than the Japanese "consumer." (This is seen as a stark contrast to the U.S. system, which is seen as oriented in support of consumers.) As a result, it is argued, Japan's resistance will be very strong to U.S. efforts to press for market opening in Japan that would encourage consumption and undercut the interests of Japanese producers. By the same token, Japan is said to be likely to continue trying to maximize the economic benefit its manufacturers can derive from increased defense and foreign aid spending. This would likely lead to strong Japanese resistance to U.S. pressure to get Japan to buy U.S. sophisticated weapons "off-the-shelf" and to U.S. pressure that Japanese foreign aid be "untied" from the purchase of Japanese goods and services.

According to this perspective, the United States is urged not to resort to pressure tactics that can be deflected by Japan, but to carefully marshal sources of U.S. leverage over Japan and enter into negotiations that would set specific milestones toward meeting U.S. interests. Thus, rather than pressing Japan for broad policy changes to encourage consumption and to open its market more to foreign goods, these advocates urge U.S.-Japanese negotiations to set specific requirements for U.S. market share in Japan or plans involving specific objectives toward reducing the U.S. trade deficit with Japan. And, rather than pressing Japan to spend more on defense and foreign aid, these proponents would urge U.S.-Japanese negotiations to set specific requirements for Japanese purchase of U.S. military equipment, for increased compensation for U.S. forces in Japan, and for types and amounts of Japanese foreign aid to individual countries important to the United States. Critics of this "managed" approach to trade, security, and aid issues doubt both its efficacy and advisability, arguing that the trade deficit and other problems will not be significantly affected by such measures.

Notes

1. For a comprehensive review of all major aspects of Japanese-U.S. relations, see "Japan-U.S. Relations: A Briefing Book," CRS Report for Congress 90-223 F. March 1990. See also the suggested readings at the end of this book.

2. See, among others, Robert Kimmitt, "The U.S. and Japan: Defining Our Global Partnership." U.S. Department of State, Bureau of Public Affairs. Current Policy No. 1221. October 9, 1989.

3. See, among others, *Wall Street Journal*, June 13, 1990.

4. Williams Watts et al., *America and Japan: How We See Each Other*. Commission on U.S.-Japan Relations for the Twenty-First Century. May 2, 1990.

5. The security relationship repeatedly got pride of place in U.S. officials' statements of overall U.S. policy toward Japan during the 1980s. Former Commerce Department official Clyde Prestowitz complained about his inability to raise economic disputes to a higher level during the Reagan administration. See his book, *Trading Places: How We Allowed Japan to Take the Lead* (New York: Basic Books, 1988).

6. CRS, "Japan-U.S. Relations: A Briefing Book," pp. 96-97.

7. See interview with a U.S. general in Japan, *Washington Post*, March 27, 1990.

8. Discussed in Watts, *American and Japan*.

9. Prominent in the former group are Clyde Prestowitz, Karel van Wolfren, and James Fallows; prominent in the latter group is Shintaro Ishihara.

10. See Watts, *America and Japan*. See also public opinion surveys reviewed in "Japan-U.S. Relations: A Briefing Book."

Japan: Partner or Competitor?

11. Coverage of the U.S.-Japan economic negotiations is provided weekly by the *Far Eastern Economic Review* and the *Asian Wall Street Journal Weekly*.

12. See, among others, Ryutaro Komiya and Ryuhei Wakasugi, "Japan's Foreign Direct Investment." *Annals of the American Academy of Political and Social Science* 513 (January 1991), pp. 48–61.

13. For an overview of U.S.-Japanese security relations, see U.S. Department of Defense, "A Strategic Framework for the Asian Pacific Rim," Report to Congress, April 1990.

14. For coverage of congressional action on these bills, see relevant issues of *Congressional Quarterly Weekly Report*.

15. See among others, Francis J. McNeil, "Reassessing the U.S.-Japan Security Relationship in the Post–Cold War Context," a report prepared for the Commission on U.S.-Japan Relations for the Twenty-First Century. (Washington, DC: Commission on U.S.-Japan Relations for the Twenty-First Century, May 1991).

16. See coverage of the controversy in *Congressional Quarterly Weekly Report* for this period.

17. See, among others, Watts, *America and Japan*.

18. Among the good recent works on Japanese politics, see Gerald Curtis, *The Japanese Way of Politics* (New York: Columbia University Press, 1988).

19. Detailed coverage of the elections, scandals and political development was provided weekly by the *Far Eastern Economic Review*.

20. See, among others, Kazu Kato. "Japan and the Environment," *Environment* 31 (July–August 1989), pp. 4–5.

21. Some recent reviews include James Tobin. "The Adam Smith Address: On Living and Trading with Japan: U.S. Commercial and Macroeconomic Policies," *Business Economics* 26 (January 1991), pp. 5–16; David Halberstram. "Coming from the Cold War," *Washington Monthly* 23 (January–February 1991), pp. 30–37; Karel Van Wolfren. "The Japan Problem Revisited," *Foreign Affairs* 69 (Fall 1990), pp. 42–55.

22. For a more recent articulation of the U.S. administration's view, see Richard Solomon. "Asian Security in the 1990s: Integration in Economics, Diversity in Defense," *U.S. Department of State Dispatch* (November 5, 1990), pp. 243–248.

4

U.S.-Chinese Relations in Adversity

There were grounds for optimism in assessing the course of Sino-American relations in the late 1980s, before the upheavals caused by the unprecedented pro-democracy demonstrations and the brutal crackdown in mid-1989. The strategic dimension of the relationship, involving close Sino-American collaboration in opposition to Soviet expansion during the 1970s and early 1980s, diminished considerably in importance as both Soviet-American and Sino-Soviet tensions eased. Yet Chinese-American relations were seen as playing a strategically important role in an emerging multipolar world. The superpowers, the United States and the Soviet Union, were expected to remain at odds and slowly to decline in power relative to other parts of the world. They were thought to be particularly interested in working closely with China and other newly emerging centers of world power (i.e., Western Europe and Japan).[1]

China's ongoing economic reform attracted increasing attention and support from developed countries and from the international financial institutions supported by them. Beijing looked forward to fruitful economic interaction, technology transfer, and training in China's relations with the United States and other Western-aligned countries. Easing Sino-Soviet tensions also opened prospects for broader economic cooperation with the Soviet bloc.

U.S. policymakers pursued the steady development of a multifaceted relationship with China. Trade ties grew to an annual turnover of $13 billion in 1988. Aside from Hong Kong, the United States was China's most important source of investment. Political ties continued to grow with frequent high-level official visits, including representatives of the United States and the Chinese armed forces. U.S. technology transfer to China was an important element in Chinese modernization plans, and there were 40,000 students from China studying at U.S. universities.[2]

The Tiananmen Square massacre and subsequent Chinese government efforts to exert tighter control over political and economic developments in China repelled American leaders and public. U.S. government reaction in the form of official criticisms and limited sanctions prompted strong Chinese government protests. Many observers in the United States and China saw prospects of a downward spiral in relations, despite extraordinary effort by the administration of President George Bush in sending two high-level missions to discuss matters with Deng Xiaoping and other senior Chinese leaders in July and December 1989.

As far as China was concerned, the basic question determining future Sino-American relations centered on whether China would persist in its previously internationally oriented development strategy or would revert to a much more narrowly circumscribed relationship with the outside world, including the United States. For the United States, the question focused on how to strike an appropriate balance in suspending ties, issuing critical statements, and otherwise showing disapproval for Chinese reversal of reforms, while sustaining U.S. interests in continuing relations with China. The answer to these questions was complicated by domestic factors, including partisan and leadership politics in both Beijing and Washington, and by a range of international factors including the radical shifts in the policies of the Soviet Union and the East European countries.

By mid-1990, there was a distinct possibility that Sino-American relations might fall to a new low as a result of a U.S. refusal to renew most-favored-nation (MFN) tariff treatment for Chinese imports and Beijing's warnings of probable Chinese retaliation. But the leaders of both sides, although circumscribed by circumstances, were anxious to sustain a basic framework of relations that would serve their respective interests. Chinese leaders still regarded relations with the United States as a critical element in their efforts to modernize China. And American leaders were reluctant to allow their revulsion with the Tiananmen massacre to isolate China in ways that could jeopardize stability in Asia and a hoped-for revival of reform in China.

Events in late 1990 and early 1991 underlined a moderating trend in relations. Without significant U.S. opposition, Japan announced in June 1990 that it would incrementally implement a large new loan program for China—beginning a trend followed by the World Bank and other international financial institutions. China appeared to be playing a constructive role in promoting a U.N. peace plan for Cambodia, and China's explicit or implicit sanction of efforts in the U.N. Security Council to secure support for the U.S.-led effort to reverse Iraq's invasion of Kuwait was especially noted by U.S. leaders. Congress allowed to stand President Bush's May 1990 waiver granting MFN treatment for Chinese imports, and there was little hostile reaction to President Bush's resumption of high-level exchanges during his meeting with the Chinese foreign minister in the White House in late 1990. With the conclusion of the Persian Gulf war, however, came an upsurge in an array of contentious issues regarding U.S. policy toward China. These issues grew toward a crescendo in mid-1991, coincident with the president's annual waiver granting MFN trade status to China and congressional deliberations over the president's action. Observers generally agreed that withdrawal of MFN status for China would represent a major further downturn in U.S. relations with China. Few could predict definitively what the outcome for U.S. policy would be.

New Challenges for Chinese Policy

The events in China that led to the Tiananmen Square massacre and the subsequent political crackdown and economic retrenchment vividly demonstrated the fault lines that ran through the Chinese leadership over a range of sensitive domestic and foreign policy questions, including relations with the United States.

Officials in Beijing who made the decision to suppress dissent forcefully recognized that much of the noncommunist world would react negatively. And they almost certainly expected some negative reactions to the intensification of China's concurrent economic retrenchment. Available evidence suggests that party leaders believed that their continued political control required such harsh measures; and at least some of them believed that sharp negative reactions from the West and elsewhere would pass without long-term consequences for China.[3] Perhaps this prediction would have come true in late 1989 if world conditions had not changed. But events in Eastern Europe and the Soviet Union upset this Chinese calculus. The dramatic changes in the Soviet bloc had a ripple effect in China. They encouraged pro-democracy forces and alarmed Chinese leaders who grew even more determined to maintain the party's monopoly of power. In addition, developments in the Soviet bloc abruptly ended hopes that Chinese leaders could avoid the "spiritual pollution" of pro-democracy ideas by expanding economic-technical contacts with the then communist-ruled European countries. By the early 1990s, the political ideas coming from Eastern Europe appeared more directly challenging to the political status quo in China than the ideas from the West.

Finally, changes in the Soviet bloc also attracted positive attention from the developed countries of the West and Japan, including the international financial institutions and businesses associated with them or located there. Thus, China's crackdown alienated foreign interests and capital; at the same time, the seemingly positive developments in Eastern Europe served as a magnet to attract these resources toward Eastern Europe and the Soviet Union.

Shifts in Global Politics

On the plane of world politics, the events of 1989-1990 began significantly to alter the balance of world forces that had been reasonably satisfactory for China, especially over the past ten years. Heretofore, the Chinese worldview had been premised on an international order heavily influenced by U.S.-Soviet competition. Because of their rivalry, the superpowers would spend resources on weapons, foreign bases, and foreign interventions that would weaken their power relative to newly rising centers of world power like Japan, the European Community, and China.

Given China's size, its strategic location, its armed forces possessing nuclear weapons, and its demonstrated willingness to use force to pursue its world interests, many observers at home and abroad saw China as holding a key position in world politics. It was one corner of the "strategic triangle" in U.S.-Soviet-Chinese relations—a critical balancing force between the United States and the Soviet Union. As such, policymakers in Washington and Moscow paid close attention to Chinese policies. Of course, the zero-sum quality of U.S.-Soviet-Chinese relations varied over time; by the late 1980's, for example, policymakers in Washington appeared confident that the slowly emerging Sino-Soviet détente would have no major deleterious effects on U.S. interests. But the fact remained that U.S.—and presumably Soviet—policymakers continued to pay close attention to how China's policy affected U.S.-Soviet competition for world influence.

By the early 1990s, however, relations between the U.S. and the Soviet Union had changed to such a degree that observers in China and elsewhere could no longer safely assume that the U.S.-Soviet rivalry would continue as an overriding international fact. Because of events in Eastern Europe and the Soviet Union, it was becoming increasingly apparent to Western leaders that the Soviet Union was unlikely to pose a major threat to the West for some time. Even though there remained a persistent danger of the reversal of Soviet policies should Soviet president Mikhail Gorbachev be toppled or under other possible circumstances, it seemed likely that the United States and its allies would find the Soviet policies more accommodating than confrontational: U.S. interest might well be better served by encouraging the accommodating Soviet policies.

Thus the dynamics of U.S.-Soviet rivalry so central to China's worldview were in the process of fundamental change. In the past, Chinese officials had portrayed U.S.-Soviet collaboration as coming at the expense of lesser powers, especially those in the Third World, including China—a concern that appeared to be reflected in recent Chinese media coverage.[4] At a time of rapidly improving U.S.-Soviet relations, both powers would probably see that their interests would be best served by avoiding any actions with countries of lesser importance (including China) that could complicate the improvement in East-West relations.

U.S.-Soviet Collaboration in Asia

Under these circumstances, both Moscow and Washington saw their interests well served by mutual accommodation in dealing with international trouble spots. In Asia, these trouble spots included Afghanistan, Cambodia, and Korea. Both sides showed interest in cooperating or working in parallel in order to ease tensions or settle conflicts in these areas.

From China's perspective, such U.S. collaboration with Moscow signaled a fundamental change in the common strategic orientation that had bound Sino-American relations since the rapprochement between Chairman Mao Zedong and President Richard Nixon. Despite their differences over a wide range of issues, China and the United States had reached common ground in the early 1970s on their fundamental opposition to Soviet expansion in Asia. This common Sino-American understanding continued with varying degrees of intensity for two decades. As the Soviet threat to both China and the United States appeared to diminish in the 1980s, both sides adjusted their policies accordingly, but kept in close touch about their respective and often parallel policies vis-à-vis the Soviet Union. Indeed, the December 9–10, 1989, trip to China by National Security Adviser Brent Scowcroft was initially described as one in a long series of U.S. efforts to keep Chinese leaders fully informed about Soviet policies as seen in the series of U.S.-Soviet arms control and summit negotiations.

Concurrent with the recent downturn in Sino-American relations, the events in Eastern Europe and the Soviet Union and resulting changes in Soviet policy challenged the anti-Soviet basis of Sino-American policy in Asia.

Beijing's Response

As Beijing faced these challenges, some U.S. officials warned of possible dire consequences for future Chinese policy toward the United States and elsewhere if the United States reacted too strongly to China's political repression and economic retrenchment. They warned particularly that Beijing might revert to its former policies of self-imposed isolation in the interest of sustaining communist party control.[5] But more moderate U.S. views gained ground as Chinese leaders seemed to be placing limits on how far they would go to reverse the generally moderate foreign policies of recent years, including China's policy toward the United States.[6] Limits were seen in several areas.

First, much of the basic framework that had governed Chinese foreign policy in the post-Mao period remained intact. Chinese leaders continued to place priority on promoting China's wealth and power. Economic development still represented a linchpin, determining their political success or failure. They did not have the prestige of Mao, who could ignore development needs in pursuit of ideological or political goals. These officials had to produce concrete results in order to stay in power. And all policies, including foreign policy, had to serve this goal. Foreign policy helped to maintain a stable security environment around China's periphery and to promote advantageous economic exchanges. The continuation of this basic framework suggested that China was not looking for trouble, but for help.

Second, broad international trends supported a continuation of moderation in Chinese foreign policy in general and policy toward the United States in particular: (1) China's leaders were aware of their need to focus on economic development and to pursue open interaction with the world in order to achieve that goal; they knew of the accomplishments of Japan and many other noncommunist East Asian states, and the negative development experiences of the rigid communist regimes in North Korea and Vietnam. (2) Despite sanctions enacted by the West and Japan, the noncommunist world, especially the countries of East Asia, made it clear that they had no intention of isolating China. (3) Soviet bloc changes meant that China could not turn to these countries for economic development support if Beijing decided to cut back economic interchange with the West.

Third, internal factors and trends called for moderation. The Chinese leadership appeared divided and in transition from one generation to another. Making significant changes in foreign policy in most areas remained sensitive politically. Past periods of similar leadership transition (e.g., 1973–1975, 1976–1978) did not see marked changes in foreign policy. Leaders who actively promoted reform, interaction with the world, and cooperation with the West were relatively quiet, but they had not been removed from power. Even so-called hardliners had proven records of relatively moderate foreign policies and related defense and domestic policies. Few appeared to favor a return to the policies of isolation, autarky, or Stalinist control that were tried unsuccessfully in the past.

Finally, the evidence of Beijing's post-Tiananmen foreign policies did not suggest a radical shift. Even the results of the economic retrenchment and political repression policies were mixed. Foreign trade and investment continued to grow, although at a less rapid rate than before the Tiananmen incident. Thousands of American and other foreign experts continued to be invited to work with the Chinese in China. The *New York Times* reported that 7,000 Chinese students came to the United States between July 1989 and January 1990.[7] Although Beijing put stricter limits on Chinese students going abroad, older Chinese or those assumed to be more likely to return to China after training continued to go abroad.

In sum, Beijing's leaders almost certainly felt beleaguered in the face of international criticism and sanctions and in response to the rapid changes in Eastern Europe and the Soviet Union. Chinese leaders were cautious in reply to their international predicament. They avoided unduly harsh responses to foreign criticism and took few tangible steps in reaction to world trends that appeared to jeopardize their basic interests. Behind China's moderation lay a complicated policy equation that saw little room for significant Chinese initiatives to improve U.S.-PRC relations.

Chinese Policy

The party and government leadership remained at an impasse over a variety of sensitive policy issues, belying an appearance of calm. Central leaders managing day-to-day affairs were hesitant or unable to show much initiative or vision regarding China's future course—a pattern reflecting the conflicting views of China's policies held by the ostensibly retired senior leaders who still wielded strong power and influence. In one view, the central officials were marking time, waiting for the seemingly inevitable competition for power and political shakeup that would occur once the octogenarian Deng Xiaoping and his contemporaries passed from the scene. In the meantime, the consensus in support of "stability" caused Chinese leaders to avoid dealing with the case of disgraced party chairman Zhao Ziyang, to avoid major leadership shifts, and to be certain that needed new appointments to the central leadership reflected a careful balance of the conservative and reformist views often at loggerheads in Beijing.[8]

Similarly, the cases of dissidents arrested after the Tiananmen massacre were handled in a way that reflected a muddled picture that resulted from conflicting reformist and conservative trends. Thus, prominent dissident Fang Lizhi was allowed to leave the U.S. embassy for exile abroad; others were tried in court proceedings in early 1991, coincident with the diversion of world attention to the Persian Gulf war. Some were treated leniently, according to Chinese spokespersons; but some received long sentences. The military achieved new prominence and gained a greater share of government resources, but its leaders were divided over the appropriate role of the army. The results of the Persian Gulf war underlined the importance of technology and training in the modern battlefield and reinforced those Chinese military leaders who warned that Maoist-oriented traditions in the army caused China to fall increasingly further behind in international security matters. Some in the military and other conservatives attempted—with little apparent effect—to use a revival of Maoist orthodoxy to fill the ideological vacuum caused by the Tiananmen massacre and worldwide decline of authoritarian Marxist regimes.

The weak and divided central government was unable to control the social and economic changes affecting coastal regions and other parts of China in close contact with the rest of the world. Dependent on revenue coming from these areas and judging that the "open door" to outside economic, technical, and other exchanges were essential to China's future, even conservative central leaders were forced to modify earlier efforts to restore centralized economic controls and to allow economic reforms to continue at varying paces. The primary emphasis on stability also caused central leaders to opt for an economic program of only moderate growth and incremental changes to the inefficient state industrial sector, which served as a serious impediment to growth and a major recipient of inefficient government expenditure.

The Chinese had more success in dealing with foreign relations around their periphery in Asia. In general, Asian neighbors pragmatically assessed China's size, strategic location, certain comparative economic advantages, and its leadership's desire to avoid additional problems abroad at a time of protracted domestic difficulties. They generally viewed the Chinese crackdown after the Tiananmen incident more as a symptom of a long repressive Chinese political system, which they must nonetheless deal with, rather than as a major turning point in Chinese behavior requiring strong countermeasures by them. Thus, they were inclined to respond in kind to China's overtures for good relations.

International financial institutions also took a pragmatic view toward China, seeing Beijing's continued economic reform efforts, its willingness and ability to pay off debts, and its continued open door economic policies as encouraging signs warranting continued outside support. China's seat on the U.N. Security Council gave Beijing a major forum in which to play a constructive international role on major issues involving the Persian Gulf war and the conflict in Cambodia—developments that added to the incentive by the United States and others to resume high-level political exchanges with China.

Despite the progress, Beijing leaders showed considerable angst about foreign affairs. In particular, China had worked for many years to establish an important role in the Persian Gulf, not only as an important arms supplier, but also as the only major power having good relations with all major contending parties in the region. Although Chinese diplomats attempted to carve an independent role for China during the Persian Gulf confrontation of 1990–1991, it was clear that China's role and importance were pushed aside by the flow of events dominated by the U.S.-led international coalition. The U.S. success and the concurrent rapid decline of Soviet power and influence in world affairs were also the sources of a broader Chinese concern as to how the United States would use its newly apparent power. Chinese commentators were divided on this issue, with some urging Beijing to work closely with other states to create means with which to balance America's enhanced power. Some in China judged that the U.S. would use its power to interfere in Chinese affairs and to press for political and economic change in China. Amid the fears of American "hegemonism" and "power politics" voiced by some in China, it was not surprising that Beijing showed few signs of taking substantial initiatives that would markedly improve U.S.-Chinese relations.

U.S. Policy

While Chinese leaders were preoccupied with internal control and adverse international trends, the initiative in Sino-American relations passed to the United States after mid-1989. President Bush succeeded initially in preserving a general U.S. consensus about China policy when he announced on June 5, 1989, the steps the United States would take in response to the Tiananmen incident. The president ordered the suspension of all government-to-government sales and commercial exports of weapons; the suspension of visits between U.S. and Chinese military leaders; and the sympathetic review of requests by Chinese students in the United States to extend their stay, among other measures.

On June 30, 1989, the president took the additional steps of directing that the U.S. government suspend participation in all high-level exchanges of government officials with China and directing that American representatives at various international financial institutions seek to postpone consideration of new loans for China.[9]

Reflecting the strong reaction by U.S. public opinion, media, and human rights organizations against China's leaders after the Tiananmen incident, many members of Congress pressed for harsher measures against China. As debate continued into the summer of 1989, however, it became clear that congressional legislation on sanctions against China would leave the president considerable room to maneuver. A lengthy amendment to the State Department authorization bill, which the Senate passed in late July, codified the sanctions against China already imposed by the president and added the following actions: it suspended new programs to guarantee U.S. investments in China; suspended export licenses for U.S. satellites scheduled for launch on Chinese launch vehicles; suspended peaceful nuclear cooperation with China; and required the president to negotiate with the Coordinating Committee for Multilateral Export Controls (CoCom) to suspend the further liberalization of export controls on technology for

China. The bill provided enough waiver authority to make it acceptable to the administration. Meanwhile, in July and August, the House and the Senate respectively passed the Emergency Chinese Immigration Relief Act (H.R. 2712), which would have made it possible for Chinese students in the United States to extend their stays for up to four years.

The Bush administration and many in Congress privately pressed the Chinese authorities to take actions that would improve the strained atmosphere in Sino-American relations. Suggested steps included easing martial law in Beijing; showing greater flexibility in the case of dissident Fang Lizhi; allowing U.S. Fulbright professors to resume work in China; halting the periodic jamming of Voice of America (VOA) broadcasts to China; and allowing the U.S. Peace Corps to begin its volunteer program in China. As gestures to China in the interest of preserving U.S.-Chinese relations, in late July 1989, the administration granted waivers to' the suspension of military sales to allow the sale of four Boeing commercial jets with navigation systems that could be converted to military use. In October 1989, the administration permitted Chinese military officers to return to work at U.S. facilities where they had been assisting U.S. engineers in upgrading China's F-8 fighter with American avionics. On November 30, the president announced that he would pocket veto the Emergency Chinese Immigration Relief Act, maintaining that the bill was unnecessary because he was ordering into practice many of its provisions.

Although there was considerable grumbling in Congress and the media over the president's "soft" approach to China, the debate over China policy reached a fever pitch after the December 9–10, 1989, visit to Beijing by a U.S. delegation led by National Security Adviser Scowcroft and the disclosure a few days later that a similar U.S. delegation had secretly visited Beijing in July 1989. The administration mustered several arguments for its initiatives, but critics in Congress, the media, and elsewhere denounced the president's actions and asked Congress to take stronger action when it convened in late January 1990. Despite the storm of criticism, President Bush continued his moderate approach during December. On December 19, he waived restrictions prohibiting export licenses for three U.S. communications satellites to be launched on Chinese launch vehicles, and he announced that he would not impose the new restrictions on Export-Import Bank funding for China that Congress had enacted earlier.

As Congress prepared to reconvene in late January 1990, amid a chorus of media comment calling for tougher action against China, it was clear that the president had miscalculated and would have to adjust his policies. For one reason, Chinese leaders had proven unable or unwilling to make gestures to the United States that were seen to be of sufficient importance to justify the president's actions. The Chinese promised not to sell medium-range ballistic missiles to any Middle East countries, but this was widely seen as a repetition of previous promises. By late February, President Bush personally expressed disappointment with China's response.[10]

It was also clear that changes in international politics and U.S. domestic politics had restricted the president's flexibility in foreign affairs in general and toward China in particular. He would have much greater difficulty than previous presidents in arguing for secret diplomacy, special treatment, or other exemptions that had marked U.S. treatment of China since Secretary of State Henry Kissinger's secret trip in July 1971.

U.S. legislators like the people they represent, traditionally place a strong emphasis on morality or values as well as realpolitik or national interest in American foreign policy. The Tiananmen massacre sharply changed American views about China.[11] The leaders in Beijing now were widely seen as pursuing practices opposed to American values. They were deemed to be unworthy of American support. Rapidly changing U.S.-Soviet relations undercut the realpolitik or national security rationale for close U.S.-Chinese relations. Thus, U.S. policy became heavily influenced by the widespread revulsion with Beijing's leaders and their repressive policies.

Adding impetus to this trend were political, economic and security changes in other parts of the world that attracted wide and generally positive attention from the American people, the media, interest groups, and legislators. Eastern Europe and the Soviet Union were increasingly following policies of political and economic reform based on the values of individual freedom, political democracy, and economic free enterprise. U.S. officials were pushed by popular U.S. opinion and other forces to be more forthcoming in negotiations and interaction with their East European and Soviet counterparts with regard to arms control, trade, foreign assistance, and other matters.

The importance of this shift in domestic U.S. opinion regarding China and the Soviet bloc countries appeared to be particularly important at this time. In the past, the executive branch had been able to argue (on many occasions quite persuasively) that domestic concerns about common values should not be permitted to override or seriously complicate U.S. realpolitik interests in the protracted struggle and rivalry with the Soviet Union. Now that the Cold War was ending and the threat from the Soviet Union was greatly reduced, the ability of the executive branch to control the course of U.S. foreign policy appeared somewhat weakened. The administration could no longer argue that the dangers of Cold War confrontation required a tightly controlled foreign policy. It had to take greater account of U.S. domestic opinion, as a result.

Partisan politics also complicated President Bush's ability to sustain a more moderate policy toward China. Partisan opponents seemed anxious to portray the president and his Republican backers as more sympathetic to the "butchers of Beijing" than to Chinese students and other pro-democracy advocates. Ironically, it appeared to be partisan politics that allowed the president to avoid an embarrassing defeat at the hands of the Democrat-controlled Congress, which took up the proposed override of the president's veto of the Chinese immigration measure as its first order of business in January 1990. By arguing for support for the Republican president from wavering Republican senators in the face of a barrage of often partisan criticism from Democrats, White House lobbyists were able to gain enough votes to sustain the president's veto on January 25, 1990.[12]

The unanticipated defeat of the Democratic leadership's override effort had a sobering effect. During the winter and spring of 1990, congressional leaders did not go out of their way to challenge the president's China policy as long as President Bush avoided major initiatives or exceptions in dealing with China. In February 1990, the president signed the State Department authorization bill that contained a version of the sanctions language passed by Congress the previous summer, and the administration delivered a hard-hitting report on conditions in China as part of its annual human rights report to Congress.

More notably, the administration adopted a low public profile on what was expected to be a major issue of controversy—the annual waiver of provisions under the Jackson-Vanik Amendment of the Trade Act.[13] The waiver is required for Chinese goods to receive MFN tariff treatment by the United States. Loss of MFN status would lead to immediate heavy duties on China's $12 billion annual exports to U.S. markets—in effect, closing much of the U.S. market to Chinese goods. The last waiver was granted in late May 1989, and the 1990 waiver was due by June 3—coincident with the first anniversary of the Tiananmen pro-democracy demonstrations and the subsequent crackdown.

Congress, the media, and various human rights groups were widely expected to attack any early administration decision to grant a waiver for China. Faced with this likelihood, the administration delayed; U.S. officials refused many opportunities to stake out a position on the issue and refused to appear at public forums addressing the question. This had the effect of forcing Congress, the media, and interest groups to address the issue themselves. After deliberations, many critics of Bush administration policy toward China nonetheless came out in favor of granting, with appropriate conditions, MFN treatment for Chinese exports.

In the following year, several basic factors characterized the American posture toward China:

- Over much of 1990–1991, policy toward China generally did not get high priority. American policymakers were preoccupied with developments in the Middle East and Soviet Union, and with pressing domestic issues.
- There appeared to be little incentive for forward movement in U.S. relations with China. In the United States, there was an array of critics with a seemingly ever lengthier bill of particulars against China. Also, there was no assurance that Chinese leaders had the power or inclination to respond positively to possible U.S. overtures. In fact, it was possible that Beijing would respond in such a way as to embarrass Americans taking such initiatives or otherwise promoting better relations.
- Some Americans emphasized the role China would play in the U.N. Security Council and elsewhere as an important actor in the new world order; and others stressed the long-term importance of China to major American security and economic interests in Asia. But these views often were overtaken by Americans concerned with Chinese practices that offended U.S. moral sensibilities on human rights, disturbed U.S. interest in checking proliferation of nuclear weapons technology and missile systems, and appeared to take unfair economic advantage of trade with the United States.

The Importance of President Bush

In this muddled climate, the main reason U.S. China policy did not stagnate and decline further had to do with President Bush. Following the Tiananmen massacre, President Bush, supported by his aides in the National Security Council, took the lead in formulating the U.S. response to the crisis. The president took charge personally in dealing with various issues during the next two years. He strove hard to maintain a balanced policy that would allow for continued U.S. involvement with the people and leaders of China.

Available evidence suggests strongly that the president relied on his own best judgments on how to proceed, based on his long experience with China and his well thought out views on the future of China and U.S.-Chinese relations.[14] Staff support for the president came mainly from the National Security Council. The president was also in close touch with his good friend and Chinese affairs adviser, James Lilley, U.S. ambassador to Beijing. The president's wife, Barbara, whom he repeatedly noted had spent more time in China than he had, almost certainly played an important role as confidant.

In the crisis atmosphere of 1989–1990, the president appeared to judge that it was important to narrow sharply the circle of officials who would manage U.S. policy toward China. In part, this was because the president was attempting to strike a difficult balance in U.S. policy. On the one hand, he was attempting to elicit positive gestures from Beijing's beleaguered leaders in the wake of the Tiananmen incident. On the other hand, he was attempting to avoid what he judged were overly punitive and counterproductive U.S. measures against China, which were being pressed on the administration by U.S. leaders in the Congress, the media, and elsewhere. In order to avoid sending the "wrong signal" to Beijing or to domestic U.S. constituencies, the president and his White House staff decided to keep tight reign on policy. Most notably, the president and his close advisers planned and executed two high-level missions to Beijing without the knowledge of most U.S. officials, and they took steps to ensure that State Department and other U.S. officials avoided comment on the most sensitive policy issue of 1990—the extension of most-favored-nation tariff treatment to China. Moreover, by holding a tight reign on policy, the president and his aides were well positioned to adjust U.S. policy should circumstances change in China or the United States.

By mid-1991, however, it was clear that the president's policy efforts had not stilled congressional debate or restored a consensus on U.S. China policy. President Bush still labored under the misperception in many quarters that he was less interested than others in human rights in China, was overly attentive to the interests of Chinese leaders, and stressed excessively China's alleged strategic importance for the United States. The common misperceptions of the president's intentions on China policy appeared likely to remain an obstacle to the formulation and execution of an effective U.S. China policy for sometime to come.

President Bush's determination to maintain firm personal control of U.S. China policy following the Tiananmen incident appeared to be rooted in his repeated affirmation that he "knows" China, is able to deal effectively with Chinese leaders, and has a proper perspective on U.S. policy toward China. In contrast, U.S. critics of the president took issue with these claims.[15] They repeatedly asserted that the president did not have a vision of future U.S. policy toward China that took into account the new realities of the post–Cold War environment and the greater importance of human rights in American foreign policy. Other charges focused on the president for allegedly being heavily influenced by advisers like Brent Scowcroft and Lawrence Eagleburger, who led the two secret U.S. missions to Beijing in 1989. Those officials were said by some critics to share views of China associated with former secretary of state Henry Kissinger that allegedly overemphasized China's strategic and economic importance and soft-pedaled U.S. interests in Chinese human rights and political reform. Behind such accusations lay broader charges regarding the president's alleged tendency to be swayed by public opinion polls, his reported proclivity to be flexible and to make compromises in order to preserve a smooth foreign policy, and his alleged reluctance to fight for the sake of principle.

What must have been particularly frustrating for the president was the fact that the public record showed that most of these criticisms were far from the mark. Thus, a careful review of publicly available White House documents shows that President Bush at the outset of his administration carefully laid out clearly the broad outlines of his administration's China policy.[16] He notably used the occasion of his February 1989 state visit to China to offer repeated and often personal reflections on the future course of U.S.-Chinese relations. At that time, the president saw the prospect of a gradually changing China—a communist nation whose growing economic and other interaction with the United States and the developed world would eventually and inevitably lead to greater economic benefit, political benefit, and improved human rights conditions for the people of China. The president judged that it was very important for the United States to be involved constructively with this process of change. This assessment was due to his view of China's size, location and strategic importance to world affairs, and of its economic potential. He judged that there were likely to be continued serious Sino-American disputes because of the wide differences in respective political, economic, and social systems. But he averred that U.S. engagement should continue, despite such inevitable differences and difficulties.

In contrast, U.S. press coverage of the president's visit highlighted two issues and virtually ignored the president's exposition of a comprehensive U.S. policy.[17] On the one hand, the visit was widely held in press coverage to be a thinly disguised U.S. effort to assess Chinese intentions and solidify U.S.-PRC relations prior to the April 1989 visit of Soviet leader Gorbachev to Beijing. The president's repeated denials in the face of press queries about the United States being interested in playing the "China card" during the visit were often interpreted as reflecting alleged concern in the administration over the thaw in Sino-Soviet ties. By far the highlight of U.S. press coverage of the trip, however, was the incident that occurred when Chinese security forces prevented the leading Chinese dissident, Fang Lizhi, from attending a U.S. embassy reception for the president, to which he had been invited. Some press coverage emphasized that President Bush was less than firm in complaining about the security forces' actions. It alleged that the president's longstanding personal ties with Chinese leaders, going back to his days as head of the U.S. liaison office in Beijing in the mid-1970s, curbed his willingness to complain about such high-handed Chinese actions. Pointed out in this regard was the fact that Chinese leader Deng Xiaoping had openly favored Bush over his Democratic challenger in the 1988 presidential elections.

To be fair, it is important to note that the president's actions and statements in Beijing could have given the impression to the press that he was not prepared to push strongly bilateral differences with Chinese leaders. President Bush repeatedly characterized the visit as a sort of sentimental journey. He noted that it was the fifth time he had returned since leaving as liaison office chief in the mid-1970s, and that his wife, Barbara, had returned six times since then. On several occasions he referred warmly to events that marked his stay in China during the 1970s, noting repeatedly that his daughter had been baptized in China. But the president also used the occasion of his visit to his former congregation in Beijing to press his case for the gradual improvement of human rights in China, and his keynote speech to the Chinese nation also emphasized this theme. The president's interest in this issue was underlined by the fact that Fang Lizhi was only one of several Chinese dissidents who were invited and some of whom actually attended the president's reception in Beijing.

The president's statements in China also took due account of the rapidly changing world order and the role of U.S.-Soviet-Chinese relations in that order. China was not seen as an important lever against Soviet power. According to the president, it was important because of its size, location, and potential impact on world development in a host of areas. In effect, the president's statements in this regard attempted to move U.S. policy away from a myopic view of China's strategic importance against the USSR to one that took account of recent trends of East-West and Sino-Soviet accommodation and served U.S. interests in an emerging world order.

Subsequently, despite all the turmoil in China and in the United States over U.S.-China policy following the Tiananmen massacre, President Bush remained steadfast in support of his vision of U.S. China policy. Critical American commentators often interpreted the president's actions as reflecting the president's insensitivity to human rights concerns, his overemphasis on China's strategic importance, and his misguided reliance on personal relations with Chinese leaders. In retrospect, a more balanced view would see that the president was consistent in his determination to see that the United States remained involved in China for the sake of human progress there; and that while China's strategic and economic importance to the United States was temporarily in decline because of the East-West détente and economic and political disruption in China, the PRC, because of a variety of geographic, demographic, and other reasons, was of long-term strategic importance to U.S. interests.

U.S. Policy Debate, 1990-1991

The storm of controversy that greeted the July and December 1989 high-level U.S. missions to Beijing caused the president and his close advisers to adjust their approach to China. Beijing leaders appeared too divided or otherwise unwilling to come up with responses to high-profile U.S. initiatives that would be sufficiently positive to justify those initiatives to American opinion. As a result, the U.S. administration appeared to lower its expectations, presumably hoping to preserve the basic framework of relations, to encourage a slow improvement over time, and to position the United States to deal effectively with the new generation of leaders likely to emerge in China during the next few years.

Events in 1990 worked to support this approach. Chinese leaders came up with a few positive gestures in mid-year, notably the release of Fang Lizhi, that appeared to justify a slow improvement in U.S. relations with China. Japan announced that it would incrementally resume its aid program in China, and the World Bank and Asian Development Bank also moved forward with their programs in China. In August came the announcement of the U.N.-backed peace plan for Cambodia, which provoked repeated U.S. statements concerning China's "constructive role." Iraq's invasion of Kuwait focused U.S. strategy on the U.N. Security Council, where China's veto power loomed large in American calculations.

Congressional critics of President Bush's decision in mid-1990 to grant the annual waiver allowing China to continue to receive MFN status were able to muster enough support in the House to vote to disapprove the extension of MFN in the waning days of the 101st Congress. But many saw the House action as mainly symbolic in importance, inasmuch as there was almost no likelihood that the Senate would take action on the measure in the last days of the session and during the Gulf crisis.[18]

Further signs of improved Sino-U.S. relations included Chinese foreign minister Qian Qichen's meetings with President Bush and Secretary Baker in October 1990. Qian also met with congressional officials. Reports of the meetings averred that congressional members were more cordial in greeting the Chinese envoy than was the president, who reportedly focused on differences on human rights questions, among others.[19] Congressional members also visited China during this period.

The broader relationship stimulated continued growth of Sino-U.S. trade, but Chinese restrictions on imports gave rise to a rapidly growing U.S. trade deficit ($10 billion in 1990) with China. About half of the economic sanctions adopted in 1989 remained in effect. China was ineligible for investment guarantees through the Overseas Private Investment Corporation (OPIC) or for concessional trade financing through the Trade Development Program. A nuclear safety cooperation program and the process for liberalizing U.S. controls on technology transfer were frozen. On the other hand, contrary to earlier sanctions, the administration had renewed China's eligibility for Export-Import Bank financing and American satellites were allowed to be launched on Chinese rockets. American tourism and investment in China both were recovering slowly from the sharp drop in the period following the Tiananmen massacre. Sino-American cultural relations followed a similar pattern. Most formal programs that were suspended by the United States were restored, although some were operating at a lower level than might have been expected. American public and leadership opinion appeared more inclined to move ahead in selected ways with China than to add to U.S. restrictions on interchange with China.

The Spring 1991 Crisis

In early 1991 there appeared to be little need for the president or senior leaders of the administration to devote significant attention to China policy. President Bush had emerged from the Persian Gulf war with overwhelming approval ratings, especially regarding his handling of foreign affairs. As far as China was concerned, the United States appeared likely to follow along with the other developed countries and the international financial institutions—slowly and incrementally improving relations with China. There appeared to be little to be gained from more dramatic U.S. initiatives toward China, whose leaders seemed unable or unwilling to respond commensurately.

The Bush administration did follow its meetings with Foreign Minister Qian by arranging for Assistant Secretary of State for Human Rights Affairs Richard Schifter to travel to China for talks in December 1990. And a senior State Department arms control specialist was slated to visit China sometime in 1991. Assistant Secretary of State Richard Solomon traveled to China in March 1991 to discuss the peace process regarding Cambodia, Middle East arms control, and other issues. Yet, the United States still did not seem ready to resume past high-level exchanges between the U.S. Commerce and Treasury secretaries and their Chinese counterparts, which used to take place annually in the past. In addition, as noted earlier, President Bush reportedly stressed human rights issues in his talks in October 1990 with Foreign Minister Qian; Assistant Secretary Schifter's visit focused on this question; and the State Department was firm on the issue in its annual human rights report released in early 1991.[20]

The situation began to change markedly during spring 1991 as U.S. critics of Chinese government behavior and Bush administration policy toward China renewed their attacks, especially in the media and in Congress. As with most Americans, the critics had focused throughout late 1990 and early 1991 on the dramatic confrontation in the Persian Gulf. The ending of the Gulf war reduced the salience of the argument that China's importance in the U.N. Security Council and its willingness to go along with U.S. leadership in the Gulf crisis pointed to a U.S. need to soft-pedal some differences with China in order to stay on reasonably good terms with the Beijing regime. Meanwhile, disclosures of Chinese policy actions in sensitive areas of human rights, trade policy, and arms sales/nuclear proliferation fed a building storm of criticism focused on the annual U.S. granting of MFN status to Chinese imports. The critics urged strong and wide-ranging conditions on, or a cut off of, this substantial American trade benefit to China. Supporters of MFN argued that such measures would harm innocent parties (e.g., the Hong Kong economy would be seriously affected), would undermine the power of those reformers in China urging greater contact with the outside world, and would lead to Chinese retaliation likely to put U.S.-Chinese relations into tailspin.

Apart from Beijing's continued suppression of human rights, the most important developments provoking renewed calls for curbing China's MFN status included the following:

- *U.S. trade deficit with China.* The deficit appeared to arise from deliberate Chinese decisions to restrict imports, especially from the United States, and to encourage exports to the United States. Part of the trade deficit was caused by China's reported infringement on U.S. copyrights and patents and its illegal export of textiles to the United States via third party countries. The deficit ballooned by early 1991—coincident with the low point of the 1990–1991 U.S. economic recession—to be second only to the U.S. deficit with Japan.
- *China's missile and nuclear proliferation.* U.S.-backed efforts after the Persian Gulf war to control the export of ballistic missiles to the Middle East were challenged by reports of Chinese efforts to sell short-range and intermediate-range ballistic missiles to Pakistan and Syria, and by China's refusal to join the Missile Technology Control Regime (MTCR) designed to limit the proliferation of such dangerous weapons systems. Concurrently, it was disclosed that China for several years had been helping Algeria to build a secret nuclear reactor, which some saw as likely to be used to produce nuclear weapons.
- *Tibet.* The April 1991 visit to Washington by the Dalai Lama triggered heavy congressional attention to Chinese oppression of Tibetans and to expressions of support for Tibetan self-determination—an anathema to Beijing. House and Senate resolutions introduced in spring 1991 declared that Tibet should be considered as an independent state—a step Beijing saw as a direct challenge to China's territorial integrity.
- *Cambodia.* Closer examination of the 1990 U.N. agreement on peace in Cambodia caused some in Congress to question sharply China's

role. In particular, they focused on China's continued support for the Khmer Rouge and decided that the United States needed to take more steps to check the Khmer Rouge, including a much tougher policy toward China. They were particularly concerned with China's seeming ability to manipulate the situation to its advantage, and to that of the Khmer Rouge, as the realization of peace seen in the U.N. plan was repeatedly delayed.

- *Prison labor; heroin traffic; arms sales; family planning; Hong Kong.* Other issues eliciting critical attention in Congress and the media at this time included charges that China exported to the United States industrial products made by political prisoners in China; that China was insufficiently vigilant in curbing heroin traffic through China to the United States; that China's use of arms sales to shore up the corrupt and repressive regime in Burma was an offense to international standards of human rights; that China continued to use coercion in family planning; and that China followed a heavy-handed policy toward Hong Kong that promoted an exodus from the territory and undermined extensive U.S. economic and political interests there.

In this atmosphere of a building crisis in U.S. policy toward China, President Bush took several steps designed to keep the policy initiative in his hands while attempting to elicit some possible gestures from the PRC. On human rights, the president in mid-April met with the Dalai Lama— the first U.S. president to do so since before President Nixon's opening to China; in late April, administration trade officers listed China among three nations targeted under Section 301 of the 1988 Trade Act, which requires U.S. retaliation against countries that do not adequately protect U.S. intellectual property; also in April, the administration refused to allow U.S. components to be exported for a Chinese satellite—a step taken in response to Beijing's reported marketing of missiles abroad. In early May, the administration sent Under Secretary of State Robert Kimmett to Beijing for talks designed to curb China's missile and nuclear proliferation and to discuss human rights and other concerns. Chinese and other observers were warned both publicly and privately that it was far from certain that the president would grant China a MFN waiver in 1991—a tactic also used in 1990 in part to elicit more forthcoming Chinese behavior on issues important to the United States. In the end, the president disclosed on May 15, 1991, that he would recommend that China continue to receive most-favored-nation status.

Senate Majority Leader George Mitchell followed the next day with a proposal granting MFN status for half a year, after which the president would have to certify that China had made improvements in its human rights, trade, and proliferation policies for MFN status to continue. Similar conditions were proposed in the House, and both chambers also saw legislators come forward with demands for an immediate cut off of trade benefits. President Bush launched a strong defense of his position with a major speech at Yale University in late May. Coincidentally, the administration announced restrictions on high-performance computer sales to China and on the launching of U.S. satellites on Chinese rockets that were related to U.S. concerns over Chinese missile sales abroad. The new restrictions were quickly dismissed by Senator Mitchell, who stressed the need for stronger restrictions on MFN privileges for China.[21]

Thus, lines were being drawn for a political debate over China policy that appeared likely to rage off and on throughout the summer. President Bush was required to make his formal recommendation by June 3, 1991, which he did, and Congress would then have sixty days to vote a joint resolution of disapproval, which could be vetoed, or China's MFN privileges would continue. But Congress followed another option. Each House passed new legislation, including in the Senate, Senator Mitchell's proposal noted above. But the vote in the Senate was not sufficient to ensure an override of an anticipated presidential veto.

Compromises appeared possible but not before various parties had an opportunity to stake out a clear position on the issue. President Bush appeared determined to sustain MFN treatment for China as a critical element in the constructive engagement he favored for U.S. policy toward China. Presumably, this would have him oppose conditions that would have a major substantive effect on U.S.-China trade. Congressional critics were determined to cut off or place stringent conditions on MFN in order to send a clear message to Chinese leaders that their human rights, trade, and proliferation policies would have to change in order for Beijing to continue to reap the economic benefits it obtains from trade with the United States. In the view of some, partisan issues of U.S. domestic politics lay behind the lines of the debate; some congressional critics attempted to portray the president and his party supporters as insensitive to concerns about human rights, proliferation, and trade equity, whereas the president's backers equated criticism of the president's China policy with the "misguided" criticism the administration faced when it moved steadily toward a military showdown with Iraq's Saddam Hussein.[22] The debate promised to be more acrimonious and protracted than that seen in 1990, and by late 1991 the outcome remained uncertain.

Notes

1. Prominent Chinese foreign policy expert Huan Xiang was a notable proponent of this view in the late 1980s. This chapter is based heavily on articles published by the author in *Current History* (September 1990 and September 1991).

2. Steven Levine, "The Uncertain Future of Chinese Foreign Policy," *Current History* (September 1989), p. 262.

3. See discussion of this view in *Crisis in China: Prospects for U.S. Policy. Report of the Thirtieth Strategy for Peace, U.S. Foreign Policy Conference* (Muscatene, IA: The Stanley Foundation, 1989).

4. See, for instance, *Liaowang* (overseas edition), no. 2 (January 7, 1990), p. 28.

5. See the statement of February 7, 1990, Deputy Secretary of State Lawrence Eagleburger before the United States Senate Foreign Relations Committee.

6. See assessment of United States views in *National Journal* (February 24, 1990), pp. 445-449.

7. *The New York Times*, January 26, 1990.

8. See, among others, Michel Oskenberg, "The China Problem," *Foreign Affairs* (Summer 1991), pp. 1-16.

9. The administration's actions and congressional responses can be monitored in *Congressional Quarterly Weekly Report*.

10. See the review of the U.S. policy toward China in the *Washington Post*, March 7, 1990.

11. See discussion in *Crisis in China: Prospects for U.S. Policy*.

12. Discussed in *National Journal* (February 24, 1990), pp. 445-449.

13. The 1974 amendment linking favorable tariff treatment to emigration performance was authored by Senator Henry Jackson (D., Wash.) and Congressman Charles Vanik (D., Ohio).

14. See author's article-length study, "American Policy Toward Beijing, 1989-1990: The Role of President Bush and The White House Staff," *Journal of Northeast Asian Studies* (Winter 1991), pp. 3-15. Sources for this study included *Congressional Quarterly Weekly Report*, 1989-1990; weekly compilation of *Presidential Documents* (Washington, DC: The White House, 1989); and interviews.

15. Actions by the administration and its critics can be monitored in *Congressional Quarterly Weekly Report*, 1989-1991.

16. See weekly compilation of *Presidential Documents*.

17. See *New York Times* and *Washington Post* coverage of the president's February 1989 visit.

18. *Congressional Quarterly Weekly Report* (April 27, 1991), p. 1045.

19. Interviews with U.S. administration and congressional officials, Washington, DC, February and March 1991.

20. See, among others, *Los Angeles Times*, January 8, 1991, p. 47; *New York Times*, May 2, 1991, p. A3.

21. Reviewed in the author's article in *Current History*, September 1991.

22. Reviewed in *Congressional Quarterly Weekly Report*, April 27, 1991, pp. 1044-1046; May 18, 1991, p. 1260; and *National Journal*, May 18, 1991, p. 1178.

5

U.S. Policy Concerning Taiwan, Hong Kong

The Changing U.S. Interest in Taiwan

During the Cold War, U.S. policy debate concerning Taiwan focused on how best to support the security and international identity of this noncommunist Asian outpost. Improved U.S. relations with the People's Republic of China (PRC) in the 1970s centered the policy debate on how best to increase U.S. ties with Beijing on the one hand, while maintaining U.S. support for "old friends" in Taiwan on the other hand.

In the early 1990s, U.S. policymakers continued to work to establish a proper balance between U.S. relations with Beijing and unofficial U.S. relations with Taipei. That effort was affected by the political turmoil in China, in the wake of the brutal PRC government crackdown on student-led demonstrations in mid-1989, and the concurrent and seemingly paradoxical increase in Taiwan people's investment in and travel to the mainland. Meanwhile, other developments affecting Taiwan's international identity, economic prosperity, and political stability posed a wider range of sometimes difficult U.S. policy issues than in the past. A large U.S. trade deficit with Taiwan, and internal political developments there, including the rise of a vocal opposition movement and the leadership succession following the death of President Chiang Ching-kuo in January 1988, added important issues to the American policy agenda. U.S. leaders were repeatedly called upon—during travel to Asia, in meetings with representatives interested in Taiwan, and when considering policy choices or legislation affecting Taiwan—to choose from among competing U.S. policy options related to these issues.[1]

The longstanding U.S. involvement with the government of Taiwan has its roots in the World War II alliance with the Nationalist Chinese administration of Chiang Kai-shek. U.S. military protection and over $5 billion in military and economic aid allowed Chiang and his one-party government to consolidate their position on Taiwan, to which they had retreated following the communist victory on the mainland in 1949. U.S. support also was instrumental in helping Taiwan develop a strong, export-oriented economy, characterized by sustained rapid growth.

Throughout four decades, the United States was Taiwan's main foreign investor and trading partner. In 1990, U.S. markets received about 30 percent of Taiwan's exports. The United States supplied a much smaller percentage of Taiwan's imports. Overall, the imbalance in U.S. trade with Taiwan led to a $19 billion U.S. trade deficit in 1987—second largest for the United States after Japan. The deficit was about $13 billion in 1988, about $12 billion in 1989, and $11.2 billion in 1990.

Taiwan's economic development is closely related to continued political stability on the island. Taiwan's per capita income in 1991 was over $8,000 per year. The economy distributed wealth in a balanced way that gave all major sectors in society an important stake in continued economic progress. The benefits of economic prosperity tended to offset the political costs of opposition to the forty years of authoritarian, one-party rule by the Chinese Nationalists. The Nationalists have continued to follow the political legacy of Chiang Kai-shek, who died in 1975. Thus, while focusing attention on the developments in Taiwan, the Nationalists insisted on governing the island as part of their mandate as the legitimate government of all of China. They called their government the "Republic of China."

American officials long criticized perceived excesses of the Nationalists' authoritarian rule, and pressed for increased political liberalization that would allow the more than 85 percent of the population whose roots on the island predated 1949 to have a greater role in running their own affairs. Some U.S. officials argued that political change in Taiwan should be very gradual in order to avoid shifts that would upset stability and economic progress, or provoke the PRC. But others warned that instability would result if political change did not keep pace with the economic dynamics and social changes of the island.

U.S. security interests in Taiwan have changed markedly from the 1950s and 1960s, when U.S. forces used the island as a forward base against Sino-Soviet communism in Asia. After the Sino-Soviet split, President Nixon's opening to Beijing, and the major pullback of U.S. forces in Asia under guidelines of the "Nixon doctrine," U.S. officials viewed the mainland government more as a strategic asset against the USSR than an adversary to be confronted in the Taiwan Strait. It was in this context that the United States in 1979 broke defense and other official ties with Taiwan in order to establish formal diplomatic relations with the PRC. The United States subsequently affirmed its security interests in Taiwan through the Taiwan Relations Act (TRA) and the continued supply of U.S. arms to Taiwan. But this reflected a moral commitment to a former ally rather than U.S. interest in using Taiwan's strategic position for broader policy ends.

U.S.-PRC-Taiwan Relations, 1979–1991[2]

The governments in both Beijing and Taipei have claimed that they represent all of China, including Taiwan. Both had agreed that diplomatic recognition of one foreclosed recognition of the other. (In 1989, Taipei began to show some flexibility on this issue under the policy rubric of "one country, two governments"—see discussion below.) On January 1, 1979, the United States switched its diplomatic recognition from Taipei to Beijing. In the U.S.-PRC joint communiqué that announced the change, the United States recognized the government of the People's Republic of China as the sole legal government of China and acknowledged the Chinese position that there is but one China, and Taiwan is part of China. The joint communiqué also stated that "within this context, the people of the United States will maintain cultural, commercial, and other unofficial relations with the people of Taiwan."

On April 10, 1979, President Carter signed into law the Taiwan Relations Act (P.L. 96–8) which created domestic legal authority for the conduct of unofficial relations with Taiwan.

American commercial and cultural interaction with the people of Taiwan is facilitated through the American Institute in Taiwan the (AIT), a nongovernmental entity. The institute has its headquarters in Washington, DC, and field offices in Taipei and Kaohsiung. Staffed largely by U.S. State Department and other officials who are temporarily separated from the U.S. government, the AIT is authorized to accept visa and passport applications and to provide assistance to U.S. citizens in Taiwan. A counterpart organization, the Coordination Council for North American Affairs (CCNAA), has been created by Taiwan. It has headquarters in Taipei and field offices in Washington, DC, and ten other U.S. cities.

On January 1, 1979, at the time of derecognition, the United States notified the Taiwan authorities of intent to terminate the 1954 Mutual Defense Treaty. That termination took effect January 1, 1980, but the United States in its unilateral statement released on December 16, 1978 (issued concurrently with the Joint Communiqué on the Establishment of Diplomatic Relations between the United States and the People's Republic of China), declared that it "continues to have an interest in the peaceful resolution of the Taiwan issue and expects that the Taiwan issue will be settled peacefully by the Chinese themselves."[3]

Since derecognition, the United States, in accord with the TRA, has continued the sale of selected defensive military equipment and defense technology to Taiwan. This has prompted often strong objections from the PRC. U.S.-PRC negotiations in 1981 and 1982 led to the August 17, 1982, U.S.-PRC joint communiqué addressing this point. In that communiqué, the PRC cited a "fundamental policy" of striving for a peaceful solution to the Taiwan question. With that Chinese policy in mind, the United States stated in the communiqué that "it does not seek to carry out a long-term policy of arms sales to Taiwan, that its arms sales to Taiwan will not exceed, either in qualitative or quantitative terms, the level of those supplied in recent years since the establishment of diplomatic relations between the United States and China, and that it intends to reduce gradually its sales of arms to Taiwan."

Future arms sales to Taiwan are to accord with the policies contained in the August 17, 1982, communiqué. In conjunction with the issuance of that communiqué, President Reagan issued a statement:

> regarding future U.S. arms sales to Taiwan, our policy, set forth clearly in the communiqué, is fully consistent with the Taiwan Relations Act. Arms sales will continue in accordance with the act and with the full expectation that the approach of the Chinese government to the resolution of the Taiwan issue will continue to be peaceful. The position of the U.S. government has always been clear and consistent in this regard. The Taiwan question is a matter for the Chinese people, on both sides of the Taiwan Strait, to resolve. We will not interfere in this matter or prejudice the free choice of, or put pressure on, the people of Taiwan in this matter. At the same time, we have an abiding interest and concern that any resolution be peaceful.[4]

U.S. commercial ties with Taiwan have been maintained and expanded since derecognition. Taiwan continues to enjoy Export-Import Bank financing, Overseas Private Investment Corporation (OPIC) guarantees, most-favored-nation status, and ready access to U.S. markets. For several years, Taiwan was the largest beneficiary of the U.S. Generalized System of Preferences (GSP) program. The Reagan administration announced in early 1988 that Taiwan and other newly developing countries would be phased out of the GSP program. The U.S. Agency for International Development (AID) mission in Taiwan closed in 1965, long before derecognition. More than $1.7 billion in U.S. economic aid was provided between 1949 and 1965.

The switch in U.S. recognition and the 1982 communiqué on arms sales to Taiwan did not remove the so-called Taiwan issue in U.S.-PRC relations. Specifically, Beijing for many years has encouraged Taipei leaders to begin talks leading to a peaceful reunification of Taiwan with the mainland. It finds that continued U.S. support, especially U.S. arms sales, reduces Taipei's interest in negotiations. It thus concludes that smooth U.S.-PRC relations will require the removal of what it sees as the continued "obstacle" of U.S. arms sales to Taiwan.

U.S.-PRC relations declined sharply as the United States took actions to protest vigorously Beijing's brutal crackdown on pro-democracy demonstrations in mid-1989. Beijing's actions curbed Taiwan's immediate interest in closer trade, investment, or other unofficial contacts with the mainland, but contacts picked up substantially later in the year.

Current Problems

Concerns over International Isolation and National Defense

The Nationalist government and public opinion in Taiwan view U.S. derecognition, restrictions on arms sales, and improvements in U.S.-PRC relations as part of broader trends that are harmful to Taiwan's international identity and national security. In particular, Taipei has faced a decline in its official standing abroad. In recent years, for example, countries such as Saudi Arabia, Bolivia, and Uruguay broke ties in order to establish official relations with the PRC, leaving Taiwan with official diplomatic relations with only about twenty-five countries. Except for South Korea and South Africa, the countries are of relatively small international importance. This diplomatic isolation complicated greatly the Taiwan government's efforts to obtain from other countries the types of advanced military equipment it feels it needs to sustain a credible defense posture against the mainland. As a result, it remains heavily dependent on the carefully calibrated flow of arms supplied by the United States. The Nationalists were successful in 1981 in persuading the Netherlands government to approve the manufacture and sale of sophisticated submarines to Taiwan's navy. (The United States has sold no new submarines to Taiwan.) But strong PRC reaction prompted a decision by the Netherlands government not to sell such sophisticated weapons to Taiwan in the future. In January 1990, a deal to sell French frigates to Taiwan was halted after extensive negotiations. A modified version was signed in 1991.

A number of other developments have reinforced trends that are adverse to Taiwan's international standing:

- Beijing successfully negotiationed entry into the main regional development bank, the Asian Development Bank (ADB). Taiwan had been an active member of the bank, but an arrangement concluded in 1986 permitted PRC entry and was seen by Taipei as downgrading Taiwan's status in the bank. Taiwan has chosen to remain a bank member, but chose not to attend meetings of the ADB until 1988.
- Beijing's economic reforms and increasingly active foreign trade have raised its standing with noncommunist countries important to Taipei. Thus, South Korea, the only East Asian country still recognizing Taiwan diplomatically, now conducts a lively trade worth $3 billion each year with the PRC. South Korea agreed in October 1990 to

exchange trade offices with the PRC. Meanwhile, Saudi Arabia purchased PRC intermediate-range missiles prior to establishing official relations with Beijing in July 1990.
- Beijing successfully concluded negotiations with the British over the future status of Hong Kong in 1984, and it has followed this with repeated overtures to Taiwan. The PRC calls for humanitarian, trade, and other contacts, to be followed by negotiations to settle Taiwan-mainland differences in the spirit of the "one country, two systems" model used by the PRC to frame the Hong Kong settlement. Taipei's response was defensive, employing a so-called "three nos" policy regarding relations with the mainland: no negotiations, no compromise, and no contacts.
- The thaw in the Cold War and Sino-Soviet relations has reduced Beijing's preoccupation with the Soviet threat and given Chinese forces greater leeway to focus on Taiwan. It has also opened the way to possible Soviet jet fighter sales to China.[5]

Offsetting Developments

Offsetting—at least to some degree—Taiwan's concerns over adverse international trends are success in trading abroad despite the absence of diplomatic relations; increased confidence in Taiwan over the direction of U.S. China policy; recent officially sanctioned contacts by residents of Taiwan to the mainland; and Taiwan's success in some recent diplomatic initiatives conducted under the rubric of "flexible diplomacy."

International Trade. Based largely on Taiwan's growing international economic importance, Nationalist administration officials have been able to work out arrangements with major trading partners that allow Taiwan and foreign entrepreneurs to travel between the island and countries that do not have formal diplomatic relations with Taipei. In the process, the officials have established a series of ostensibly unofficial bureaus, similar to but not as extensive as unofficial arrangements used in relations with the United States. Taipei also is modifying past prohibition on trade with the Chinese mainland, as it permits over $3 billion of Taiwanese goods that pass each year through Hong Kong, Japan, and other countries on the way to the PRC. Taiwan's investments on the mainland through indirect channels reportedly reached $520 million in 1988 and were increasing rapidly in 1989 and 1990. By 1991, Taiwan investment in the mainland amounted to about $2 billion.[6]

U.S. China Policy. Taiwan leaders and public opinion seem assured, at least for the present, that the United States is unlikely to move in directions that would seriously jeopardize Taiwan's interests. In particular, they judge that U.S. administration leaders have reduced the importance they previously placed on developing closer relations with the PRC. Indeed, the impasse in U.S.-PRC relations over human rights issues related to Beijing's mid-1989 crackdown on popular dissent underlined this trend. As a result, the United States is seen to have less incentive to accommodate continued PRC demands for further cutbacks in U.S. ties with Taiwan.

They also are reassured by the fact that the United States policy regarding Taiwan has, for several years, been consistent with the so-called six assurances, which they see as essential for preserving Taiwan's interests vis-à-vis the mainland. The six assurances involve U.S. promises not to: (1) set a date for ending arms sales to Taiwan; (2) hold prior consultation with Beijing on U.S. arms sales to Taiwan; (3) play any mediation role between Beijing and Taipei; (4) revise the Taiwan Relations Act; (5) alter the U.S. position regarding sovereignty over Taiwan; and (6) exert pressure on Taiwan to enter into negotiations with the PRC.

An exception to this view had involved Taiwan's concern about the increasing U.S. military sales to the PRC, which were viewed as compromising Taiwan's ability to maintain an acceptable balance of power in the Taiwan Strait. (These sales were suspended in June 1989.) Taipei appears generally satisfied with continued U.S. arms supplies to Taiwan and the reported progress being made in Taiwan's development of a new fighter aircraft. U.S. reports disclosed in 1986 that the fighter is being developed in consultation with U.S. military contractors, but does not involve direct U.S. government support. In December 1988, Taiwan unveiled its first "Indigenous Defense Fighter."

Travel to and Contacts with the Mainland. In November 1987, the Red Cross Society in Taiwan was authorized to begin processing applications for Taiwan citizens who wished to visit the mainland for family reunions. In March 1988, Taiwan authorities announced many mainland publications and movies would be available in Taiwan and that mail to and from the mainland would be permitted through authorized channels. The authorities also said they were considering opening officially sanctioned trade contacts with the mainland and, in late 1988, they authorized some Taiwan citizens to travel to internationally sponsored meetings on the mainland. By 1989, more than 400,000 people from Taiwan had traveled to the mainland and the number was growing in 1990. Taipei sent a cabinet minister to attend the Asian Development Bank meeting in Beijing in May 1989. On May 15, 1990, President Lee Teng-hui seemed to end Taipei opposition to official contacts with Beijing. He said Taipei was willing to open a dialogue with Beijing on the basis of "one country, two governments," a stance opposed by Beijing. President Lee established a National Unification Council in October 1990 that was to help revise Taipei's policy toward the mainland. Economic and cultural contacts and exchange of personnel via the respective Red Cross societies were allowed by Taipei by October 1990. In late 1990, a Mainland Affairs Council was established at the ministerial level in Taipei, and a Foundation for Exchanges Across the Taiwan Straits was set up to deal with practical issues that arise given the extensive exchanges across the straits.

Flexible Diplomacy. Taiwan in 1989 showed greater flexibility in conducting diplomacy abroad, even with countries having active relations with the PRC. President Lee Teng-hui visited Singapore in March 1989, even though Singapore—out of deference to the PRC—referred to him as "President Lee from Taiwan," rather than Taipei's preferred designation, "President Lee from the Republic of China." Subsequently, some Taiwan officials supported the idea of "one country, two governments" to describe the mainland-Taiwan situation and called on other countries having ties with the PRC to upgrade their relations with Taiwan. Beijing criticized Taiwan's stance but some Western and Third World governments began to increase the size and scope of their contacts with Taiwan. Meanwhile, Taipei was successful in increasing trade and other contacts with other countries; and some small countries (Grenada, Liberia, Belize, Lesotho, Guinea-Bissau, and the Central African Republic) reestablished formal diplomatic relations with Taiwan. On January 1, 1990, Taiwan asked to join GATT as a separate "customs territory"—a move that angered the PRC, whose application for GATT membership awaits approval by the international economic organization. On August 31, 1990, Taiwan announced an interest in a "one country, two regions" formula for China, but Beijing opposed the idea.

Economic Prospects[7]

Prospects for continued healthy economic growth in Taiwan are reasonably good. The economy grew rapidly (over 10 percent in 1986 and 1987, and 7 percent in 1988 and 1989; growth slowed to about 5–6 percent in 1990). In the mid-1980s, declines in world oil prices and the high value of the U.S. dollar relative to Taiwan's currency helped to encourage economic growth. So did the continued growth in the U.S. economy. Taiwanese entrepreneurs were able to cut production costs and compete more effectively in foreign markets, resulting in export-driven growth that continued into 1988 and 1989, albeit at rates somewhat less than 1986–1987.

Taiwan's economy remains vulnerable to rises in oil prices, decline in the U.S. economy, and international protectionism, especially in the United States. Half of Taiwan's GNP derives from exports, and about 30 percent of these exports go to the United States. (Leading exports to the United States include wearing apparel and footwear, toys, and various electronic products.) In recent years, Taiwan government officials have attempted to accommodate increased U.S. pressure on trade issues. They met many of the U.S. administration demands for greater market access for U.S. goods and services. They accepted without serious protest U.S. decisions in the late 1980s to "graduate" (i.e., remove) Taiwan exports from the Generalized System of Preferences (GSP), which allows goods from developing countries to enter the United States duty-free.

The government also responded to U.S. complaints by taking stronger measures to protect U.S. copyrights and other intellectual property rights. A key change was the Taiwan government's willingness to arrest, try, and punish those who violate existing law. (In the past, such culprits often received only light sentences, if they were prosecuted at all.) As a result, Taiwan was seen to be changing its past reputation as a center for international counterfeiting. Also, Taiwan allowed the value of its currency relative to the U.S. dollar to rise over 30 percent in the late 1980s.

The U.S. trade deficit with Taiwan remained over $10 billion for almost a decade. The deficit continues despite Taiwan government efforts to encourage more purchases of U.S. products and to promote diversification of Taiwan's export markets. As a result, Taiwan officials and businesspeople have remained worried that the United States may take stronger action, such as a revival of provisions, seen in the U.S. House-passed omnibus trade bills of the 99th and 100th Congresses, which aimed to reduce rapidly the U.S. trade imbalance with Taiwan and other countries. They felt that U.S. action that focused on sharply reducing the trade deficit with Taiwan, through legislated action or other steps, would crimp severely Taiwan's ability to export to the U.S. market in the future and would cause a wrenching readjustment of Taiwan's economy. They were somewhat relieved when Taiwan was not named in recent years among those countries subjected to special U.S. negotiations under provision 301 of the U.S. Trade Act to end unfair trade barriers overseas.

Internal Politics

Political problems for the island have centered on the succession of President Chiang Ching-kuo, following his death on January 13, 1988, and the rise of an increasingly vocal and politically active opposition movement.[8]

Leadership Succession. President Chiang Ching-kuo had ruled Taiwan with preeminent authority following the death of his father, Chiang Kai-shek, in 1975. Some observers in Taiwan and abroad claimed that Chiang's death would create a power vacuum at the top levels of Taiwan's administration that would make it difficult for the Nationalists to reconcile competing bureaucratic and political interests as it faced international and internal difficulties in the period ahead.

In the aftermath of Chiang Ching-kuo's death, the authorities handled succession smoothly and stability was maintained. Vice President Lee Teng-hui, a "Taiwanese," was sworn in to finish the several years remaining in Chiang's term. Lee was not thought to have a powerful political base in his own right, but was receiving the support of reformers and others in the Nationalist party led by Lee Huan; in the government ministries; and in the military, led by officials such as Hau Pei-tsun. On January 27, 1988, Lee was elected acting chairman of the Nationalist party, and was elected to the post of Nationalist party chairman at the Nationalist party's Thirteenth Congress in July 1988. That Congress saw major changes in the top party and government bodies, providing a much greater role for Taiwan natives in senior positions.

A behind-the-scenes struggle for power was reported in the months leading up to the election of Lee Teng-hui as president by the National Assembly in March 1990. Although the Nationalist party nominated Lee for the post and Nationalist party members dominated the Assembly, evidence of opposition to Lee was seen in the actions of other potential candidates and their supporters. Subsequent to Lee's election, the president selected Defense Minister Hau Pei-tsun as premier. This surprise move upset some in Taiwan concerned with Hau's reputation as a "no-nonsense" military leader, but it acted to outflank more conservative opponents of Lee within the Nationalist party.

Internal Political Opposition. The political opposition in Taiwan recovered from a serious setback it suffered in 1980 when several key leaders were arrested and given prison sentences as a result of their alleged involvement in a violent clash between antigovernment demonstrators and police in the city of Kaohsiung. The opposition successfully challenged the ruling Nationalist party in a number of key races in the December 2, 1989, elections in Taiwan.

The overthrow of Philippines president Ferdinand Marcos and rising political opposition to government authority in South Korea in 1986 stimulated Taiwan political opposition leaders to try to overcome persistent internal divisions in order to hold rallies and to press the government for greater political reform. They focused demands on a call for an end to martial law (in effect since 1949), and the right to form opposition political parties. (Their goals were actively supported by Taiwanese-American groups and by several U.S. members of Congress.) Predictably, the opposition's new prominence raised political tensions on Taiwan, as many government supporters strongly rejected opposition demands.

Opposition politicians claimed to better represent the people on Taiwan whose roots go back to before 1949 (over 85 percent of the total population). They pointed out critically that the Nationalist party administration was still dominated at its senior level by "mainlanders"—people who came to Taiwan from the Chinese mainland in 1949. In response, Nationalist party representatives claimed that they well represent the majority of people on Taiwan. They noted in particular that over 80 percent of the party rank-and-file are people whose roots in Taiwan go back to before 1949.

The Nationalist government is concerned that the oppositionists will try to appeal to "separatist" tendencies among non-mainlanders in Taiwan. Some officials suspect that the oppositionists will push to have Taiwan declared an independent state. They warn that such action would not only challenge the Nationalists' claim to represent the government of all of China, but also would likely provoke Beijing to strong action to support its claim that Taiwan is part of China. The oppositionists rebut the charge of promoting separatism. But they emphasize that "the people of Taiwan" should determine the island's "future status."

In September 1986, opposition leaders announced that they had formed a formal opposition political party, the Democratic Progressive Party (DPP). Although the Nationalists considered the action illegal under terms of martial law, they took no repressive action and allowed oppositionists to campaign in the December 1986 elections under their new banner. At the polls, the DPP candidates received about 22 percent of the vote, an increase over the 17 percent opposition politicians received in the last such elections in 1983.

Martial law ended July 15, 1987, and opposition leaders shifted their focus to calls for an overhaul of Taiwan's National Assembly, Legislative Yuan and Control Yuan—important legislative bodies still dominated by mainlanders elected over forty years ago. Following Chiang Ching-kuo's death, President Lee Teng-hui reaffirmed his commitment to reforms that would legalize opposition parties and restructure the parliamentary bodies. On February 28, 1988, Lee publicly urged older members of the National Assembly to consider retirement. He also reportedly pushed for a revival of an "on-again, off-again," Nationalist party dialogue with the opposition, which was formally resumed on February 10, 1988. The opposition, for their part, urged in mid-1988 that a new unicameral legislature be selected by direct ballot; that the president be elected directly by the people; and that any negotiations between Taiwan and the PRC await the establishment of a "truly democratic" political system in Taiwan.

In late 1989, political attention focused heavily on the parliamentary and other elections slated for December 2, 1989. The elections—the first island-wide balloting since martial law was officially lifted in 1987—were for national-level parliamentary bodies and local posts. The elections helped to make the national legislative bodies more representative of the people in Taiwan, although the majority of the representatives in those bodies continued to be individuals elected from mainland Chinese constituencies prior to 1949. As it turned out, the DPP won several key races and garnered about 35 percent of the popular vote—a big advance over its showing in 1986. In 1990, President Lee Teng-hui pardoned a few dissident leaders still in jail or under restrictions for past political actions and convened in June a National Affairs Conference comprised of ruling party and dissident politicians and dignitaries from other fields. President Lee promised to implement the conference suggestions for political reform, which included constitutional and legal reforms long favored by the opposition. By early 1991, President Lee's plans and other government actions forecasted the following changes in Taiwan:

- May 1991, an end to the "emergency," "temporary" provisions that have governed Taiwan's administration for over forty years of ostensible civil war with the mainland. (The National Assembly voted to end these in April 1991 and President Lee approved the change in May.)
- End of 1991, retirement of all members of Taiwan's parliamentary bodies who were elected on the mainland in the late 1940s and have held their seats without election since that time.
- End of 1991, election of a new national assembly.
- Spring 1992, revise the constitution.
- 1992, elections for new parliamentary bodies.
- 1993, direct election of the president.

A basic question underlying the political reform was the ability of the government to control the pace of political change and the pace and scope of Taiwan economic investment in the mainland. In particular, by late 1991, it was clear that Taipei was unable to thwart opposition party efforts to promote openly the idea of Taiwan independence and that the government was having a difficult time encouraging Taiwan investors to avoid "over exposure" on the China mainland. Part of the problem had to do with a widely held view that the Nationalist government leaders held divided views on these questions, with President Lee holding more moderate views and Premier Hau Pei-tsun favoring a tougher line.

Competing U.S. Policy Choices

The recent developments affecting Taiwan's international identity, security, prosperity, and political stability pose a wider range of difficult U.S. policy choices than in the past. U.S. policy debate no longer is focused on how best to support the security and international identity of this noncommunist Asian outpost. Improved U.S. relations with China in the 1970s, prompted the United States to increase U.S. ties with Beijing on the one hand, while maintaining U.S. support for "old friends" in Taiwan on the other hand.

Today, U.S. policymakers continue to work to establish a proper balance between U.S. relations with Beijing and Taipei. But Taiwan's international trade patterns and internal political developments are important issues for American policy. Competing U.S. policy options related to Taiwan's identity, security, prosperity, and internal politics raise often difficult choices for U.S. policymakers who deal with Taiwan-related affairs.

Meanwhile, other issues sometimes emerged to affect the U.S.-Taiwan relationship. Thus, some Americans looked to Taiwan for support for multilateral efforts to pressure Iraq to withdraw from Kuwait. In the event, Taipei announced on August 8, 1990, that it would follow the economic sanctions against Iraq. This came six days after the invasion and the U.S. imposition of sanctions, five days after Japan imposed sanctions, and two days after the U.N. Security Council (including the PRC) voted in favor of sanctions; it reportedly followed a formal U.S. request for Taiwan to join the sanctions. Taipei announced in September 1990 that it would provide $30 million in assistance to Jordan, Egypt, and Turkey. Taipei reportedly offered more aid as part of a U.S. "economic action" plan to deal with the crisis but was turned down by the Bush administration, presumably out of sensitivity to PRC reaction.[9]

U.S.-PRC-Taiwan Relations

Strong U.S. supporters of the Nationalist government, encouraged by that government's vigorous public relations efforts, remain an important and well-organized force in American politics. Generally, they see U.S. interests as best served by following policy options that support, or are compatible with, the concerns of the Nationalist administration. In particular, they encourage U.S. policy to take strong action to support Taiwan's international identity and security in the face of the communist mainland. Specifically, they would like the United States to:

- Back strongly Taipei's position vis-à-vis the PRC in international organizations such as the Asian Development Bank and the GATT.
- Support Taiwan's efforts to raise its international profile under the rubric of flexible diplomacy.
- Use the Taipei administration's preferred title, the "Republic of China."
- Supply weapons more advanced and in larger quantities than those currently supplied by the United States.
- Firmly rebuff PRC efforts to obtain U.S. support for negotiations between the PRC and Taiwan.

A contrasting set of policy choices has come from Americans concerned with sustaining and developing economic, political, or military ties with the PRC. They stress that the United States should avoid actions regarding Taiwan that they judge would provoke a negative PRC response. Thus, they support strict compliance with the U.S. commitment to reduce arms sales to Taiwan. They also judge that the U.S. position in the Asian Development Bank, GATT, or other public forums should not identify Taiwan as the "Republic of China." Some in this group advocate U.S. support for PRC efforts to encourage greater contacts with Taiwan, even though the Taiwan administration sometimes opposes such contacts.

Trade Issues

Americans concerned with the large U.S. trade deficit call for strong action (possibly including limitations on foreign access to U.S. markets) to improve the U.S. trade balance. They recognize that such action could negatively affect the economic prosperity and related political stability of a number of important U.S. trading partners, including Taiwan. But they judge that the United States has little choice but to take firm measures to protect its own markets and economic advancement. A contrasting view comes from U.S. supporters of the Nationalist government, Americans concerned with promoting greater political democracy amid continued economic prosperity in Taiwan, and free-trade advocates who tend to oppose measures designed to restrict foreign exporters' access to U.S. markets. They emphasize the negative results for U.S. interests in Taiwan and in a free international trading system that they believe would result from such restrictive trade legislation or administrative actions.

Political Liberalization

Americans strongly concerned with promoting democracy abroad have joined with small but well-organized groups of Taiwanese-Americans to push for greater U.S. efforts to promote political liberalization in Taiwan. They argue that greater U.S. pressure is needed to force the Nationalists to reduce political restrictions and allow the development of a truly multiparty democratic political system in Taiwan.

An opposing view comes from those Americans who identify closely with the Chinese Nationalist administration and urge U.S. support for Taipei's gradual and incremental efforts to develop greater political liberalization on Taiwan. Meanwhile, Americans keenly interested in closer U.S. relations with the PRC sometimes note a possible tradeoff for U.S. interests stemming from greater political liberalization in Taiwan. They judge that such liberalization might lead to a separate identity for Taiwan vis-à-vis the mainland, and they see such separation deepening the already serious U.S.-PRC differences over Taiwan.

Hong Kong's Transition to PRC Rule: U.S. Policy Concerns[10]

The Sino-British Agreement on Hong Kong

The colony of Hong Kong was acquired from China in three segments by Great Britain under the terms of three treaties in the nineteenth century: the 1842 Treaty of Nanking, by which Hong Kong Island (32 square miles) was ceded in perpetuity; the First Convention of Peking in 1860, by which Kowloon peninsula and Stonecutters' Island (3.75 square miles) were ceded in perpetuity; and the Second Convention of Peking in 1898, by which the New Territories (365 square miles, consisting of a mainland area adjoining Kowloon and 235 adjacent islands) were leased to Britain for ninety-nine years beginning July 1, 1898. The latter treaty called for the New Territories—90 percent of Hong Kong's land area—to revert to China in 1997; this approaching deadline prompted Britain in 1982 to begin what turned out to be twenty-two rounds of negotiations with China on Hong Kong's future, ending with a draft accord in September 1984.

China has consistently viewed all of Hong Kong as sovereign Chinese territory being ruled illegally by a foreign government because of the three "unequal" treaties—a view China expressed formally to the United Nations in 1972. China's adherence to this view during the Sino-British negotiations made it clear that continued British administration of the New Territories after 1997 would not be acceptable to the PRC. Moreover, the British government believed that those portions of Hong Kong ceded to Britain in perpetuity were not viable as an entity separate from the New Territories, which were scheduled to revert to China. Consequently, the agreement as finally drafted will formally restore to Chinese sovereignty and administration in 1997 the entire area now under British administration, including leased and permanently ceded land.

The accord contains detailed assurances to China that certain elements of Hong Kong's current situation considered essential for its secure economic future—such as local administrative autonomy, convertibility of the Hong Kong dollar, British-style laws and institutions, and recognition of existing land rights—will be maintained for fifty years after 1997. Policies set out in the agreement were included in a Basic Law subsequently passed by the National People's Congress of the People's Republic of China.

U.S. Financial and Political Stake in Hong Kong[11]

Hong Kong is a major center for U.S. investment, trade, and contact with China and the rest of Asia. More than 800 U.S. corporations, with investments of about $6 billion, are located in Hong Kong.

Hong Kong also is a transportation and communications hub for Asia. Its airport is served by more than thirty airlines. Hong Kong is the busiest international port in terms of containers handled. The number of visitors (almost 20 percent U.S.) to Hong Kong has also increased steadily over the last twenty years.

Hong Kong is an important and growing market for American products. U.S. exports of agricultural commodities to Hong Kong, for example, have totaled more than 10 percent of all of Hong Kong's food and commodities imports. Hong Kong imported over a fifth of all U.S. fresh produce sold overseas. Other opportunities for U.S. exports to Hong Kong include textile fabrics, office equipment and computers, telecommunications equipment, environmental control equipment, and hotel and medical equipment.

The future of Hong Kong also has implications for U.S. interests on Taiwan. China has explicitly linked its Hong Kong policy with its goal of reunification with Taiwan. Thus, if China can resume sovereignty over Hong Kong smoothly, with little or no apparent deterioration of the territory's socioeconomic system, its claim might be strengthened that the same nondisruptive results could be achieved were China to reunify Taiwan. Conversely, if China is seen as being too heavy-handed in its administration of Hong Kong or if the socioeconomic order there deteriorates, PRC claims that Taiwan's reunification would not adversely affect U.S. interests on the island could lose credibility. The Tiananmen Square massacre of June 1989 triggered mass demonstrations in Hong Kong and legislation in the U.S. Congress linking U.S. policy toward China with PRC policy toward Hong Kong. The U.S. Congress continues to show periodic interest in the territory, although there has been no repeat of the dramatic June 1989 demonstrations that elicited strong American attention.

Determinants of Hong Kong's Future

The success or failure of Hong Kong's transition to Chinese rule and U.S. interests there will be determined by the behavior of three separate groups: (1) policies of the Chinese leadership, (2) reactions of Hong Kong investors, business executives, and the general populace, and (3) actions by the international community.

Chinese Policies

What Chinese leaders do and say about Hong Kong will be the most important element in shaping the territory's future, not only after 1997, when China resumes sovereignty, but in the intervening years as it acquires greater influence. Some Americans and other observers believe that China will be inclined to pursue discreet and moderate policies toward Hong Kong that would be conducive to maintaining the territory's prosperity and stability. A more intrusive policy, in this view, would jeopardize important economic and political interests there.

In terms of trade, Hong Kong has remained China's most lucrative export market. The favorable trade balance that China maintains with Hong Kong, along with money sent by Hong Kong residents to relatives in the PRC, provides China with an estimated 30-40 percent of its annual convertible exchange, assets that most believe are critical to the success of China's modernization efforts. Hong Kong also serves as China's largest re-export center.

China also has sizable direct investments in Hong Kong that would seem to reinforce the incentive for preserving the strength of the territory's economic system. Meanwhile, China is interested in using Hong Kong's current economic system for experiments in capitalist ideas that would be difficult to carry out in its own socialist economy, such as the listing of state-owned enterprises on Hong Kong's Hang Seng stock exchange.

Politically, China would also seem to have sufficient incentives for wanting to perpetuate stability and prosperity in Hong Kong. In particular, a successful transition in Hong Kong could serve as evidence that Taiwan has nothing to fear from PRC administration. There is also the important matter of Chinese nationalism to consider. Years of past humiliation at the hands of foreign imperialistic powers—symbolized by the three treaties that made Hong Kong a British colony—create in China an emotional patriotic fervor when the question of Chinese sovereignty arises. Thus, resumption of sovereignty over Hong Kong and a successful transition to PRC rule could give China an opportunity to regain important international prestige.

Nevertheless, American and other observers also judge that there are other Chinese interests or potential developments in China that might prompt Beijing to adopt more assertive policies that could seriously disrupt the status quo in Hong Kong. For instance, a few observers maintain that China does not need to prolong Hong Kong's current system to receive foreign exchange income because when China resumes sovereignty it will become the beneficiary of all of Hong Kong's foreign exchange earnings, particularly through the holdings of the Bank of China. Moreover, the standards of economic success in China are seen to be very different from those in the West. The case of Shanghai, an economic disaster by Western standards after its takeover by Chinese communists, is nevertheless pointed to as "proof" of proficient economic management by some Chinese leaders. Indeed, Shanghai supplies the PRC government with a large portion of the revenue for its national budget. Furthermore, China's leaders often have been motivated more by ideological or political considerations than by economic ones. Beijing's warnings to demonstrators in Hong Kong after the Tiananmen Square massacre appeared to reflect this trend. Thus, the preservation of Hong Kong's vibrant economy may be of less importance to the PRC than certain domestic political considerations. Looking to the future, some believe that leadership instability will arise in China following the death of Deng Xiaoping and disrupt some of the more pragmatic policies—including Beijing's posture toward Hong Kong—associated with the elderly Chinese leader.

Events Within Hong Kong

The success or failure of Hong Kong's transition depends also on actions taken by Hong Kong business executives, investors, and residents. So far, their actions have shown a mixed pattern. Although the economy continues to grow, there are persisting trends of emigration and capital sent overseas by the well-to-do members of the society. Moreover, some Hong Kong political organizations have supported dissent in the PRC and resisted PRC policies—adding to PRC–Hong Kong frictions.

Actions by the International Community

The future of Hong Kong will be influenced by actions taken by the international community, particularly such key actors as the United States, Japan, and Taiwan. As an international financial center, Hong Kong depends on a stable world economy, and its own economy can generally be expected to ebb and flow with the global economic tide. As a result, Hong Kong is especially vulnerable to international sentiments for protectionist trade policies.

U.S. Options

U.S. efforts to help preserve Hong Kong's stability and prosperity have remained limited mainly to occasional positive statements by U.S. officials regarding future economic growth in the territory and quiet diplomatic consultations designed to foster an atmosphere of moderation and calm over the Hong Kong issue. After the Tiananmen Square massacre, Congress inserted provisions in support of Hong Kong's autonomy into several pieces of legislation. Suggested options involving a possibly more active U.S. role have been offset by perceived negative side-effects of such actions.

One U.S. option would be to intercede strongly with Chinese leaders, using U.S. influence to advocate policies toward Hong Kong that would take U.S. interests into account. Nevertheless, even if handled carefully, such a maneuver could backfire, because the PRC has always been sensitive to matters involving its sovereignty. Any appearance that the United States was attempting to interfere might seriously offend Chinese leaders and adversely affect U.S.-Chinese relations. In particular, Beijing might resent such American action coming at a time when PRC leaders still see the United States repeatedly affronting Chinese sovereignty with arms sales to Taiwan. Moreover, U.S. willingness to discuss Hong Kong's status with the PRC could put the United States into the compromising position of appearing also to be willing to bargain with Beijing over Taiwan's future.

A second option available to U.S. policymakers is to play a greater role in Hong Kong's political affairs prior to 1997, encouraging Hong Kong's officials and residents to demand a greater voice in their own government on the theory that more active participation now could mean greater autonomy in the future. Advocates of this view point to increased political activity in heretofore apathetic Hong Kong as evidence that Hong Kong's citizens are interested in self-government and may respond to U.S. encouragement in this area. However, this option could seriously complicate Sino-American relations by setting the United States directly against PRC plans for the territory, and it could set a precedent for a similarly activist U.S. approach for political organization and self-determination in Taiwan—a position strongly opposed by both the Nationalist government in Taipei and the Communist government in Beijing. Those advocating a stronger stand on Hong Kong's future have expressed support for use of U.S. trade sanctions involving Hong Kong should China's rule contribute to a serious decline in Hong Kong's status quo. According to these observers, the U.S. trade relationship is so important to Hong Kong's economic survival that trade sanctions would be an effective means of influencing events there. In particular, the United States could threaten to reduce the benefit Beijing derives from the territory and thereby prompt the Chinese to follow a policy in Hong Kong more compatible with U.S. interests. Others, however, have pointed out that trade sanctions against other countries in the past have rarely proven successful in influencing policy. Moreover, for the United States to protect its significant economic interests in Hong Kong by imposing economic sanctions would seem to be counterproductive.

Notes

1. For background, see the suggested readings at the end of this book. Particularly useful are: Ralph N. Clough, *Island China* (Cambridge, MA: Harvard University Press, 1978); Thomas B. Gold, *State and Society in the Taiwan Miracle* (Armonk, NY: M.E. Sharpe, Inc., 1986); Ramon Myers, ed., *A Unique Relationship: The United States and the Republic of China Under the Taiwan Relations Act* (Stanford,

CA: Hoover Institution Press, 1989); Denis Fred Simon, *Taiwan, Technology Transfer, and Transnationalism: The Political Management of Dependency* (Boulder, CO: Westview Press, 1988); Robert G. Sutter, *Taiwan: Entering the 21st Century* (Asia Society: University Press of America, 1988); and Hung-mao Tien, *The Great Transition: Political and Social Change in the Republic of China* (Stanford, CA: Hoover Institute, 1989).

2. Among recent reviews, see John Copper, *China Diplomacy: The Washington-Taipei-Beijing Triangle* (Boulder, CO: Westview Press, 1991).

3. For quotations and other citations, see U.S. Department of State Bureau of Public Affairs, *Background Notes, Taiwan* (1984 and 1988.)

4. Ibid., 1984.

5. The implications of the reported jet sale were the subject of lively discussion at Taiwan affairs conferences held in the Washington, DC, area in mid-1991. See, among others, *Defense News*, May 13, 1991, p. 1.

6. See, among others, President Lee Teng-hui's interview in *Washington Times*, July 10, 1991.

7. For useful background, see U.S. Department of Commerce, *Foreign Economic Trends and Their Implications for the United States* (Taiwan: December 1990.)

8. *The Far Eastern Economic Review* provides periodic coverage of significant political developments in Taiwan. The government's perspective is often seen in the *Free China Journal*, and an opposition perspective is seen in *The Taiwan Communiqué*, published by the International Committee for Human Rights in Taiwan.

9. See, among others, *Free China Journal* (September 20, 1990), p. 1.

10. For useful background, see, among others, Frank Ching, *Hong Kong and China, For Better or For Worse* (New York: Asia Society and Foreign Policy Association, 1985) and Kerry Dumbaugh and Michael Ipson, *The United States and Hong Kong's Future: Promoting Stability and Growth* (New York: National Committee on U.S.-China Relations, 1990).

11. See, among others, U.S. Department of State. Bureau of Public Affairs, *Background Notes* (Hong Kong: November 1988).

6

Korean-U.S. Relations

Broad U.S. security interests on the Korean peninsula relate to the longstanding U.S. concern to deter aggression, ease tensions, and avoid great-power confrontation. Changes in Chinese and Soviet policy over the past decade have allowed for substantial progress in efforts to reduce the chance of major conflict in Korea. Notably, the Soviet Union established full relations with South Korea and China established a formal trade relationship; both allies of North Korea have repeatedly counseled Pyongyang to take measures to reduce tension and avoid the chance of conflict. Contrary to North Korea's wishes, Moscow and Beijing have indicated their refusal to block South Korea's efforts to enter the United Nations. Pyongyang had held out for a demand that the North and South enter the international body as representing one unified nation, but North Korea was forced to acquiesce to separate delegations when it became clear in 1991 that Moscow and Beijing would not veto Seoul's application to join.[1] Both Koreas joined the United Nations in September 1991.

The decline in Soviet and Chinese material support worsened already poor economic conditions in North Korea, and presumably sapped Pyongyang's ability to threaten the South. The continued firm U.S. security backing for South Korea reinforced this trend. However, North Korea maintained a formidable military force, in a high state of readiness, that required constant vigilance by South Korea and its U.S. ally. Meanwhile, it was widely reported in 1991 that North Korea would soon reach the stage in its nuclear program where it could move to develop its own atomic weapons. Also disturbing were reports of North Korean ability to deliver mass destruction weapons through surface-to-surface ballistic missiles and other means. It was uncertain whether or not strong international pressure would persuade Pyongyang to offer credible safeguards regarding its nuclear program and place limits on other weapons systems of mass destruction. Not only were the United States, China, and Russia following parallel tracks to encourage such an outcome, but Japan seemed determined to use the incentive of much needed Japanese economic aid and trade relations for North Korea to encourage Pyongyang to come to terms on these issues that would be supportive of greater stability in Northeast Asia.[2]

A major uncertainty remained the status of North Korea's leadership. Kim Il Sung had dominated the regime in North Korea since its inception over forty years ago. In 1991, he was seventy-nine years old and reportedly not in the best of health. His son and designated successor reportedly had a less stable personality and less support within powerful security, party, and other constituencies in Pyongyang. Thus, many observers predicted serious political unrest in North Korea once Kim Il Sung dies. The implications for stability on the peninsula appeared serious and wide ranging.

The United States had strong interest in reducing North Korea's potential to threaten regional stability, and U.S. opposition to North Korean human rights, economic, and other policies resulted in continued severely restricted formal contact. The longstanding U.S. policy of following South Korea's lead in policy toward the North also restricted U.S. contacts until there was more substantial progress in North-South Korean relations. The main official channel of U.S.–North Korean contacts was a series of talks held by the political counselors of the U.S. and North Korean embassies in Beijing. U.S. policy toward North Korea was also heavily influenced by North Korea's emerging nuclear program. Better U.S. ties were held out, at least implicitly, as a possible response should North Korea put its nuclear program under tight safeguards and sustain a moderate policy toward the South. As part of its broader review of tactical and short-range nuclear weapons, the United States decided in late 1991, in consultation with South Korea, to remove nuclear weapons from South Korea.

Along with continued U.S. concern about North Korea's potential to disrupt Northeast Asian stability, U.S. policy issues regarding Korea tended to focus on evolving concerns in U.S.–South Korean relations. In recent years, U.S. relations with South Korea have become more complicated as U.S. policymakers face a series of often interrelated economic, security, and political policy questions. The United States wants to foster a better balance in economic and military ties with South Korea, taking account of South Korea's new prosperity and economic competitiveness, while sustaining American interest in stability and prosperity in South Korea. The United States also continues to support progress toward democracy and political pluralism in South Korea, even though it may complicate South Korean decision making on economic, military, or other issues important to the United States. Differences among U.S. policymakers arise over how fast and in what ways the United States should work for changes in U.S.–South Korean relations. Among the varied policy approaches available to U.S. leaders are those that emphasize greater U.S. efforts to push the Koreans out of practices seen as detrimental to U.S. interests; policy approaches that are more cautious in applying U.S. pressure on individual issues in U.S.-Korean relations that would risk seriously disrupting the bilateral relationship, which is seen as important for the United States; and policy approaches that highlight what the United States can do to help remedy strains in U.S.-Korean relations, apart from applying varying degrees of pressure on Korean leaders.

U.S. Interests in South Korea

U.S. interests in South Korea date back to before the Korean War and involve a wide range of security, economic, and political concerns.[3] The United States has remained committed since the 1950–1953 Korean War to maintaining peace on the Korean peninsula. This commitment is widely seen as vital to the peace and stability of Northeast Asia. In particular, the U.S. security guarantee supports U.S. military, economic, and other interests in Japan and strengthens U.S. ability to manage complex relationships among the four major powers—the Soviet Union, China, Japan, and the United States—whose interests converge on the peninsula.

The United States agreed in the 1954 Mutual Security Treaty to defend South Korea from external aggression. U.S. security assistance to South Korea in the early 1980s amounted to between $150 million and $230 million in Foreign Military Sales (FMS) credits annually. Beginning in FY1987, South Korea was "graduated" from the aid program and no longer receives FMS credits. The United States maintains over 40,000 troops in South Korea to supplement the 600,000 strong South Korean armed forces. This force is viewed as needed to deter North Korean military adventurism and repeated terrorist attacks. For example, a 1983 North Korean bomb assassination attempt against South Korean President Chun Doo Hwan in Rangoon, Burma, killed several senior South Korean officials. North Korean agents were also responsible for blowing up a South Korean airliner in November 1987.

The United States has played a major role in fostering South Korea's remarkable economic growth. The Bank of Korea estimated that U.S. economic assistance to South Korea, from 1945 to 1971, totaled $3.8 billion. South Korea has entered the ranks of the newly industrializing countries, with a per capita income of over $4,000 per year. Dependent on foreign trade, South Korea has tried to diversify its foreign markets but still relies on the U.S. market to absorb about 35 percent of its exports. The United States is South Korea's largest trading partner. South Korea is the United States' seventh largest trading partner and is the fourth largest market for U.S. agricultural products. Annual bilateral trade amounted to $15.7 billion in 1985, $18.6 billion in 1986, $24.7 billion in 1987, and $31.8

billion in 1988. The figures for the U.S. trade deficit with South Korea $4.3 billion in 1985, $6.8 billion in 1986, $9.3 billion in 1987, and $9.6 billion in 1988. The U.S. trade deficit with South Korea declined to $6.3 billion in 1989 and $4.1 billion in 1990.

The United States has long viewed South Korean political stability as crucial to economic development, maintaining the security balance on the peninsula, and preserving peace in Northeast Asia. Rather than accept the political status quo, however, U.S. officials in the administration and Congress have pressed the South Korean administration with varying degrees of intensity to gradually liberalize its political structure, broaden the popular base of its government, and release political prisoners. Thus, for example, U.S. officials took the lead in persuading the Chun government in 1981 not to carry out the death sentence imposed on opposition political leader Kim Dae Jung, to allow Kim to seek medical treatment in the United States, and to permit him to return to South Korea in 1985. A political crisis in Seoul during 1987 provoked mass demonstrations calling for greater freedom and democracy, which were strongly backed by U.S. congressional resolutions and administration actions supporting the demands for greater democracy and warning against the use of the military to suppress popular dissent.

Economic Issues

"Unfair" Economic Practices[4]

There are several perceived causes of the recent U.S. trade deficits with Korea and other countries. They involve the results of the recent macroeconomic policies of the United States and other major economic powers, Third World debt, a perceived decline in U.S. ability to compete with its trading partners, and unfair trade and economic practices of U.S. trading partners. Congress has taken the lead in the Omnibus Trade Act of 1988 (P.L. 100-418) and other measures in pressing for a more active U.S. effort to promote change in perceived unfair trading and other economic policies of foreign competitors. In the case of Korea, the United States has focused in recent years on better access to the Korean market. Under heavy pressure from the United States and other trading partners, the Korean government has instituted a series of sometimes sweeping changes designed to loosen restrictions on imports and foreign investment and better protect foreign intellectual property rights (copyrights and patents). Thus, Korean officials claim that the government has already reduced to a small fraction the number of products whose importation were restricted by the Korean Foreign Trade Act; that tariff cuts taken or planned will reduce average tariffs by 1993 to a level comparable to those in the United States and the West; and that markets for insurance, telecommunications, and maritime transportation are gradually opening. They also note that, responding to U.S. demands that Korea's currency adjust to international economic realities, the Korean currency rose more than 30 percent in value relative to the U.S. dollar over three years; and that South Korea has instituted a system to protect U.S. and other foreign intellectual property and is attempting to meet U.S. charges that the system is not enforced fairly.

The United States still seeks removal of numerous formal and informal restrictions on foreign economic activity in South Korea to make U.S. firms more competitive. U.S. representatives focus on the opening of the Korean markets and the opening of the Korean business system to reduce restrictive regulation and promote a transparent and supportive business and regulatory environment. Korea's often closed agriculture markets remain a primary objective. Other priorities include access to the Korean market for services, such as financial services and telecommunications, in which U.S. companies are competitive, and the ability to compete with fewer restrictions in the domestic Korean market, including public sector procurement. The United States wants more improvement in protection of intellectual property rights and greater deregulation of foreign direct investment into Korea.

At the end of April 1989, the U.S. government released the annual National Trade Estimate Report on Foreign Barriers. The report outlined the trade practices of thirty-four countries that restrict U.S. exports. Based on this report, the U.S. Trade Representative designated "priority countries" and "priority practices" under the so-called Super 301 provision of the 1988 Trade Act.

When the priority list was made public at the end of May 1989, Korea was not included. Korea successfully avoided the designation as a Super 301 "priority country" by agreeing to a number of U.S. objectives, including reductions in import tariffs on some 200 agricultural products; elimination of import restrictions on selected food products; liberalization of grain and livestock imports; liberalization of the foreign investment process; and elimination of restrictions and performance obligations for foreign investors. Korea also made commitments for stronger protection of intellectual property rights. By making prior concessions and avoiding designation as an unfair trading country, Korea helped weaken the perception held by some in the United States that it represents a "second Japan." Korea's actions also gained it some goodwill on Capitol Hill. The U.S. decision to exclude Korea from "Super 301" consideration was a close call. U.S. decision makers continue to watch carefully to see how Korea implements its many recent pledges (the U.S. Trade Representative placed Korea on its "priority watch list" for intellectual property rights violations).

In late 1990, U.S. officials were particularly critical of a government-sponsored "austerity" plan that had the effect of sharply limiting sales of some U.S. products in the South Korean market.

U.S. Restrictions on Korean Imports

Reflecting the interests of U.S. textile, steel, and other industries challenged by an influx of imported goods in recent years, the administration has instituted a series of restrictions affecting textile and steel imports into the United States. As a major exporter of these products, Korea has been affected by these decisions. Korea is the second most important supplier of foreign-made textiles in the United States and has a steel industry highly competitive in international markets. Koreans complain that these arrangements are restrictive. Coming at a time of strong U.S. pressure to open Korea's markets, the restrictions are also said to reflect an apparent "double standard" in U.S. trade policy.

Security Issues

U.S.–South Korean security ties have long been determined by the two countries' judgments of their respective security needs, which are based principally on the prevailing military balance on the Korean peninsula and in Northeast Asia. Persisting pressure on U.S. government resources in recent years has restricted the amount of money available for defense and has prompted U.S. policymakers in Congress and the administration to press well-to-do or newly prosperous allies (like South Korea) to share more of the allied defense burden. U.S. policymakers also have become more cautious than in the past in arranging for the transfer of defense technology to allies (as part of weapons coproduction or other security programs) that might enhance the capabilities of foreign competitors of U.S. manufacturers in the years ahead. Meanwhile, U.S.-backed political liberalization in South Korea in recent years has allowed some rising criticism of the U.S. military presence and practices in South Korea. Such criticism, along with reassessment of threats from the North in a period of broader détente in East-West relations, have prompted some in Congress to call for a scaling down of the U.S. presence. Recent issues focus on proposals to withdraw some U.S. forces from South Korea; to place restrictions on a proposed U.S.–South Korean coproduction arrangement for a new jet fighter for the South Korean air force; and to lower the profile of the U.S. military presence and command structure. At the same time, many U.S. officials were interested in South Korea's efforts to support multilateral efforts in opposition to Iraq's invasion of Kuwait in August 1990.

U.S. Troop Withdrawal

In June 1989, Senator Dale Bumpers and five other senators introduced legislation (S. 1264) calling for a gradual withdrawal of 10,000 U.S. ground forces in Korea by 1992. He noted that South Korea is strong enough economically to fill whatever gap would be caused by the U.S. withdrawal, and that the cost of U.S. forces in South Korea ($2.5 billion) is something the United States can ill afford while Korea runs a large trade surplus with the United States and spends somewhat less proportionately on defense than does the United States. He pointed out that South Korea is much richer and has twice the population of North Korea. Senator Carl Levin earlier in June had also called for a scaling back of U.S. forces in Korea, and press reports indicated that the Bush administration was also considering some adjustments in U.S. forces. The defense authorization bill for 1990–1991 (H.R. 2461), which was reported on November 6, 1989, called for U.S.–South Korean consultations on possible U.S. troop withdrawals and greater South Korean sharing of the allied defense burden on the peninsula. It did not specify any reduction of U.S. troops. As part of its consideration of the defense appropriations bill (H.R. 3072) on September 26, 1989, the Senate defeated by a vote of 65 to 34 a proposal to order the withdrawal of 3,000 U.S. troops from Korea and called instead for the administration to "reassess" U.S. deployments there.

During a February 1990 visit to Korea, Defense Secretary Richard Cheney reportedly told the South Koreans that the United States wants to withdraw 5,000 noncombatants from South Korea by 1993. (Bush administration plans were later adjusted to call for a withdrawal of 7,000 forces by 1993.) On September 12, 1990, the House defeated an amendment to H.R. 4739 that would have withdrawn 13,000 of the 43,000 U.S. troops in Korea over the course of three years. In May 1991, the House passed the FY1992 defense authorization bill (H.R. 2100), which positively referred to Korea's burden-sharing efforts, and defeated an amendment that would have cut U.S. forces in Korea by one third.[5]

Issues for U.S. policy include how such proposals would affect the tenuous balance on the Korean peninsula and U.S.–South Korean relations. Some U.S. officials judge that North Korea has shown little sign of relaxing its forward deployed force posture, and that Northern forces have advantages in numbers, location, firepower, and readiness that can only be deterred by a strong U.S. presence. They add that South Korea is one of a few U.S. allies that spends on defense close to the same level of GNP (4.4 percent of GNP for 630,000 troops) as does the United States; and Seoul has contributed heavily (estimated by the Koreans at about $2.2 billion— U.S. officials judge this as an inflated estimate, although the U.S. government has not arrived at an official estimate of its own)[6] for the maintenance of U.S. forces in South Korea. Finally, this view holds that to avoid sending the "wrong signal" to Pyongyang about U.S. intentions and to avoid exacerbating strains in U.S.–South Korean relations, careful U.S.–South Korean consultations are required before any U.S. troop withdrawal is considered.

U.S. Military Profile in South Korea

The large and prominent U.S. military presence in South Korea has been a source of criticism on the part of some South Koreans. The criticism has added to friction between the two countries. Solutions have focused on provisions and proposals to lower the profile of U.S. forces in South Korea. Specific steps have included a recent U.S.–South Korean agreement to move a large U.S. base, containing an eighteen-hole golf course, from downtown Seoul to a less crowded area and to consider changes giving South Korean officers greater prominence in the current U.S.-led Combined Forces Command—the command structure that generally governs the operation of U.S. and South Korean forces in defense of South Korea. In March 1991, a South Korean general was appointed for the first time as head of the allied side at the military armistice talks at Panmunjom. In June 1991, it was disclosed that a South Korean general would take over command of the combined U.S.-ROK ground forces. Other proposed adjustments are designed to redress Korean complaints about perceived inequities in treatment of Americans and Koreans under the U.S.–South Korean Status-of-Forces Agreement (SOFA) and about perceived intrusive and culturally offensive segments in U.S. armed forces television broadcasting.

The FY1990 military construction appropriations bill (H.R. 3012), which passed Congress on October 27, 1989, deleted all but $14 million of the $84 million requested for construction in South Korea. In October 1990, Congress passed H.R. 5313, which eliminated military construction requested in Korea. The FY1990 defense authorization bill (H.R. 2461), which was reported November 6, 1989, called on the Pentagon to come up with a five-year plan that, among other things, would address relocation of U.S. bases and adjustments in U.S.–South Korean military command relations. The FY1991 defense appropriations bill (H.R. 5803) cut 25 percent of the amount requested by the administration to pay foreign nationals employed at U.S. bases. On January 4, 1991, U.S. and ROK officials signed a new status-of-forces agreement that gave the ROK wider jurisdiction on offenses committed by U.S. forces in Korea.

The FX-Korean Fighter Aircraft Program

U.S. senators John Heinz and Alan Dixon introduced legislation (S.Res. 154) in July 1989 objecting to provisions of a reported U.S. plan to help

South Korea produce a new jet fighter, known as the "FX" or Korean Fighter Program (KFP). They were particularly concerned with the possible transfer of U.S. technology under the agreement which, in their judgment, could help South Korea develop an aircraft industry competitive with the United States, and with reported provisions in the planned agreement that would require the U.S. contractor to agree to "offset" the amount of the Korean purchase by purchasing a comparable amount of Korean products. On July 19, 1989, the Senate approved (S.Res. 154) as an amendment to the State Department authorization bill (S. 1160). In August, the Defense Department reportedly warned U.S. manufacturers and the South Korean government against offering excessive offsets in the pending deal. On December 20, 1989, South Korea said it had selected the McDonnell Douglas Corporation's F/A-18 as the new Korean fighter. On July 19, 1990, the Bush administration reportedly submitted a formal notification to Congress on the deal, and it reportedly provided the two congressional foreign policy committees a draft memorandum of understanding outlining the administration's position on offset arrangements and technology transfer. On October 15, 1990, an amendment sponsored by Senator Dixon was attached to the defense appropriations bill that called for Congress to receive copies of the "memorandum of understanding" before the fighter deal could go through. Senator Dixon dropped the amendment on October 23, 1990, after the administration approved release of the memorandum to him and other members of Congress. On March 28, 1991, South Korea announced that it had ended negotiations with McDonnell Douglas and had placed an order worth $5.2 billion with General Dynamics involving 120 F-16 fighter planes. Senator Dixon and others voiced concern over the terms of the deal and, at their request, U.S. General Accounting Office (GAO) investigations were begun in May and June 1991.

Iraq-Kuwait Crisis

According to press reports of August 8, 1990,[7] the U.S. government expressed regret over what it saw as South Korea's low-key initial reaction to Iraq's invasion of Kuwait. South Korea had a large economic stake in Iraq and Kuwait involving Iraqi debts, outstanding construction projects, and orders for tankers. South Korea announced a restrictive ban on trade with Iraq and occupied Kuwait on August 9. The Bush administration's subsequent plan to call on others to provide financial and other support for the multilateral effort to press for Iraqi withdrawal from Kuwait reportedly involved South Korean aid amounting to $450 million. By January 31, 1991, South Korea had pledged $500 million to the costs of Desert Shield/Storm and to frontline states, a 154-member military medical unit, and five C-130 planes and related personnel.

Political Issues

From one perspective, U.S. support for democratization in South Korea has been a great success for U.S policy. Unlike the authoritarian leaders of the past, the current president, Roh Tae Woo, was popularly elected, even though he received only 36 percent of the vote in an election in late 1987. (The opposition vote of over 50 percent was split between two opposition candidates, Kim Dae Jung and Kim Young Sam.) The election in April 1988 for the 299-seat National Assembly gave President Roh's party control of 125 seats and the three main opposition parties control of, respectively, 72 seats (Kim Dae Jung), 58 seats (Kim Young Sam), and 35 seats (Kim Jong Pil).

Past restrictions on press and individual freedoms have been relaxed, and a number of political prisoners released. Korean opposition leaders criticized what they saw as a resurgence of human rights abuses in South Korea in 1989. Over forty U.S. members of Congress reportedly sent a letter to President Bush in September 1989 asking him to raise discussion on the human rights situation with President Roh during the latter's visit to Washington in October 1989.[8]

A major political reorganization took place in early 1990 as Roh Tae Woo, Kim Young Sam, and Kim Jong Pil merged their parties into one, the Democratic Liberal Party (DLP), which commanded over 200 seats in the 299-seat National Assembly. The merger left Kim Dae Jung's Party for Peace and Democracy as the only significant opposition party. Initial power-sharing arrangements in the new DLP went smoothly, but by mid-1990 there were widespread reports of factional differences within the party and popular discontent with the DLP and its leaders. This was accompanied by continued active labor strikes and an upsurge in antigovernment demonstrations led by students and others. On April 9, 1991, Kim Dae Jung's party merged with another opposition group to form the "New Democratic Union Party," with Kim as the party leader.

An upsurge of radical student demonstrations, including several suicides, in spring 1991, came at a time of low popularity for the Roh Tae Woo government and popular discontent over inflation, housing, and other issues. But the students were unable to garner much support from middle-class Koreans. Roh released some prisoners, reshuffled government leaders, and took other steps to deal with the crisis.

The United States welcomes the politically more democratic and fluid situation in South Korea even though it poses several important considerations for U.S. policymakers. The situation complicates the ability of the South Korean government to accommodate U.S. demands on the trade, defense, or other issues that are politically unpopular in South Korea, because opponents may well exploit the issues in local, regional, and national elections slated over the next few years. It makes it difficult for the Roh Tae Woo government to successfully counter anti-American charges made by vocal critics, especially in the South Korean universities and the press, regarding the alleged U.S. role in the division of Korea after World War II; the alleged U.S. complicity in the bloody crackdown by South Korean forces of Korean dissidents in the city of Kwangju in May 1980; and the alleged longstanding U.S. policy of supporting authoritarian rule in South Korea. It prompts the South Korean government to make politically popular initiatives toward communist neighbors, and especially North Korea, that may run the risk of promoting an imprudent sense of relaxation on the peninsula. On the one hand, President Roh's popular "Nordpolitik" has been welcomed by the Bush administration and resulted in the establishment of closer South Korean relations with several communist countries, including Hungary, Yugoslavia, Poland, Bulgaria, and the Soviet Union (formal diplomatic relations) and China (trade ties). Nevertheless, this has not appreciably reduced the threat from North Korea. As a result, some observers in the United States and South Korea caution that the allies should not be lulled into reducing a vigilant defense posture. Finally, it raises the possibility of more serious political and economic instability in South Korea. Labor strife over the past two years has been unprecedented; demands for wage increases have outstripped productivity gains in many areas; declining economic competitiveness could lead to an economic downturn, which—when combined with a new government, vocal opposition politicians, and a large anti-establishment press and intellectual community—could result in instability detrimental to South Korea's security and continued prosperity.

U.S. Policy Approaches

Broad American policy goals remain clear despite the rapid changes affecting circumstances in South Korea and U.S.-South Korean relations. The United States wants to foster an appropriate balance in economic and military ties with South Korea, taking into account South Korea's new prosperity and economic competitiveness, while sustaining American interest in South Korea's stability and prosperity. The United States also will continue to support progress toward democracy and political pluralism in South Korea, even though such progress may complicate South Korean decision making on a number of issues important to the United States. U.S. policymakers also will likely continue efforts at consultation and negotiations with South Korean counterparts to build a greater consensus on both sides of the Pacific as to the value of the U.S.-South Korean relationship. Differences among U.S. policymakers arise over how fast and in what ways the United States should work for changes in U.S.-

South Korean relations. Among the varied policy approaches available to U.S. leaders, there are those that emphasize greater U.S. pressure to push the Koreans out of practices seen as detrimental to U.S. interests. Koreans are said to be unlikely to change without strong pressure, and the changes that are sought are said to be of sufficient value for U.S. economic, security, or political interests as to warrant the use of U.S. pressure despite possible adverse South Korean reactions. Moreover, pressure on Korea regarding economic, defense, and political issues is also thought to have a useful effect on U.S. allies, close trading partners, or other states. Specific tactics include private U.S. pressure applied in negotiations, such as those associated with the "Super 301" process; public U.S. criticism of Korea's restricted market access for certain U.S. goods and services; advocacy of greater South Korean financial support for the U.S. troop presence in South Korea, gradual reduction of the U.S. troop presence, and/or expansion of South Korean military capabilities to fill some of the roles now performed by U.S. forces in South Korea; and private and public U.S. efforts to encourage South Korea to buy U.S. jet fighters "off the shelf" rather than require elaborate coproduction and offset arrangements that could add to foreign competition for U.S. arms exporters and could reduce the positive impact of such sales on the U.S. trade balance.

Other policy approaches are more cautious in applying U.S. pressure on individual issues. Advocates of such policy approaches believe that the benefits of greater U.S. pressure on Korea regarding economic, defense, or political issues might not be worth the disruption they could cause to close U.S.–South Korean ties. They are particularly concerned that the cumulative effect of recent U.S. prodding on economic, defense burden-sharing, and political liberalization questions might prove to be too much for the still weak South Korean government to handle gracefully. The result could be growing anti-American feeling in South Korea that could fuel a mutual desire for withdrawal of U.S. forces; or the result could be political instability among the competing political factions in South Korea. Such outcomes are seen as dangerous in the face of North Korea's threat and as contrary to the longstanding U.S. interest in stability on the peninsula.

Meanwhile, there are policy approaches that highlight what the United States can do to help remedy strains in U.S.–Korean relations, apart from applying varying degrees of pressure on Korean leaders for economic, security, or other changes. Some stress that the U.S. trade deficit with Korea would improve markedly following serious U.S. efforts to cut the U.S. government's spending deficit and to promote policies that effectively encourage greater savings, technological development, productivity, and educational competence in the United States. It is also suggested that U.S.–South Korean trade relations would be effectively treated within multilateral arrangements like the General Agreements on Tariffs and Trade (GATT), where South Korea and the United States could adjust their policies without appearing to be giving in to outside pressure.

Some urge U.S. policy adjustments to foster a more collaborative relationship that remains sensitive to South Korean feelings. This could be pursued by raising the stature of the Korean commander in the Combined Forces Command, by highlighting South Korea's economic role in various economic forums being proposed for the Pacific Rim countries, or by other measures. U.S. officials could work harder than in the past to consult with South Korean counterparts and to engage the South Korean press and intellectuals to create a more positive image for U.S.-Korean relations than at present.

An issue cited for possible close U.S.-ROK cooperation concerns the desirability of reunification of North and South Korea. Even though the Bush administration supports President Roh's "Nordpolitik" and is on record favoring Korean unification, press, students, and intellectuals in South Korea sometimes tend to perceive that the United States is less than enthusiastic about "Nordpolitik." Joint Bush-Roh administration efforts to change this perception could build closer cooperation and improve the U.S. image in the South. A highlight in this regard was seen in the fact that President Roh met President Gorbachev on June 4, 1990, in San Francisco, following Gorbachev's meeting with President Bush in Washington.

Notes

1. The *Far Eastern Economic Review* and *Asian Wall Street Journal* provide useful coverage of significant recent events affecting developments in Korea. For background on these events, see, among others, Council on Foreign Relations/The Asia Society, *Korea at the Crossroads: Implications for American Policy* (New York: The Asia Society, 1987); Karen Elliott House, "Where Communism Still Thrives," *Wall Street Journal*, June 6, 1991; Byung Chul Koh, *A Midterm Assessment of the Roh Tae Woo Government* (New York: The Asia Society, 1990); and Robert Sutter and Han Sungjoo, *Korea-U.S. Relations in a Changing World* (Berkeley, CA: University of California, 1990).

2. See, among others, the reports in the *Washington Post*, published by senior diplomatic correspondent Don Oberdofer during an extensive visit to Korea, Japan, and China in May–June 1991.

3. See, among others, U.S. Department of State, Bureau of Public Affairs, *Background Notes* (South Korea: April 1987).

4. See, among others, U.S. Department of Commerce, Foreign Economic Trends and Their Implications for the United States (South Korea, annually updated).

5. See *Congressional Quarterly Weekly Report* for coverage of this and other legislative action.

6. Interviews with the author, Washington, DC, November 1990.

7. Replayed in U.S. Foreign Broadcast Information Service (FBIS), *Daily Report, Asia and Pacific*. (August 9, 1990).

8. See coverage in FBIS *Daily Report, Asia and Pacific*. (October 2, 1990).

7

Policy Concerns in Indochina: A Peace Settlement in Cambodia and Possible Normalization with Vietnam

By the end of the 1980s, the decade-long conflict in Cambodia caused by Vietnamese military occupation of the country had entered a new stage, and negotiations for a peace agreement had become more active. Vietnam withdrew most—if not all—of its forces from Cambodia. Vietnamese officials and representatives of the country's client government in Phnom Penh expressed some flexibility regarding a compromise political settlement of the Cambodian conflict. This was strongly encouraged by their main international supporter, the Soviet Union. The three resistance groups (those led by the Khmer Rouge, Prince Norodom Sihanouk, and former prime minister Son Sann) and their main international backers in China, the Association of Southeast Asian Nations (ASEAN), and the United States responded with varying degrees of flexibility.

All parties in the conflict appeared to see their interests as better served by making some adjustment in their positions, rather than by sticking to the intransigence of the previous ten years. They held repeated deliberations, including an international conference on Cambodia that began in Paris on July 30, 1989; but obstacles to a peace agreement remained. They centered on guaranteeing Vietnam's military withdrawal and achieving a peace agreement in Cambodia that would neither allow the return of the genocidal practices of the Khmer Rouge, nor permit Vietnam to continue domination over Cambodia. Significant progress toward a peaceful settlement was made in 1991, leading to a reconvening of the major international conference in Paris, where a peace accord was signed in October 1991. The accord called for a strong U.N. peacekeeping role, partial demobilization of combatants, a cutoff of foreign military supplies and U.N.-sponsored elections leading to the creation of a new Cambodian government by 1993. But significant concern was raised about the ability of the United Nations to carry out these large tasks and about the willingness of Cambodian factions, especially the Khmer Rouge, to be bound by the terms of the agreement.

In the wake of the peace accord, U.S. policy continues to face dilemmas in Cambodia.[1] Most notably, the United States wants to help push back Vietnamese expansion in Indochina and to support the positions of its treaty ally Thailand and other friends in ASEAN. But the United States strongly opposes the Khmer Rouge and fears that Vietnamese withdrawal may result in expanded scope for the Khmer Rouge and their brutal rule. In the past, U.S. policy dealt with these competing pressures by adopting a low posture that followed the lead of ASEAN. The United States provided small amounts of nonlethal assistance to the two noncommunist resistance forces led by Prince Sihanouk and Son Sann, but it has refused any support to the third and most powerful member of the resistance groups, the Khmer Rouge. As the Vietnamese began to withdraw and the search for a peace agreement intensified, U.S. policymakers in the Bush administration and Congress proposed steps to strengthen the two noncommunist resistance groups led by Sihanouk and Son Sann, to block the return to power of the Khmer Rouge, and to relieve human suffering in Cambodia.

But U.S. policymakers strongly disagreed on the appropriate steps necessary to reach these goals and support broader foreign policy objectives. Policy issues facing them at the start of the 1990s included the following:

- What are the most effective means for the United States to follow in order to curb the supply of weapons to the Khmer Rouge, or to otherwise ensure that these Cambodian communists are not allowed to return to a dominant position of power in Cambodia?
- Should the United States strengthen the influence of the two noncommunist resistance forces that maintained a loose alignment with the Khmer Rouge against the Vietnamese-backed communist government in Phnom Penh?
- What is the effect on U.S. influence in the Cambodian situation of the absence of normal U.S. relations with Vietnam? What are the pros and cons of normalizing relations with Hanoi and what are the main procedures that would have to be considered in such normalization of relations?
- What is the appropriate U.S. policy toward China, Russia, Japan, and other powers in regard to a Cambodian settlement? Is there possible common ground among them that could help to foster a settlement that would be in the interests of the United States? Is the United

Nations or some other forum appropriate for these powers to meet to discuss Cambodia?
- How do U.S. policy interests in a Cambodian settlement and possible normalization of relations with Vietnam fit in with broad U.S. economic and humanitarian concerns, including resolution of longstanding interests over U.S. prisoners of war and missing in action (POWs/MIAs) from the Vietnam War and the large refugee populations coming from Vietnam and Cambodia?

In the new more fluid situation in Indochina, U.S. support was actively sought by various proponents of Cambodian peace plans. And U.S. leverage was seen as more important than in the past. This leverage stemmed from several factors:

- The United States was one of five members of the U.N. Security Council and a key financial backer of U.N. operations, including U.N. peacekeeping operations as part of a Cambodian settlement.
- U.S. covert and overt aid to the noncommunist Cambodian resistance was a key element in the international support received by those two groups.
- Ending the U.S. diplomatic and economic embargo against Vietnam was seen to be of profound importance to Hanoi leaders in their efforts to break out of their diplomatic-economic isolation that had resulted from their invasion of Cambodia. It was seen to be the main incentive that could be offered by the United States in order to encourage Hanoi to press its client regime in Phnom Penh to be flexible over a future Cambodian settlement, humanitarian issues, and other questions.
- The United States exerted influence on the lending policies of the international financial institutions and had some influence on the lending policies followed by other possible sources of economic assistance to Indochina, notably Japan.
- The United States remained an ally of Thailand, the key ASEAN conduit of support for all three Cambodian resistance groups and base for the 300,000 displaced Cambodians who provided the new recruits for the resistance.
- Despite the downturn in U.S.-Chinese relations following Beijing's hard crackdown on dissent in mid-1989, the United States sustained limited high-level communications and possibly considerable influence with China, the main backer of the Khmer Rouge resistance forces.
- Radical change in Eastern Europe and internal instability in the Soviet Union reinforced President Gorbachev's need for greater outreach to

the West. This appeared to give the interests of the United States greater importance in Soviet calculations of policies in areas of past controversy in U.S.-Soviet relations. In particular, it seemed to promise a Soviet approach toward a settlement in Cambodia and evolution in Indochina more in accord with U.S. interests.

This chapter reviews recent efforts to reach a Cambodian peace agreement, assesses the positions and interests of the contending parties, and examines U.S. policy dilemmas and possible options. Because U.S. policy toward the Cambodian problem is closely related to the state of U.S.-Vietnamese relations, the chapter concludes with an examination of U.S.-Vietnamese relations: it reviews developments since 1975 and assesses competing U.S. policy approaches.

A Settlement in Cambodia: U.S. Interests, Options, and Policy Debate[2]

American policy has had several longstanding interests in Cambodia. These interests are often at odds with one another, and U.S. policymakers have disagreed about what steps are appropriate to strike a proper balance to serve these interests and broader U.S. policy objectives.

On the one hand, the United States—along with China, Thailand, and other members of ASEAN—has wanted to push back the Soviet-supported Vietnamese expansion in Cambodia. The Vietnamese army, with Soviet support, invaded Cambodia in December 1978 and toppled the Khmer Rouge government then in control of the country. The Vietnamese set up in Phnom Penh a client regime, the State of Cambodia (SOC), known prior to 1989 as the People's Republic of Kampuchea (PRK), and backed it with Vietnamese troops. The Soviet Union provided military and economic assistance.

For many years, U.S. policy followed the lead of its treaty ally Thailand and other members of ASEAN, and of China, in giving political support and modest amounts of nonlethal military support to the armed resistance against the Vietnamese occupiers and their Cambodian client government. U.S. policy avoided all contacts with the Khmer Rouge, the strongest of three loosely connected groups resisting the Vietnamese, which received support mainly from China. It focused support on the two noncommunist resistance groups, led by Prince Sihanouk and former prime minister Son Sann.

On the other hand, U.S. policy also has opposed strongly the Khmer Rouge. When it ruled in Cambodia in 1975–1978, the Khmer Rouge carried out radical social policies and a bloody reign of terror that resulted in over one million deaths. Though driven from power by the Vietnamese, the

Khmer Rouge regrouped along the Thai-Cambodian border and have grown in size and strength as an insurgency opposing the Vietnamese and their client regime, the SOC. Pol Pot and other senior leaders responsible for the atrocities of the 1970s have remained central to Khmer Rouge policies and practices up to the present.

By the late 1980s, the Vietnamese faced a protracted military stalemate in Cambodia, declining Soviet support, and deteriorating economic conditions in Vietnam brought on in part by U.S.-led international economic and political restrictions on contacts with Vietnam. Hanoi withdrew most, if not all, of its forces from Cambodia by late 1989 and became an active participant in international negotiations to achieve a peaceful settlement of the Cambodian conflict.

As the Vietnamese withdrew, peace negotiations became more active—a trend helped by the broader U.S.-Soviet thaw in relations that accelerated in 1989–1990. The Bush administration became actively involved in brokering a settlement. Bush administration policy in 1990 emphasized the importance of peace negotiations led by the five permanent members of the U.N. Security Council. The five powers reached a general agreement on principles to govern a peace settlement in January 1990, announced a more detailed plan for peace in August 1990, and held further talks during the year. During these talks, details of the peace plan were worked out among the competing Cambodian groups and interested international parties. The so-called Perm Five plan was endorsed by the four contending Cambodian parties (i.e., the Vietnamese-backed communist State of Cambodia in Phnom Penh, and the three loosely aligned resistance groups, the communist Khmer Rouge and the noncommunist resistance groups led by Sihanouk and Son Sann. But, despite hopeful negotiations and occasional diplomatic breakthroughs, the Cambodian groups were unable for some time to overcome an impasse over the distribution of political power in Cambodia and other issues. Attention focused in part on the composition and role of the "Supreme National Council." The Council serves as an interim political arrangement and a repository of Cambodian sovereignty while the United Nations administers Cambodia until elections are held and a new Cambodian government is formed, according to terms of the Perm Five plan. More specifically, the SOC, and its Vietnamese supporters, was concerned with giving up its military power and political authority to U.N. administration, in the face of what it saw as inadequate safeguards against the threatening power of the Khmer Rouge.

The Bush administration also attempted to strengthen the two noncommunist resistance groups through U.S. covert and overt assistance and other means. The United States provided over $3 million of overt nonlethal aid annually to the noncommunist resistance from 1985 to 1988; in FY1989 the amount was $5 million and in FY1990 the amount was $7 million. A reportedly larger amount of covert U.S. nonlethal aid was also provided. Such support was designed to continue to pressure Vietnam and its Phnom Penh client to compromise on a Cambodian peace settlement; it also helped in an attempt to sustain the two noncommunist resistance groups as a viable noncommunist force in a post-settlement Cambodia, especially vis-à-vis the more powerful forces of the communist State of Cambodia and the communist Khmer Rouge.

Many in the U.S. Congress believed that the Bush administration struck the right balance in attempting to support the return to peace in Cambodia through the Perm Five plan, continued nonlethal support to the noncommunist resistance, and maintenance of the U.S. economic and political restrictions against the SOC and its Vietnamese backer. During 1989 and 1990, however, there emerged in Congress a growing group of vocal and powerful critics who endeavored to push for changes in U.S. policy on Cambodia. These critics judged that the terms and slow progress of the Perm Five peace plan enhanced the legitimacy of the Khmer Rouge and failed to check its rising power and influence in Cambodia. U.S. aid to the noncommunist resistance was seen to play into the hands of the Khmer Rouge and weaken the Cambodian faction best equipped to offset Khmer Rouge power, the State of Cambodia. The critics pressed for a cutoff of U.S. aid to the noncommunist insurgents, and the opening of aid, trade, and other contacts with people under the administration of the SOC.

In the face of this political pressure, administration officials and supporters in Congress modified policy and continued to emphasize support for the Perm Five plan, assistance to the noncommunist resistance, and restricted U.S. interaction with Phnom Penh and Hanoi. Arrangements reached during 1990 reflected new U.S. attempts to restrict the power and influence of the Khmer Rouge, to provide U.S. aid to people under Phnom Penh's rule as well as to the noncommunist insurgents, to phase out the U.S. covert aid to the insurgents, and to open official contacts with both Phnom Penh and Hanoi over a Cambodian settlement.

Events in late 1990 and early 1991 appeared likely to continue the debate between Bush administration supporters and critics. The debate lay behind-the-scenes during much of this period on account of U.S. preoccupation with the Persian Gulf crisis. The defeat of Iraq and the requirements of the authorization and appropriations process saw renewed attention devoted to Cambodia by March 1991. There was widespread concern that the Perm Five peace plan had reached an impasse. Backed by Vietnam, the SOC remained reluctant to give up its military power and political authority, asserting that it felt threatened by rising Khmer Rouge power. Concurrently, the Khmer Rouge reportedly was expanding its political influence in the Cambodian countryside and had come up with economic enterprises that would help sustain itself if outside support were cut off. A series of State Department and U.S. General Accounting Office (GAO) reports required by law or requested by the Senate Foreign Relations Committee detailed the extent of cooperation between forces of the noncommunist opposition and the Khmer Rouge; revealed the amount of U.S. aid flowing to the noncommunist resistance through the auspices of the McCollum Amendment—200 tons of surplus U.S. Department of Defense commodities provided under that program from 1987 to 1989 were not counted as part of the U.S. overt aid to the noncommunist resistance at that time; and disclosed that the $100 million U.S. contribution to the U.N. border relief operations from 1983 to 1989 represented about 30 percent of the total cost of the program, which helped to feed, shelter, and provide basic medical care for the 300,000 displaced Cambodians located in camps along the Thai border, including the 70,000 Cambodians located in camps controlled by the Khmer Rouge. By early 1991, there was considerable congressional grumbling over the fact that the administration had yet to conduct a U.S. aid "needs" assessment involving the people under control of the SOC, and that the allocation of U.S. assistance between the noncommunist resistance and the needy Cambodians under SOC control appeared to favor the former and oppose the latter.[3] Subsequent progress in peace talks during mid-1991 and the conclusion of a peace accord in Paris in October 1991 eased the immediate concerns in the debate. But observers were uncertain as to the likely long-term outcome of peace talks and their implications for the United States. In particular, critics of the administration's position focused on the ability of the Khmer Rouge to reenter Phnom Penh under terms of the peace accord and warned of stronger U.S. measures needed to restrict the power of the Khmer Rouge.

The strong debate between administration supporters and congressional critics provided the backdrop for a third, less clearly articulated viewpoint on the Cambodian crisis. There are many Americans who share the strong moral concerns voiced by the administration backers and detractors regarding the desirability of restoring peace and territorial integrity to Cambodia and restricting the power of the Khmer Rouge. But they tend to believe that the United States should be more realistic in acknowledging American ignorance of the forces at work inside Cambodia; the limited influence of the United States among the local and regional actors with a basic stake in the situation in Cambodia; and America's continuing difficulty in dealing decisively with sensitive issues related to the U.S. experience in Indochina.

This point of view often emphasizes the difficult questions U.S. leaders face in attempting to overcome fundamental dilemmas in U.S. policy: How could a proper balance be established between the desire to prevent Vietnamese domination of Cambodia and the opposition to the spread of

Khmer Rouge influence? When will conditions in Cambodia and progress in U.S.-Vietnamese bilateral humanitarian issues reach a point where the United States can move decisively to normalize relations with Vietnam? How should the United States assess the sometimes conflicting signals coming from its ally Thailand and other members of ASEAN about an appropriate U.S. policy toward Cambodia and Vietnam? How does U.S. policy toward Cambodia fit in the midst of changes in Asia brought about by the collapse of communist regimes in Eastern Europe; the rise of a more collaborative than contentious U.S.-Soviet relationship; and a decline in positive U.S. attention to China as result of differences since 1989? Proponents of this viewpoint also focus on what they see as the checkered record of U.S. policy in recent years, where American attention has been pushed toward one "solution" after another, only to find each solution to be less than satisfactory. For example, some in the United States thought in the mid-1980s that active U.S. support for Son Sann's noncommunist resistance forces represented a good way to encourage the formation of a viable noncommunist alternative to the two more powerful Cambodian communist groups, the Khmer Rouge and the PRK. Closer examination and battlefield experience showed severe leadership and morale problems in Son Sann's organization. U.S. attention then focused on Prince Sihanouk and his forces. The prince was seen by some, including senior leaders in the Reagan administration, to have great residual popular support in Cambodia; he could provide an effective check to the Khmer Rouge and to the PRK in a future Cambodian government. Closer examination of the prince's mercurial behavior and his ties to China raised suspicions about his ability to play a meaningful independent role.

As the Vietnamese troops withdrew from Cambodia in 1989, American leaders gave more attention to the possible growth of Khmer Rouge power and influence. Some called for U.S. efforts to normalize with the SOC and with Vietnam in the interests of strengthening forces that would prevent a Khmer Rouge revival and possible takeover in Cambodia. But subsequent developments, including reports of continuing substantial Vietnamese military presence in Cambodia, raised doubts about the credibility of Phnom Penh and Hanoi concerning the degree of residual Vietnamese influence in Cambodia.

In 1990, U.S. hopes focused on meetings of the five U.N. Security Council members on establishing a framework for a settlement in Cambodia. Closer examination showed that the powers, even if they could agree among themselves, had difficulty in persuading the competing Cambodian factions to come to terms.

It is added that, in American domestic politics, the legacy of the U.S. experience in the Vietnam War still impedes U.S. policy toward Indochina. For example, the Bush administration's effort in 1989 to provide lethal assistance to the noncommunist resistance in Cambodia was stopped by those who argued that such commitment could start a military involvement similar to that seen in earlier U.S. involvement with South Vietnam. Others argue that Hanoi has been repeatedly perfidious in past interactions, continues to hold remains of MIAs, and should receive no benefits from the United States until Washington's conditions are fully met. More broadly, U.S. politicians appear hesitant to revive the emotional feelings and possibly antagonistic debate that could be associated with a more assertive U.S. role in policy toward Cambodia and Vietnam. The potential risks of coming out politically bruised or battered from initiating such a debate are seen as large, by at least some American leaders.

This does not mean that Americans, even those who are skeptical of finding a realistic solution in Cambodia, are unconcerned about the suffering caused by war in Cambodia, the possible return to power of the Khmer Rouge, the poverty that prevails in both Cambodia and Vietnam, and the continued outflow of people from both countries. But the many uncertainties surrounding the situation in Cambodia and potentially divisive feelings over Indochina make some pessimistic that U.S. officials will ever build a consensus behind an assertive U.S. policy that goes further than the recent mix of U.S. actions.

Looking to the future, events in Cambodia and Southeast Asia could work to the advantage of the current U.S. efforts. A consensus has been reached among the U.N. Security Council members and their respective clients in Cambodia; a ceasefire has been established; U.N.-monitored elections could be held and the results respected. The Khmer Rouge is seen as the main source of potential disruption. If China agrees to cut off supplies and otherwise presses the Khmer Rouge, it is possible that they might fall into line or be isolated as a dissident resistance movement. The achievement of a settlement in Cambodia has presumably helped to open the way to U.S. normalization with Vietnam.

It is also possible that a resurgence of Khmer Rouge power or other events in Cambodia could impel U.S. leaders to take a more decisive leadership role to prevent a return to power of these reviled Cambodians. Pressure in Southeast Asia for establishing more normal relations with Hanoi and Phnom Penh could build to a point where the United States might move ahead with its own normalization efforts, even if the peace settlement in Cambodia should fail. Other scenarios are possible. For the present, however, it appears that U.S. administration leaders have focused hopes on the October 1991 settlement. Meanwhile, U.S. policymakers remain very attentive to developments in the region, watching for events (such as a resurgence of Khmer Rouge power, or a change in Thai or other ASEAN positions) that might prompt adjustment or change in U.S. policies. They continue to play a strong role in efforts to deal with humanitarian issues such as the return of MIA remains, refugee departures from Vietnam, and assuring proper care and handling of Indochinese refugees, migrants, and other displaced persons.

Possible U.S.-Vietnamese Normalization[4]

The Vietnamese troop withdrawal from Cambodia coincided with a more forthcoming Vietnamese stance over the issue of the approximately 2,300 American POWs/MIAs in Indochina and other humanitarian concerns. These developments revived discussion in the U.S. Congress and elsewhere between opposing groups who have generally similar goals but who differ on the appropriate U.S. policy to reach these goals. One group holds that U.S. interest in obtaining a full accounting for U.S. POWs/MIAs and restoring peace and stability in Indochina and Southeast Asia requires continued firm U.S. pressure on Vietnam. An opposing view says that success in reaching these goals requires greater U.S. flexibility and accommodation toward Vietnam. The Bush administration gave new attention to this issue when it announced on July 18, 1990, that it would seek contacts with Hanoi to reach a peace agreement in Cambodia and, in September 1990, that it would open official contacts with the Vietnamese-backed government in Phnom Penh. In 1991, the Bush administration laid out a detailed "road map" for normalization, welcomed Hanoi's willingness to allow a U.S. office in Vietnam to handle POW/MIA issues, and announced a grant of $1 million in humanitarian aid to Vietnam. The October 1991 Cambodian peace agreement appeared to open the way to a gradual U.S. normalization with Vietnam in accordance with the Bush administration's "road map."

U.S.-Vietnamese Relations Since 1975[5]

U.S.-Vietnam diplomatic and economic relations have remained essentially frozen for over a decade. After the communist victory in South Vietnam in April 1975, the United States ended diplomatic relations with Saigon and subjected all economic relations with South Vietnam to the same restrictions that already applied to North Vietnam. These restrictions consisted principally of a virtually total embargo on all commercial and financial transactions with Vietnam, a blocking of all Vietnamese assets in the United States, and a ban on U.S. exports to Vietnam.

The Hanoi government called for talks with the United States on establishing diplomatic relations and demanded that the United States fulfill the provisions of the January 1973 Paris peace agreement, including a provision that pledged U.S. postwar aid for Vietnam's reconstruction. The administration under President Gerald Ford rejected Vietnam's demand for aid on grounds that Hanoi had massively violated the Paris peace agreement in launching its final military assault against South Vietnam. It also said that there could be no normalization of relations without a full accounting of Americans missing in action during the war and until Vietnam's long-range intentions in Southeast Asia became more clear. The United States vetoed Vietnam's application for membership in the United Nations on three occasions during 1975–1976.

Policy Initiatives During the Carter Administration

The Carter administration took several steps to improve relations with Vietnam in 1977, but these efforts were progressively frustrated by growing evidence in 1978 that the Vietnamese government was deliberately expelling hundreds of thousands of its citizens and was making military preparations to invade Cambodia. On March 2, 1977, the administration relaxed slightly its restrictions against trade. Restrictions on U.S. travel to Vietnam were allowed to expire on March 18, 1977. President Carter sent a commission, led by Leonard Woodcock, to Vietnam in March 1977 to discuss matters affecting mutual interests.

The administration agreed to talks on establishing normal diplomatic relations in May and June 1977. During these talks, U.S. negotiators announced that the United States would no longer veto Vietnam's application for U.N. membership. (On July 20, 1977, the U.N. Security Council recommended by consensus without formal vote that Vietnam be admitted to the United Nations.) The U.S. side proposed that diplomatic relations quickly be established between the United States and Vietnam, after which the United States would lift export and asset controls with Vietnam. But the Vietnamese said in response that they would not agree to establish relations or to furnish information on U.S. MIAs until the United States pledged to provide several billion dollars in postwar reconstruction aid. They later modified this position and provided some limited information on MIAs, even though U.S. aid was not forthcoming.

The U.S. Congress, for its part, responded unfavorably to the Carter administration initiatives and the Vietnamese response. Members were particularly opposed to Vietnam's insistence on receiving U.S. aid. In the latter part of 1977, both Houses went on record as strongly opposing U.S. aid to Vietnam.

Developments in 1978 had a long-term negative effect on U.S.-Vietnamese relations. Vietnam expelled hundreds of thousands of its citizens (many of Chinese origin) as refugees throughout Southeast Asia; aligned itself economically and militarily with the USSR; and invaded Cambodia, deposing the pro-Chinese Khmer Rouge regime, and imposing a puppet Cambodian government backed by 200,000 Vietnamese troops. The Carter administration halted consideration of improved relations with Vietnam. It worked closely with the members of ASEAN to condemn and contain the Vietnamese expansion and to cope with the influx of refugees from Indochina. The United States was particularly concerned with helping to support Thailand, a U.S. ally and the country most seriously affected by the Vietnamese invasion of Cambodia. U.S. officials also worked closely in this regard with other affected regional powers, notably China.

Developments During the Reagan and Bush Administrations

The Reagan administration opposed normal relations with Hanoi until there was a verified withdrawal of Vietnamese forces from Cambodia, a position amended in 1985 to include a verified withdrawal in the context of a comprehensive settlement. Administration officials also noted that progress toward normal relations would remain difficult until Vietnam cooperated in obtaining the fullest possible accounting for U.S. POWs/MIAs. During annual votes at the United Nations, the United States supported the coalition government representing the guerrillas resisting the Vietnamese occupation. In 1985, Congress took the initiative and authorized the administration to provide annually up to $5 million of economic or military assistance to noncommunist Cambodian guerrillas resisting the Vietnamese occupation. The administration actually provided over $3 million of nonlethal aid in FY1986, FY1987, and FY1988, $5 million in FY1989, and $7 million in FY1990. It also reportedly provided even more covert aid to the noncommunist resistance groups during that time. For FY1991, Congress passed and the administration signed legislation after considerable discussion and debate to phase out covert aid and to provide $20 million in overt aid to Cambodia, including the noncommunist resistance groups but also including those in need who were under the rule of the Vietnamese-backed government in Phnom Penh. The administration requested about $25 million in aid for FY1992.

In a sharp break from past practice, the Bush administration decided on July 18, 1990, to seek contacts with Hanoi to reach a peace agreement in Cambodia and to end U.S. support for the coalition government representing three guerrilla forces, including the Khmer Rouge, which represented Cambodia in the United Nations. In September 1990, the administration also began official contacts with the Vietnamese-backed government in Phnom Penh.

Regarding the issue of the POWs/MIAs, since a visit to Hanoi by a U.S. presidential delegation led by presidential envoy John Vessey in 1987 (discussed below), Vietnam returned over 200 sets of remains said to be those of U.S. MIAs. Some but not many were confirmed as those of Americans. From 1974 to 1989, Vietnam returned the remains of about

240 Americans. There is a persistent belief in the United States that Hanoi holds many more remains. A Vietnamese refugee testified before Congress in the late 1970s that the remains of several hundred Americans were stored in a Hanoi warehouse mortuary. Belief that living Americans are still in Vietnamese captivity also has grown in recent years amid reports from former U.S. government officials and others testifying to this possibility. Hanoi denies that it holds living Americans or the remains of U.S. MIAs. The Reagan administration released a report in January 1989 that noted the difficulty involved in ever obtaining a full accounting of MIAs in Indochina.

President Bush's inaugural address alluded to the POW/MIA issue, pledged that assistance in this area would be long remembered, and called on Americans to put the divisiveness of the Vietnam War behind them. On July 28, 1989, President Bush said:

> We look forward to normalizing our relations with Vietnam, once a comprehensive settlement has been achieved in Cambodia. That settlement must include genuine power sharing with the non-Communist Cambodians led by Prince Sihanouk and in internationally verified troop withdrawal. But Hanoi must clearly understand that, as a practical matter, the pace and scope of this process will be directly affected by the seriousness of their cooperation on POW/MIA and other humanitarian issues.[6]

Highlighting a new stage of U.S.-Vietnamese contacts, the two foreign ministers met in New York on September 29, 1990. The Vietnamese foreign minister subsequently met with John Vessey and promised new cooperation on MIA matters. In April 1991, the United States laid out a detailed "road map" for normalization with Vietnam, welcomed Vietnam's willingness to host a U.S. office in Hanoi to handle POW/MIA affairs, and pledged $1 million for humanitarian aid to Vietnam.[7] At the Paris conference on peace in Cambodia, October 1991, Secretary Baker held talks with his Vietnamese counterpart on the normalization of U.S.-Vietnamese relations.

These significant developments in U.S.-Vietnamese contacts developed from numerous bilateral contacts since the latter 1980s, which focused largely on exploring signs of Vietnamese flexibility concerning humanitarian issues dividing the two countries, especially the accounting for the U.S. POWs/MIAs.

In 1985, Vietnam prompted increased U.S. interest when it returned the remains of thirty American war dead, allowed the United States for the first time to carry out a jointly monitored excavation of a suspected B-52 crash site near Hanoi, and promised to settle the MIA issue by 1987.

In January 1986, a high-level U.S. official delegation went to Hanoi for two days of talks with senior Vietnamese officials. U.S. officials also spoke with the Vietnamese in Hanoi, at the United Nations, and elsewhere regarding other humanitarian issues of concern to the United States. Discussion focused on U.S. efforts to: (1) facilitate emigration from Vietnam of relatives of Vietnamese-Americans or permanent Vietnamese residents of the United States; (2) regularize the flow of Vietnamese immigrants to the United States and other countries under the so-called Orderly Departure Program managed by the U.N. High Commissioner for Refugees; (3) resolve the issue of the estimated several thousand Amerasian children (whose fathers are Americans and whose mothers are Vietnamese) who reportedly wish to emigrate from Vietnam to the United States; and (4) obtain release from Vietnamese prison camps and the opportunity to immigrate to the United States of an estimated many thousands of Vietnamese who worked for the United States in South Vietnam or were otherwise associated with the U.S. war effort there.

The pace of U.S.-Vietnamese contacts over the MIAs and these other humanitarian issues slowed during 1986 and 1987.

On August 1-3, 1987, an official U.S. delegation led by retired U.S. General and former Chairman of the Joint Chiefs of Staff John Vessey, a special representative of President Reagan, visited Hanoi to discuss humanitarian issues. This marked the first such high-level U.S. visit to Vietnam since Leonard Woodcock traveled there for President Carter in 1977. Subsequently, significant progress was made on resolving MIA cases and on the other humanitarian issues noted above. In October 1989, General Vessey returned to Hanoi for a second visit to encourage forward movement on humanitarian issues, and the Vietnamese foreign minister met with Vessey in Washington a year later. The April 1991 announcement of Vietnam's acceptance of a U.S. POW/MIA office in Hanoi came during a visit by Vessey to Vietnam.

U.S. Interests and Policy Objectives

Americans have a long history of strong differences over how to handle U.S. relations with Vietnam; but at present, proponents and opponents of greater U.S. flexibility toward Vietnam share many common policy objectives. In particular, they want to assure a settlement in Cambodia that restores stability to Southeast Asia, secures the interests of Thailand and the other members of ASEAN, and checks the past militant expansion of Soviet and/or Vietnamese influence in Southeast Asia. The United States has a strong interest in the strategically and economically important communication routes that converge at the Straits of Malacca and other passageways in the region. The Soviet presence at U.S.-built bases in

Vietnam—including Soviet bombers, fighter aircraft, submarines, and surface warships—diminished in late 1989, but had been seen to pose a potentially serious challenge to U.S. access to those routes. U.S. trade has grown to a point that ASEAN, taken as a unit, is one of the top ten U.S. trading partners. U.S. interest in working with ASEAN members to check Soviet-backed Vietnamese expansion proceeded in parallel with U.S. cooperation with other Asian regional actors concerned with Soviet and Vietnamese influence, notably China and Japan.

At the same time, Americans on both sides of the issue want to prompt Vietnam to fully account for U.S. POWs/MIAs; facilitate orderly emigration procedures for Vietnamese relatives of U.S. residents and citizens; and release and allow to emigrate Vietnamese associated with the U.S.-backed government of South Vietnam. Americans also have a strong interest in improved human rights conditions in Vietnam and some Americans are interested in possible trade and other economic opportunities. Americans hope to accomplish U.S. objectives at minimal cost to the United States and oppose past Vietnamese calls for several billion dollars in U.S. war reparations.

Vietnam's Predicament[8]

Proponents and opponents of greater U.S. flexibility toward Vietnam also agree generally that Vietnam faces grave difficulties caused by internal mismanagement and external pressures resulting in particular from its military occupation of Cambodia. The Vietnamese are thought to be more inclined than in the past to change policy in accord with U.S. interests. External pressures against Vietnam's occupation of Cambodia have taken several forms:

- China invaded parts of northern Vietnam for a month in early 1979, and occasionally threatened to do so again—a threat backed up by the 300,000 Chinese troops in military regions near the Vietnamese border. Beijing also provides the main portion of military support to the coalition of Cambodian resistance forces opposing the Vietnamese occupation. (The bulk of the Chinese assistance has gone to the communist Khmer Rouge guerrillas, whose estimated 35,000 fighters make up over half of the forces in the coalition of Cambodian guerrillas.)
- ASEAN led international political condemnation of the Vietnamese occupation, including past annual votes on the Cambodian issue in the United Nations. ASEAN members also provided political support to the coalition government representing the Cambodian guerrillas,

and some military support to the noncommunist members of that coalition.
- At the United Nations, Hanoi's efforts to have the international body recognize the Vietnamese-backed Phnom Penh government as the legitimate representative of Cambodia were turned aside.
- As a result of the Vietnamese policy in Cambodia, most noncommunist countries restricted foreign assistance, trade, and investment with Vietnam.

The Vietnamese were able to sustain their position in Cambodia in large part because of continued Soviet economic and military support. (The Soviet Union was estimated to have supplied $3 billion of assistance annually to Vietnam. The level of Soviet and Soviet bloc aid fell off rapidly due to the changes taking place in Eastern Europe in 1989-1990.)

The low Vietnamese international political standing and their inability to attract trade, aid, and investment outside the Soviet bloc affected Vietnam's economy, which remains very poor with low per capita income ($200 in 1987). In 1988, Vietnam appealed for international food aid because of a disastrous shortage of rice and other food grains in northern Vietnam. There were persisting reports of Vietnamese dissatisfaction with their heavy dependence on the USSR and the allegedly ham-handed Soviet aid and political efforts in Indochina. From time to time, Vietnam attempted to break out of its isolation by hinting at flexibility on Cambodia or other issues.

Coincident with an across-the-board change of the top level of Vietnamese leaders during 1986-1987, the pace of international discussions on Cambodia increased. In May 1988, Vietnam announced the start of a withdrawal of 50,000 troops from Cambodia. On July 25, 1988, Indonesia convened a "cocktail party" in which representatives of the three opposition Cambodian forces and the Vietnamese-backed Phnom Penh government, along with the Vietnamese foreign minister, met face-to-face for talks.

Meanwhile, Mikhail Gorbachev tried to portray a more flexible and moderate image on Asian affairs and improved relations with Vietnam's major adversary, China. China, too, improved its ties with the Vietnamese-backed government in Laos, acknowledged the change in Vietnam's military position in Cambodia, and moderated its stand on a possible peace agreement concerning Cambodia. Cambodia was discussed at the Sino-Soviet summit in May 1989. In January 1989, Chinese and Vietnamese envoys met in Beijing, and secret high-level Sino-Vietnamese talks were reportedly held in China in September 1990.

In February 1989, a second meeting of representatives of the Cambodian groups, the Indochinese countries, and the ASEAN countries was held in Indonesia but ended without major progress toward a settlement. A major international peace conference on Cambodia began in Paris on July 30, 1989, but was suspended on August 30, 1989. On September 26, 1989, Vietnam said its withdrawal of troops from Cambodia was "complete." Another conference among the Cambodian groups ended in failure on March 1, 1990. Mixed results marked a conference in Tokyo in June 1990. In a marked departure from past practice, the Bush administration began talks concerning peace in Cambodia with Vietnamese officials in New York on August 6, 1990. Subsequent developments included the announced U.N. peace plan on Cambodia in late August, the start of U.S. official contacts with the Vietnamese-backed Phnom Penh government in early September, and the concurrent agreement of the four Cambodian parties to the U.N. peace plan. But as is noted in the previous section, difficulties continued to hamper the U.N. peace plan in 1991.

U.S. Policy Options

In light of the recent internal and external developments regarding Vietnam and U.S.-Vietnamese relations, U.S. policymakers renewed discussion over what kind of policy the United States should pursue to achieve its bilateral interests in Vietnam and long-term security, economic, and other concerns in Southeast Asia. In Congress, some prodded the administration to show greater flexibility in using diplomatic and economic overtures to encourage change in Vietnam's policies in accord with U.S. interests. But others disagreed. They opposed such U.S. initiatives unless the Vietnamese meet preconditions involving a full accounting for POWs/MIAs and withdrawal from and a peace settlement in Cambodia.

Greater U.S. Flexibility Toward Vietnam

Proponents of this view hold that, given Vietnam's current difficulties and the recent flurry of activity over a possible Cambodian settlement, U.S. interests in settling the POW/MIA and other humanitarian issues and in restoring peace and stability in Cambodia and Southeast Asia are more likely to be served by a policy that balances U.S. pressure against Vietnam with diplomatic and economic overtures. Such initiatives could include the establishment of a U.S. technical office, interests section or some other diplomatic presence in Vietnam, the easing of the American economic embargo, or the provision of small amounts of food aid or other assistance. (Vietnamese officials have said they would welcome such U.S. moves.)

According to this group, the U.S. gestures could result in several benefits. They could establish a positive atmosphere in U.S.-Vietnamese relations that is more conducive to further Vietnamese flexibility on the POW/MIA question and other humanitarian issues than the past practice of U.S. pressure. The Vietnamese leadership is perceived as highly nationalistic, and unable and unwilling to compromise in the face of unmitigated outside pressure. By balancing continued pressure with some positive gestures, it is argued, the United States would allow the Vietnamese to "save face" as they seek to end Vietnam's international isolation through accommodation with the United States over humanitarian issues.

U.S. flexibility could also encourage the Vietnamese to support a compromise settlement in Cambodia acceptable to them and the United States. According to this view, such a settlement would involve the withdrawal of Vietnamese forces from Cambodia, restrictions on the Khmer Rouge, and the establishment of an ostensibly neutral coalition government that would not be threatening to Vietnam, Thailand, or other members of ASEAN. (Some advocates of restoring U.S. ties with Vietnam feel that the Vietnamese role in Cambodia, while regrettable, is preferable to a return to power of the communist Khmer Rouge.) Such a settlement, in turn, could prompt China to moderate its hard posture toward Vietnam—a development that would remove Vietnam's main reason for a close strategic alliance with USSR/Russia.

And, U.S. trade or investment with Vietnam could encourage greater Western and Japanese involvement in the Vietnamese economy. It could reduce the economic imperative behind Hanoi-Moscow relations.

This course of events, it is argued, would see a notable improvement in U.S.-Vietnamese relations, a relaxation of tensions in Indochina and Southeast Asia, a possible reassertion of Vietnamese independence and nationalism against Russia, possible improved internal conditions in Vietnam, and a curb on Russian access to military bases in Vietnam. The latter is seen as important to the United States in light of the instability that surrounds continued U.S. access to bases in Southeast Asia as a result of the uncertain situation in the Philippines.

Opposition to Greater U.S. Flexibility Toward Vietnam

These observers oppose U.S. efforts to improve relations or ease tensions with Hanoi unless the Vietnamese withdraw their forces from and play a constructive role in a peace settlement in Cambodia, and offer a full accounting of American POWs/MIAs. In particular, they argue strongly against establishing a U.S. liaison office or interests section in Hanoi or easing the U.S. economic embargo until Hanoi meets U.S. conditions on Cambodia and the POWs/MIAs. They also argue against providing U.S. aid requested by Vietnamese officials.

According to this view, Vietnam would move to exploit unilateral U.S. gestures to improve relations and ease pressure in ways detrimental to

U.S. interests. In particular it is claimed that such U.S. gestures could make the Vietnamese more intransigent on the POW/MIA issue. For example, it could confirm Vietnam's belief that holding remains of U.S. service personnel gives Hanoi considerable leverage over the United States, rewarding and reinforcing Hanoi's demonstrated tendency to use this leverage cynically, to gain greater concessions from the United States. Thus, under these circumstances, it is argued, the Vietnamese might be expected to stress past demands for U.S. reconstruction aid as a precondition for a full accounting on POWs/MIAs.

Such steps would also make it more difficult for the U.S. government to persuade groups in the United States, Japan, Western Europe, and international organizations who are inclined to offer assistance to Vietnam to avoid such assistance. Some who are deterred for the present by the strong, U.S.-backed pressure against Vietnam might change their policy if U.S. policy changed. Increased international aid, it is argued, will increase Hanoi's resolve to continue repressive and expansionist policies.

Easing U.S. pressure against Vietnam under current circumstances could exacerbate important differences of opinion among Asian states opposed to the Vietnamese occupation of Cambodia.

At bottom, proponents of this view judge that whatever signs of Vietnamese flexibility have appeared regarding Cambodia and humanitarian issues have been prompted largely by the continued U.S.-backed pressure against Vietnam. To be effective, the United States must continue to apply this pressure until Vietnam meets U.S. conditions. Easing up now, they assert, would only further complicate U.S. efforts to get a full accounting for POWs/MIAs and to restore stability and peace to Cambodia and Southeast Asia.

Notes

1. Among the sources on the situation in Cambodia and the U.S. policy debate, see Dick Clark, ed., *The Challenge of Indochina: An Examination of the U.S. Role* (Aspen, CO: Institute for Humanistic Studies, 1991); Kenneth Conboy, *Staying the Course for Bringing Peace to Cambodia* (Washington, DC: Heritage Foundation, May 2, 1991); Christopher Madison, "Cambodia Divisions," *National Journal* (May 4, 1991), pp. 1051–1054; Stephen Solarz, "Cambodia and the International Community," *Foreign Affairs* 69, no. 2, (Spring 1990); Robert Sutter, *The Cambodian Crisis and U.S. Policy Dilemmas* (Boulder, CO: Westview Press, 1991); and Nate Thayer, "Cambodia: Misperceptions and Peace," *Washington Quarterly* (Spring 1991), pp. 79–191.

2. This section is based on the author's chapter in Dick Clark, ed., *The Challenge of Indochina*

3. The lines of argument in the debate are seen in Christopher Madison, Cambodia Divisions, *National Journal* (May 4, 1991), pp. 1051–1054. For regular

coverage, see *Congressional Quarterly Weekly Report*. Also, a particularly useful source is the *Indochina Digest*, published weekly by the Indochina Project, Washington, DC.

4. This discussion is based on the author's review of U.S.-Vietnamese relations seen in the *Cambodian Crisis and U.S. Policy Dilemmas*, pp. 52–56.

5. For a useful review, see, among others, U.S. Department of State, Bureau of Public Affairs, *Background Notes, Vietnam* (May 1990). See also, Robert Sutter, *The Cambodian Crisis*, pp. 79–106.

6. These and other statements are replayed in Robert Sutter, *The Cambodian Crisis*, pp. 52–56.

7. See coverage in *Indochina Digest*.

8. For background, see article by Nayan Chanda and summary by Frederick Z. Brown in Dick Clark, ed., *The Challenge of Indochina*.

8

Relations with ASEAN in 1990: The Issue of the Philippine Bases

Issues in U.S. relations with the countries of ASEAN focused on questions related to the situation in Indochina (treated above) and to the controversy seen in the protracted U.S. negotiations with the Philippines over continued U.S. military bases there (see discussion in this chapter). Other security questions complicating U.S. relations included repeated calls by some ASEAN members, especially Malaysia, for the creation of a nuclear weapons-free Zone of Peace, Freedom and Neutrality (ZOPFAN) in Southeast Asia—a proposal that is widely held to run up against U.S. interests in free access to and transit of lines of communications in the region; persisting reservations by at least some ASEAN leaders regarding U.S. encouragement of Japan to play a greater role in its self- defense and to bear more of the allied defense burden—which could open the way to a heightened Japanese security profile in the region; and U.S. disagreements with efforts by ASEAN countries to turn back Vietnamese boat people and other migrants.[1]

Economic issues have become more heated as some ASEAN countries have advanced into the ranks of the newly industrializing countries (NICs). Singapore has long been considered a NIC, and Thailand, Malaysia, and Indonesia are increasingly seen as among the NICs. Entrepreneurs, industrialists, and government officials in these ASEAN states have worked hard amid growing international competition to assure continued access to the U.S. market, the largest single market for ASEAN's manufactured exports. U.S. consumers welcome the products, but pressures for reciprocity have resulted in increasingly vigorous U.S. government efforts to assure "fair" as well as "free" trade. Although the United States has specific

---

The section on Philippine base negotiations is excerpted with permission from a manuscript prepared by Larry Niksch, Specialist in Asian Affairs, Congressional Research Service, The Library of Congress, Washington, D.C.

problems with each country of ASEAN, it is with Thailand that the irritations have generated a political backlash that has affected the broader set of relations. U.S. insistence on Thai adoption of legal protections for intellectual property, pharmaceutical patent protection, tobacco and cigarette imports, etc., all backed by the threat of Section 301 of the 1988 Trade Act, has spurred economic nationalism. This nationalist backlash has moved the issues to the political agenda, out of the hands of the bureaucratic technicians.

Efforts to create multilateral mechanisms to coordinate economic policies and reduce bilateral frictions have seen varying degrees of interest in ASEAN and the United States in broader Pacific Rim economic groupings. The Bush administration gave special emphasis to the Asian Pacific Economic Council, an intergovernmental group, modeled on the Europe-inspired Organization for Economic Cooperation and Development (OECD), to offer a forum of like-minded Pacific Rim countries to deal with pressing economic questions. Some in ASEAN favored a more narrowly defined economic grouping centered on Japan and excluding the United States. This appeared to reflect Japan's increasingly dominant role as the main source of financial aid, technology, and sophisticated imports for the ASEAN countries. Any exclusionary "blocs" were opposed by the United States.

Philippine Base Negotiations

On September 16, 1991, the Philippine Senate rejected a U.S.-Philippine agreement to renew U.S. base rights. The new agreement would have extended U.S. base rights for ten years beyond the expiration date of the current agreement (signed in 1947), which ended on September 16, 1991, and would have ended the U.S. military presence at Clark Air Force Base. This confirmed a Bush administration decision not to resume operations at Clark because of the damage done to it by the volcanic eruption of Mt. Pinatubo in 1991. The United States would have retained operational control over Subic Bay Naval Base. The amount of U.S. financial compensation in aid was set at $203 million beginning in U.S. fiscal year 1993.

The Philippine Senate's rejection could be reversed, however, through either an initiative-referendum process, which is provided in the Philippine constitution, or the election of a new Philippine president and Senate in May 1992. But, major legal and political obstacles also exist that could prevent a reversal. By late 1991, a compromise was reached that requires U.S. withdrawal within three years.

The bases played an important role in supporting the U.S. military presence in the Western Pacific and the Indian Ocean–Persian Gulf region. They were vital to several past U.S. force buildups in those regions. Since

1986, the bases also played a sometimes direct role in U.S. support for democratic political development in the Philippines, including notably the employment of U.S. fighter aircraft to back the Aquino government in December 1989 against an attempted coup d'etat.

The Bush administration reportedly favored an extension of base rights up to ten years after 1991 followed by a U.S. withdrawal. U.S. officials stated that the United States would withdraw in 1991–1992 if it could not secure an adequate agreement. U.S. critics of the administration's policy emphasized a declining Soviet threat and the need to cut defense spending in advocating a U.S. pullout from the Philippines in 1991.

In June 1991, Mt. Pinatubo, a volcano dormant for about 600 years, erupted and spilled layers of volcanic ash over Clark and Subic. The activity continued into July. The damage was heavy at Clark, just ten miles away from Pinatubo. The Pentagon ordered a total evacuation of Americans from Clark and an evacuation of dependents and nonessential U.S. civilian workers from Subic. The U.S. and Philippine governments put the negotiations on hold, as the Pentagon and the Bush administration assessed the cost of the physical damage, the future stability of Mt. Pinatubo, and whether the new situation would necessitate a change in the American negotiating position. The assessment found that it would cost over $500 million to repair the damage at Clark Air Force Base. Experts also concluded that Mt. Pinatubo could stage periodic eruptions over at least the next three years. These two factors led the Bush administration to conclude that the operation of Clark was no longer feasible.

Filipino attitudes toward the bases are sharply divided. General public attitudes are more favorable, but this is countered by opposition among the Manila and urban elite. These divisions are reflected within the Aquino administration and the Philippine Senate, which decides whether to ratify any new agreement. Opponents of the Aquino administration, military renegades, and communist insurgents demand an ouster of the United States and threaten violence against Americans.

Negotiations began September 17, 1990. They covered a range of potentially contentious issues: promises of aid linked to base rights; spending by the U.S. military for Filipino supplies and services; possible joint user arrangements; operational control over U.S. combat operations; the storage or transit of U.S. nuclear weapons; and criminal jurisdiction over U.S. service personnel.

As the United States withdraws in the 1990s, the U.S. Congress will have to decide how to adjust the U.S. military base structure in the Western Pacific. There are other base alternatives, but each option would be less efficient and more costly. The U.S. will also reset U.S. policy, including aid levels, toward the Philippines.

Background on the Philippine Bases

U.S. rights to military bases in the Philippines are embodied in an agreement signed on March 14, 1947, between the U.S. and Philippine governments. The agreement leased to the United States for ninety-nine years over fifteen bases and military facilities in the Philippines. It gave the United States full operational control over the bases and the military units stationed on them. A separate agreement initiated U.S. military assistance to the Philippines. The two governments signed a Mutual Defense Treaty in 1951, which entered into force in August 1952. In the treaty, each party promises to "act to meet the common danger" of an armed attack on the other party "in accordance with its constitutional process." The treaty specifies that an armed attack includes "an armed attack on the metropolitan territory of either of the parties, or on the island territories under its jurisdiction in the Pacific, or on its armed forces, public vessels or aircraft in the Pacific."

Since 1947, the U.S. and the Philippine governments have negotiated a number of revisions of the bases agreement. These resulted in the relinquishment of certain facilities or land areas to the Philippines and a shortening of the original term of the leases from 2040 to 1991. A 1959 revision states that the use of the bases for U.S. military combat operations would be the subject of prior consultation of the Philippine government except for military operations conducted in accordance with the U.S.-Philippine Mutual Defense Treaty and the Southeast Asia Collective Defense Treaty (to which the United States and the Philippines are signatories). The prior consultation, however, does not confer a veto power to the Philippine government over U.S. combat operations. The Philippine government opposed the U.S. use of Clark Air Force Base for bombing missions against North Vietnam during the Vietnam War; the United States did not use Clark for the staging of such missions.

The two governments negotiated a key revision to the 1947 accord in 1979, an amendment for a five-year period (U.S. fiscal years 1980–1984). A second amendment, signed in 1983, covered 1985–1989, and a third, concluded in 1988, covered the last two years of the 1947 agreement (U.S. fiscal years 1990 and 1991). The key policy issue brought into these amendments was a pledge by the U.S. administration to make "best efforts" to secure specified amounts of military and economic aid for the Philippines during the years covered by the amendments. The U.S. "best efforts" pledge was for $500 million under the 1980–1984 amendment; $900 million in conjunction with the 1985–1989 amendment; and $952 million for the two years of 1990 and 1991. The "best effort" pledges and American performance in actually providing the aid has been a key source of controversy between the Philippines and the United States.

TABLE 8.1   U.S. Aid to the Philippines (In $U.S. millions)

	FY1990	FY1991 (Requested)
Development Aid	62.2	40.0
Food Aid	33.6	13.7
Economic Support Fund	124.0	120.0
Military Aid	142.7	202.6
Multilateral Assistance Initiative	160.0	160.0
Total	522.5	536.3

Source: U.S. Library of Congress, Congressional Research Service, *Philippine Bases, Negotiations*, Issue Brief 90142, October 22, 1991, p. 4.

This particularly has been a source of controversy since the 1988 negotiations. The Philippine government demanded much larger amounts of aid in the 1988 talks than the United States was willing to pledge. Moreover, the U.S. allocation of bases-related aid for FY1990 was at least $87 million below $481 million—half of the $952 million promised for the FY1990–FY1991 period—with little prospect for the amount being made up in FY1991 aid. The United States, however, did provide $160 million in additional economic aid in FY1990 under the Multilateral Assistance Initiative, a multination aid program for the Philippines launched in July 1989. Table 8.1 shows U.S. aid allocated for FY1990 and requested by the Bush administration for FY1991.

The Bases in U.S. Policy

The U.S.-operated bases have played an important role since the 1940s in supporting the U.S. military presence in the Western Pacific and the use of those forces as an instrument of American foreign policy. The United States until recently operated five facilities in the Philippines: Subic Bay Naval Base, Clark Air Force Base, the Cubi Point Naval Air Station, the San Miguel Naval Communications Center, and Camp John Hay. Camp John Hay was turned over to the Philippine government on July 1, 1991.

Subic Bay, supplemented by Cubi Point and San Miguel, is the major support base for the U.S. Seventh Fleet. Approximately 65 percent of the Seventh Fleet's repair work is performed at Subic. Petroleum storage facilities, aircraft parking spaces, a general supply and parts depot, and ammunition storage facilities provide an extensive logistics network. San Miguel is the principal communications center for the Seventh Fleet. Antisubmarine aircraft operate from Cubi Point and track Soviet naval movements over the Southwest Pacific and eastern Indian Ocean.

Clark Air Force Base had the capacity to handle several tactical fighter squadrons and bombers. It was the primary service and refueling facility for C-5A and C-130 aircraft that transport supplies to U.S. forces in the Western Pacific and Indian Ocean. The Crow Valley training range regularly hosted exercises of all U.S. air units in the Western Pacific and was one of the most sophisticated in the world for training in combat-like situations.

The Philippine bases have supported buildups of U.S. forces and surges of American military operations ranging from the Persian Gulf to Northeast Asia. Subic is the principal facility in backing up any rapid buildup of Seventh Fleet strength. This occurred in the Vietnam War, and more recently in the U.S. naval buildup in the Persian Gulf in 1987–1988. Most ships deployed to the Gulf and western Indian Ocean were refueled and reprovisioned at Subic. Over 75 percent of the ships deployed to the Persian Gulf came from the Seventh Fleet during that period. Clark Air Force Base also played such a role in the Persian Gulf buildup through its service to C-5A transports ferrying supplies to Diego Garcia, the main U.S. military base in the Indian Ocean.

The United States initially did not use the bases significantly in the much larger buildup of forces in the Persian Gulf in 1990. Starting in December 1990, however, several naval task forces and transport aircraft bound for the Gulf were refueled and supplied at Subic and Clark; and this activity increased when the United States initiated military operations against Iraq. Subic could have provided important support to a permanent U.S. force in the Persian Gulf, an issue which the United States is negotiating with the Gulf states in the aftermath of the war with Iraq.

The United States has used the bases twice to support Corazon Aquino in the context of stated U.S. policy of promoting democracy in the Philippines. During the February 1986 revolution against the Marcos government, the U.S. government allowed rebel forces to use certain facilities at the bases. U.S. aircraft from Clark provided air cover for pro-Aquino forces during an attempted military-led coup d'etat against the Aquino government in December 1989. It generally is believed that U.S. air cover was a key factor in the government's defeat of the rebels.

The bases also play an indirect role in the U.S. policy of assisting the Philippine government in counter-insurgency against communist insurgents. In accordance with the U.S.-Philippine Mutual Defense Treaty, the United States has assumed primary responsibility for the defense of air and sea areas adjacent to the Philippines. This has allowed the Philippine government to concentrate its own resources on ground forces related to the communist insurgency. A study by the Philippine National Defense College estimated a savings of $123 million annually by not having to spend more money on air and naval forces.

The U.S. government bases pump money into the Philippine economy. Since 1986, this has assisted the Aquino government's efforts to spur economic growth. This money has been generated through wages paid to about 68,000 Filipino workers at the bases, contracts for construction and other services issued to Filipino firms, payments for off-base housing and utilities for U.S. personnel, procurement of local materials and supplies, and spending by U.S. personnel and dependents. According to statistics supplied by the U.S. Defense Department for FY1988, these kinds of expenditures totaled $531.5 million compared to less than $400 million in FY1987. State Department officials have stated that expenditures probably increased in later years.

The Bush administration had favored an agreement that would extend base rights at least ten years beyond 1991. Administration officials had spoken of the United States retaining access to Philippine-run bases after the new agreement expired; but in the talks in early 1991, the administration appeared to have pressed for the new agreement to allow the possibility of a future negotiation of an accord that would extend U.S. operational control further into the next century.

The Department of Defense stated in its April 1990 report on U.S. strategy in the Pacific that the Philippine bases would contribute to an American military presence in the Pacific, even if the level of U.S. forces should decline because of improved U.S.-Soviet relations and reductions in defense spending. Pentagon and other Bush administration officials and some private experts on East Asia emphasized that, regardless of a decline in the immediate Soviet threat, the United States has long-term interests to protect, and that a military presence would help to maintain a balance of power with China, Japan, and the Russia; prevent outbreaks of regional conflicts; protect key sea lanes; support a military presence in the Persian Gulf; influence the economic and trade policies of key trading partners; and support democratic political development in the region. However, Bush administration officials said that the United States would withdraw from the Philippines in 1991 if it could not secure a satisfactory extension agreement or if the Philippine government asked the United States to leave.

American critics of the Bush administration included some members of Congress, several academics, and experts from certain "think tanks." They called for more rapid reductions in U.S. forces in the Western Pacific, including a withdrawal from the Philippines. They pointed out that there are potential alternatives to the Philippine bases that could support American forces. They argued that the Soviet threat had ended and that the countries of the region should assume the burden of defense rather than rely on the United States. They contended that the United States has minimal interests in deterring regional conflicts, in protecting sea lanes that primarily benefit Japan, and in promoting democracy; and that large bases are not necessary for these purposes. Some critics continue to speak negatively about the Philippine government's performance and prospects for democracy there, and warn that the bases could become untenable if the Philippine political situation becomes chaotic.

Although the U.S. Defense Department and the Bush administration maintained that Subic and Clark were of equal strategic importance, many outside experts argued that Subic is more important in terms of the scope of its functions and that these functions would be more difficult to duplicate elsewhere and would cost much more. A number of experts argued that the U.S. negotiating position should have emphasized retaining long-term base rights for Subic, but should have offered to turn over operational control of Clark to the Philippine government relatively soon after 1991.

Filipino Attitudes Toward the Bases

Popular Views

There are three general lines of sentiment among Filipinos toward the United States and the bases. One is a close identification with and a generally positive view of the United States among average Filipinos. This stems from the historical relationship—the Philippines' status as the United States' only major colony during the first forty-five years of this century—when the Philippines adopted many institutions and aspects of culture modeled after those of the United States. It also is influenced by the family ties of over ten million Filipinos who have relatives in the United States. Public opinion polls in the 1988–1990 period have shown either a majority or large plurality of Filipinos in favor of an extension of U.S. base rights after 1991. This sentiment reportedly has grown because of U.S. assistance in rescue efforts after an earthquake in the Philippines in July 1990 and increasing Philippine political and economic difficulties.

A second attitude is a "nationalist" position that the Philippines should reduce U.S. influence and establish an "independent identity." This is a more critical reaction to the Philippines' former status as a U.S. colony and subsequent American influence in the country. This attitude is prevalent among the elite of Manila and other big cities, intellectuals, the press, and some politicians. Public opinion polls show a sharp division within the Manila and urban elite on the bases. Anti–base rights rhetoric dominates the expression of opinion among this segment.

A third view is that the Philippines deserves a high priority in U.S. foreign policy and the United States has a "moral obligation" to help the Philippines because of the history of the relationship, the importance of the bases to U.S. security interests, and the fragile state of Philippine democracy in the face of armed rebellions and economic difficulties. This concept of a "special relationship," a phrase often used in Filipino and American rhetoric, influence Filipinos to believe that the United States should provide considerable financial and other benefits in return for base rights. Polls have shown that many who favor a continuation of base rights qualify this by linking future base rights to continued or expanded U.S. benefits.

Government Views

President Aquino stated on September 17, 1990, that she wanted "the orderly withdrawal" of U.S. forces, but she did not specify a timetable. Since then, Philippine government positions have shifted several times on the timetable, the disposition of Clark Air Force Base, and U.S. access to base rights after the transfer of U.S. operational control to the Philippines. This reflects divisions within the government and apparently the inability of President Aquino to mold these divisions into a unified position. By February 1991, the government had adopted proposals calling for the termination of U.S. rights to Clark and Subic after seven years and for a U.S. compensation package totaling $825 million annually. However, the government accepted proposals from Finance Secretary Jesus Estanislao that would include in the compensation package other kinds of U.S. assistance than just foreign aid. By June 1991, the government began to show more flexibility on the duration issue.

The Philippine Senate had a crucial role in deciding the issue. The 1987 Philippine constitution stipulates that any agreement extending base rights must be in the form of a treaty subject to ratification by the Senate by a two-thirds majority (sixteen out of twenty-three senators). Conversely, it would require only eight senators to prevent ratification. In 1991, eleven or twelve senators were on record as opposed to an extension. The initial reaction in the Senate to the new agreement was negative, even among senators viewed as moderates. Beginning in May 1991, President Aquino began speaking of a period of consultation with the Filipino people before she would submit the agreement to the Senate for ratification. This opened the possibility that such a consultation could run into the Philippine election campaign for all Senate seats up for election in May 1992. Subsequently, the September 16, 1991, Senate vote and subsequent developments focused attention on a compromise that allowed U.S. forces to withdraw over a three-year period.

Views of Subversive Opposition Groups

Another important segment of Filipino opinion are the groups in armed revolt against the Aquino government: the Communist Party of the Philippines (CPP), the military dissidents of the Reform Armed Forces Movement (RAM), and the Young Officers Union (YOU). The CPP has as a major policy goal the ouster of the United States from the bases. Communist leaders believe that a U.S. military withdrawal would result in a sharp decline in overall U.S. support for the Philippine government; in the CPP's view, this would weaken the ability of the government to combat the communist insurgency and possibly lead to a military coup d'etat that would bring in a repressive, unpopular regime and thus give the CPP an opportunity to increase its popular support. To bring pressure on the United States, the communists began selectively to assassinate U.S. military personnel and other Americans in 1987. By August 1990, the CPP had killed nine Americans. In May 1990, the CPP issued a statement threatening the United States with "the agony of attrition" if it did not withdraw.[2]

The RAM-YOU forces took an ambivalent attitude toward U.S. base rights prior to the U.S. military intervention against them during the December 1989 attempted coup d'etat. They have called for an end to base rights, undoubtedly to remove the United States as an obstacle to their goal of toppling the government. The Young Officers Union has denounced "U.S. imperialism" and has threatened to launch armed attacks against the bases. Since August 1990, the communists and military renegade groups have set off bombs at or near a number of offices of American business firms in Manila.[3]

Issues in the Negotiations and the Agreement

Timetable for Termination

In view of the Senate rejection of the agreement, the timetable for a U.S. withdrawal from Subic Bay is unclear. The 1947 bases agreement provides that either party may terminate the agreement by announcing a one-year notice of termination. The Philippine government had issued such a notification in May 1990, but revoked it after the Senate vote. The Philippine constitution states that after the expiration of the bases agreement in September 1991, no foreign bases shall be allowed except under terms of a new treaty. In short, there are different ways to interpret the length of time the U.S. Navy could stay at Subic Bay after September 16, 1991, in the absence of a new bases agreement. Statements by the Aquino administration after the Senate vote indicate that the time frame would be at least until September 1992.

Money Issues

In the 1988 negotiations on base rights for 1989–1990, and in the recent talks, U.S. aid/compensation for base rights was a controversial issue. The Philippine government believed that the United States could provide more compensation than the amounts specified in connection with past amendments, and it cited generous additional U.S. aid to Israel after the Persian Gulf war as an example. Officials have said that the United States should provide a binding commitment of aid rather than another "best efforts" pledge. They have accused the United States of reneging on the pledge in the 1988 amendment to provide $962 million over the FY1989–FY1990 period. Filipino officials assert that the United States gives the Philippines low priority in aid allocations in relation to recipients of much larger amounts of aid like Israel and Egypt.

The Bush administration has argued that budget constraints on foreign aid limit the amount of compensation/aid that it can provide the Philippines. It also cites the emergence of new aid recipients in Eastern Europe and Central America as imposing new restraints. The U.S. side has offered another "best efforts" pledge, but State Department officials have stated that the U.S. "best efforts" pledges do not bind Congress to approve the specific amount of money requested for the Philippines. U.S. officials have pointed to the Multilateral Assistance Initiative as another source of U.S. aid to the Philippines ($160 million in FY1991).

In addition, there is growing opposition in Congress to linking foreign aid with U.S. base rights. Committees with legislative responsibility for foreign aid have criticized the practice in recent statements. This sentiment was fueled by the improvement in U.S.-Soviet relations and the resultant view that the United States will not need the extensive overseas base structure that it has had since the Cold War began. The congressional view also is influenced by burden-sharing sentiment that is critical of allies for not bearing a greater proportion of joint defense responsibilities. Congressional critics also cite the Philippine government's slow utilization of existing aid as a reason not to increase aid.

At the onset of the talks, the Philippine government proposed a U.S. compensation package of $825 million annually, consisting of: (1) a cash grant of $400 million, which the Philippine government would use to underwrite the issuance of bonds that would be sold to foreign buyers; proceeds from the bond sales would be used to pay off part of the Philippines' nearly $29 billion foreign debt; and $425 million in "non-budgetary" form that would not come out of U.S. aid budgets. Philippine officials spoke of trade credits/concessions, increased purchases of Filipino goods by the U.S. military, transfers of surplus U.S. military equipment to the Philippines; and cancellation of a portion of the Philippine government's debt to the U.S. government.

The Bush administration offered $360 million annually in traditional aid: military assistance, economic support funds, and development assistance. It quickly rejected the $400 million cash grant/bond underwriting proposal. The U.S. offer was well below the $481 million specified in the 1988 agreement.

In late April and May 1991, the two governments closed some of the gap. The Philippine government dropped the $400 million cash grant/bond underwriting proposal and called instead for the same amount in military assistance ($100 million) and economic support funds ($300 million). The Bush administration reportedly offered $150 million annually in surplus military equipment and an additional $100 million in yearly U.S. military purchases of Filipino products.

The new agreement specification of $203 million in compensatory aid reflected the Bush administration's view that the loss of Clark Air Force Base necessitated a major reduction in compensation to the Philippines. The agreement did contain references to other kinds of assistance or U.S.-facilitated international assistance, but it set no specific amounts.

Duration and Scope of Extension Agreement

Initial statements by U.S. and Filipino negotiators suggested the possibility of general agreement on a "phase out" formula under which an extension agreement would specify a termination of base rights within a certain period after 1991. The Philippine position called for a seven-year agreement for Subic and Clark.

The Bush administration position sought an extension over at least a ten-year period. Beyond this minimum position, the Bush administration wanted the United States to have the opportunity to negotiate with the Philippines a further base rights agreement at the end of the post-1991 accord. This would open the possibility of continued, full U.S. base rights even beyond the ten-year period.

The new agreement was close to the U.S. position. It set base rights to Subic at ten years and contained language that opened the possibility of negotiations over base rights beyond the period of the accord.

Impact of U.S. Military Withdrawal

A termination of U.S. base rights would compel the United States to alter its use of other facilities in the Western Pacific. One option is to gain access to facilities in other friendly East Asian countries and Australia. The United States has negotiated with Singapore over access to airfields and ship repair docks, and several other countries have facilities that could provide support. The Singapore negotiation, thus, could forecast discussion with other governments. Brunei reportedly has offered access to its facilities. The United States already had limited access to naval bases and air bases in Australia. Such alternatives could provide peacetime repairs of ships and aircraft and normal refueling and resupply, including refueling cargo flights to Diego Garcia. According to several studies, none of these facilities, either individually or collectively, could replace Subic and Clark in terms of space for stockpiling weapons, parts, and fuel, or in capacity for repair work. Thus, they could not support a major buildup of American forces in Southeast Asia or the Indian Ocean–Persian Gulf comparable to the role of the Philippines bases. They also would not replicate the training facilities in the Philippines. Labor costs would be higher than in the Philippines.

U.S. island possessions to the east of the Philippines could provide other alternatives. Air force and naval bases exist on Guam; there is underutilized capacity at airfields and room for expansion of ship repair facilities. The Defense Department leases extensive land on Tinian and Saipan, part of the Commonwealth of Northern Mariana Islands. Palau has an extensive natural harbor. The United States might enlarge bases and build new ones in these locations. Cost estimates provided by the U.S. Defense Department range between $4 billion and $10 billion for new construction. Labor costs and some other costs would be much higher than in the Philippines, and workers would be in short supply in some locations. Strong public opposition to U.S. bases exists in Palau, especially over the issue of nuclear weapons. Transport between widely separated base sites in these islands and access sites such as Singapore would be expensive and time consuming.

In view of a declining Soviet threat and pressures to cut U.S. defense spending, the Bush administration decided for the present not to spend large amounts of money for new and/or expanded bases. Under this option, the United States will rely on existing bases in Japan and Guam for its Western Pacific presence, perhaps supported by limited access to facilities in Singapore and Australia. The navy might have to pull some of its units back to Hawaii, where there are underutilized bases. Logistics capabilities in the Western Pacific for support of Indian Ocean–Persian Gulf operations would drop considerably.

The impact of a withdrawal on U.S.–Philippines relations is uncertain. Bush administration officials have spoken of "hard feelings" if the talks failed to extend base rights. Criticism of the Aquino government has grown in the U.S. Congress over the bases issue, President Aquino's "snub" of Secretary of Defense Cheney during his February 1990 visit to Manila, and the perceived inability of Aquino to affect domestic reforms. Filipino political leaders, who favor an early termination of base rights, assert that removal of the bases would remove a contentious issue between the two countries and place the relationship on a more mature basis. Another view holds that a termination of base rights in 1991 would bring about a downturn in relations for a period, but that a healing process would follow.

The impact of a U.S. withdrawal on the stability of the Philippine government and prospects for continued democracy could be considerable. U.S. military intervention appeared to save the Aquino administration from being overthrown in the December 1989 attempted coup d'etat, and nearly all close observers believe Aquino's position has weakened since then (polls show a drop in public approval of Aquino to below 50 percent)—a recent blow being the downturn in the already shaky economy caused by rapidly rising oil prices. (The next presidential election is scheduled for 1992.)

One thing seems certain. The RAM-YOU forces would view a U.S. withdrawal as a green light to plan another coup attempt without the prospect of American military intervention against them. To beat back another coup attempt, the Aquino administration would have to retain the support of loyalist military officers. Many of them probably support an extension of base rights along the lines of Secretary of Defense Fidel Ramos' proposal for an extension until 1998; and they could turn more critical of Aquino if a termination of base rights in 1991 threatened a discontinuation of the U.S. military aid program, which provides most of the weapons and equipment available to the Philippine armed forces.

A U.S. withdrawal would eliminate the bases as a source of contention between the Aquino administration and its opponents. However, the sources of popular support for the communists and the RAM-YOU forces lie mainly in their criticism of the inability of the Aquino administration to affect domestic social and economic reforms and reduce corruption in government. Moreover, the anti-base rights nationalists likely would turn their attention to their other themes, such as opposition to U.S. and other foreign investment and repudiation of Philippine repayment of the foreign debt.

A related question is whether the Philippine government could devise new policies that would keep the confidence of other donor governments, foreign lending banks, and foreign business investors. Many aid officials and foreign business people cite the risk of political turmoil and violence as the chief disincentive to involvement in the Philippines. U.S. policy has been influential in building international financial support for the Philippines, including the Multilateral Assistance Initiative. A U.S. military withdrawal in 1991, and any U.S. decision to downgrade other aspects of support, would increase the perception of political risk in the Philippines, according to U.S., Japanese, and other foreign business people.

Some foreign officials and business people assert that the Philippine government could keep international confidence during and after an American withdrawal in 1991 if it adopted policies and procedures more favorable to foreign investors, improved efficiency in utilizing aid funds, and implemented domestic reforms. They stress, however, that a rise in violence or a successful coup d'etat would result in diminished involvement by foreign investors, bankers, and aid-giving countries.

Impact of an Extension of Base Rights

The United States would face a different set of issues if circumstances were to arise where Washington and Manila agreed to an extension of base rights. These issues would vary, too, according to whether an extension accord was open-ended—allowing for another negotiated extension at a future date—or whether it specified termination at some point within five to ten years (the phase-out formula), which now appears to be the more likely scenario, if base rights are extended at all.

Strategically, an extension would give the United States more flexibility in dealing with military-related issues in the Western Pacific in the 1990s. These include how to reduce the overall size of the American armed force structure if East-West relations continue to improve; the kind of position to take on the issue of arms reductions in the Western Pacific (especially if U.S.-Soviet-Japanese negotiations take place); and the kind and extent of U.S. influence over Japanese defense policy in the 1990s. The United States would have a more stable position to project military power into the Indian Ocean–Persian Gulf and support existing forces there.

This flexibility would be greater if an extension agreement were openended. If it contained the phase-out formula, the United States would face several of the military strategic issues described above in the U.S. military withdrawal in 1991 scenario. The U.S. government would have additional time to make and implement decisions and allocate any money connected with adjustments in the Western Pacific force-base structure.

Within the Philippines, an extension of base rights would present at least two issues. One would be whether the United States again would intervene militarily against dissidents seeking to overthrow the Philippine government by force. A continued American presence might help to deter another coup attempt, in light of the U.S. action in December 1989. However, it would hardly guarantee that another coup attempt, or a future series of attempts, would not occur.

A second issue would be the policy to adopt if the communists continued to assassinate Americans and/or if the CPP or the RAM-YOU forces staged attacks or sabotage operations against the bases. This could affect the U.S. diplomatic presence in the country, the status of U.S. dependents, the role of the U.S. military in base security, and American business operations.

Notes

1. Among useful assessments of developments in ASEAN and U.S. relations with those countries, see Donald E. Weatherbee, *ASEAN after Cambodia: Reordering Southeast Asia* (New York: The Asia Society, June 1989).

2. Cited in U.S. Library of Congress, Congressional Research Service, "Philippine Bases Negotiations," Larry Niksch, (Washington, DC: October 22, 1991, CRS Issue Brief 90142, p. 8).

3. Ibid., 1991.

9

Australia, New Zealand, and the Pacific Islands

U.S. interest in secure access through Oceania—a vast region including Australia, New Zealand and the small island countries in the central and southern Pacific Ocean—and in the stability and development of the region grew markedly in the late 1980s and appear greater today than at any time since the end of World War II. The Asian-Pacific basin has become increasingly important for U.S. economic development and security concerns. U.S. policy in the region has become complicated by several factors: opposition in Oceania to U.S. policy regarding transit of nuclear weapons-capable warships and aircraft, U.S. association with French nuclear weapons testing and colonial administration in Oceania, U.S. fishing and farm export disputes with countries in the region, U.S. plans to destroy chemical weapons in the Pacific, and other issues. From time to time, the Soviet Union attempted to exploit U.S. vulnerabilities and expand Soviet influence among Pacific island countries.

The United States faces a series of trade-offs between measures (involving naval deployments, foreign assistance, fishing, farm export policy, and other matters) that would improve relations with the governments and peoples of Oceania and measures that would further other interests at the expense of the U.S. position in the Pacific.[1]

U.S Interests in Oceania

Following the end of World War II, the United States generally viewed developments in Oceania as favorable to American interests. For the most part, democratically elected governments controlled the region, encouraged free market economic development, and were friendly toward the United States. These governments served U.S. interests by allowing U.S. warships and aircraft to be based in, stop at, and pass through their territory, and by rebuffing repeated Soviet efforts to gain influence in the region. As a result, the United States enjoyed secure lines of communication through Oceania to Asia, the Indian Ocean, and the Persian Gulf.

At present, the United States maintains military bases in the U.S. territory of Guam. There are three major "joint facilities" used by the United States in Australia. The United States also leases an important missile test site at Kwajalein, in the Marshall Islands, and leases territory for possible future military use in the Commonwealth of Northern Mariana Islands. The United States is reported to be considering additional sites for military bases in the region as possible alternatives to the U.S. bases in the Philippines.

To secure its strategic and other interests in the region, the United States continues extensive government spending programs in Guam, American Samoa, and former trust territories under U.S. administration in Micronesia. Elsewhere in the Pacific, the United States has relied mainly on the diplomatic and aid efforts of Australia, New Zealand, Japan, and Great Britain to represent its interests. The United States spent annually about $17 million in aid to South Pacific countries in recent years, whereas Australia and Japan provide larger amounts of aid ($300 million and $93 million, respectively, in 1989) to help these poor island countries maintain basic government services and promote economic development. U.S. trade with Oceania represents only a small fraction of overall U.S. foreign trade. The region's economic significance for the United States derives partly from its fishing resources. American tuna-fishing fleets use regional fishing grounds, including those areas claimed as exclusive economic zones (EEZs) by some island states. Other American interests include a desire to support the democratically elected governments of the region and to assist the small Pacific island nations in their efforts to develop economically.

Opposition to Nuclear Weapons: Impact on the ANZUS Alliance

New Zealand

In 1984, New Zealand elected a Labor party government that strongly opposed the presence of U.S. or other states' nuclear weapons in Oceania. It initiated a policy of denying access to New Zealand's ports for warships that are nuclear-powered or carry nuclear weapons. Because 40 percent of the U.S. naval combatant ships are nuclear-powered, and it remains U.S. policy neither to confirm nor deny the presence of nuclear weapons in navy ships, the new policy effectively halted U.S. ship visits to New Zealand. The United States responded to New Zealand's restrictions by cutting back on military, intelligence, and other bilateral exchanges. As a result, the U.S.–New Zealand leg of the forty-year-old Australia–New

Zealand-U.S. (ANZUS) alliance—an important strategic framework for allied interests in the South Pacific—became moribund. The United States and Australia have continued to function as defense allies under the ANZUS framework, as do Australia and New Zealand, even though the link between the United States and New Zealand is broken. On June 4, 1987, the Labor government successfully pushed through New Zealand's Parliament legislation banning nuclear weapons from New Zealand.

On March 1, 1990, Secretary of State Baker met in Washington with New Zealand's foreign minister—the first ministerial contact since 1985. Another first was seen a year later when President Bush spoke with New Zealand's prime minister, who telephoned to congratulate the president on the allied victory in the Persian Gulf war. The New Zealand government in 1991 publicly supported in principle U.S.-backed collective security arrangements in the South Pacific. In June 1991, a U.S. government helicopter and crew successfully conducted a dangerous rescue of a New Zealand engineer from Antarctica.

The U.S.-New Zealand dispute is often seen as harmful to U.S. interests in New Zealand, Australia, and throughout the region, but the immediate impact on bilateral U.S. interests appeared to be small. Direct U.S. involvement in New Zealand is small. Bilateral trade amounts to less than $2 billion in value each year. The United States maintains no military bases in New Zealand. It uses facilities there as a staging area for government-supported activities in Antarctica.

U.S. administration officials have maintained that military exchanges, exercises, and related activities such as ship visits are particularly important foundations for an alliance relationship with New Zealand. They have argued that New Zealand should share the burden of collective defense in part by hosting U.S. warship visits, and they have criticized New Zealand policy as a challenge to the burden-sharing arrangements that prevailed until recently. If undeterred, the New Zealand policy might be adopted by neighboring Australia, the Philippines, Japan, or other countries where U.S. military access is more important than in the case of New Zealand. In Australia, an important anti-nuclear faction in Prime Minister Bob Hawke's Labor Party favors a similar policy on U.S. ship visits to Australia. New Zealand has developed extensive military, economic, and political ties with the smaller South Pacific states. These countries may side with New Zealand in a dispute with the United States over nuclear policy.

The U.S. administration's policy runs up against the strongly anti-nuclear feeling of many people in the region. Although public opinion in Oceania tends to want to continue cooperation with the United States and the West, it had feared that this long peaceful region could become a focal point in East-West nuclear confrontation. More recently, there is growing concern about the environmental impact of nuclear activities by larger powers in the region. In particular, it is widely believed that continued French underground nuclear testing in French Polynesia could result in radiation leaks and other environmental damage to nearby territory, fish, and other maritime resources.

Australia

The Australian Labor party government of Prime Minister Bob Hawke was caught in the middle of the dispute between the United States and New Zealand over U.S. ship visits. On the one hand, many in Australia, including important but minority elements of the Labor party, have been sympathetic with the New Zealand government's position. They also have encouraged the Australian government to choose an option open to signatories of the South Pacific Nuclear Free Zone Treaty (discussed below) whereby warships capable of carrying nuclear weapons would be prohibited from visiting the country's ports. On the other hand, the Australian government remains closely tied to ANZUS and the United States for security and economic reasons. (The United States is Australia's second largest trading partner.)

The United States has valued Australia's position as a regional leader. That country uses economic aid, diplomatic interchange, and military assistance to foster stability and development throughout the South Pacific. Australia is also important as a way station for transiting U.S. warships and aircraft and as a host for joint military facilities. (Australia's role is seen in the United States as all the more important on account of New Zealand's stance.)

Consistent with established Australian government policy, the United States is not permitted to establish nuclear weapons–capable bases in Australia. Moreover, since 1982, U.S. strategic bombers using Australian territory during exercises have been required to be unarmed. Anti-nuclear sentiment in Australia was also influential in Prime Minister Hawke's decision in 1985 to break an earlier commitment to allow the United States to use facilities in Australia to test a strategic nuclear capable missile, the MX missile. Nevertheless, U.S. warships have not been required to disclose whether they have nuclear weapons aboard when they visit Australian ports. Further, Australia still hosts joint military facilities that provided early warning against Soviet missile attacks, gathered intelligence on Soviet missile tests, and provided communication links for U.S. naval forces in the Pacific and Indian Oceans. The Hawke government has backed the U.S. position in response to New Zealand's policy on nuclear ship visits, has supported the maintenance of ANZUS, and has continued Australian defense ties with New Zealand under the ANZUS framework.

TABLE 9.1 Members of the South Pacific Forum

	Size (sq. km.)	Population	Economy ($ per capita GDP)
Australia	7,600,000	17,288,044	14,900
Cook Islands	240	18,000	2,200
Federated States of Micronesia	720	107,000	1,500
Fiji	1,837	740,000	1,840
Kiribati	690	71,000	525
Marshall Islands	181	48,000	1,500
Nauru	20	9,300	10,000
New Zealand	268,676	3,300,000	12,000
Nuie	259	2,672	1,080
Papua New Guinea	461,691	3,913,000	725
Solomon Islands	29,785	347,000	500
Tonga	997	102,000	850
Tuvalu	26	9,300	530
Vanuatu	14,763	170,000	860
Western Samoa	2,934	190,000	620

Source: U.S. Central Intelligence Agency, *The World Factbook, 1991* (Washington, DC: 1991).

The U.S. government supports Australia's defense policy. Some U.S. observers are concerned that anti-nuclear sentiment, government budget constraints, and other factors are moving the Australian government toward a less expensive, more narrowly defined regional orientation in its defense policy and related foreign assistance programs. In particular, budget and other pressures prompted the Hawke government to reduce defense spending to below 3 percent of GDP and to cut back on foreign aid commitments to South Pacific countries. U.S. critics view this perceived shift as detrimental to the U.S. interest in collective security efforts in the Asian-Pacific region.

South Pacific Nuclear Free Zone

In August 1985, Australia, New Zealand, and the other members of the South Pacific Forum, a regional body of then thirteen (now fifteen) South Pacific states, reached agreement on a treaty declaring the South Pacific to be a Nuclear Free Zone. (See Table 9.1 for a listing of the fifteen members of the Forum and data on their size, population, and economy.) The treaty has three protocols that the Forum has asked the United States and other nuclear powers to sign.

The treaty reserves for each South Pacific country the right to decide whether to limit naval and air access to its territory, but it poses several potential problems for the United States. In particular, it precludes the establishment of U.S. bases that could have nuclear weapons in Australia, New Zealand, and the Pacific island states south of the equator. (U.S. officials strongly emphasize that the United States has no interest in such nuclear-capable bases.) By signing the protocols, the United States could be seen as supporting the text of the treaty, which contains strong criticism of continued French nuclear testing in French Polynesia. Signing the protocols could prompt other countries in critical world areas to demand U.S. endorsement of nuclear free zones in other regions of the world. Further, New Zealand's Labor government used the occasion of the signing of the treaty to initiate legislation in the New Zealand Parliament supporting the Labor party government's policy to ban the visits of nuclear-powered ships or ships carrying nuclear weapons to New Zealand ports.

The Soviet Union and China signed the protocols of the treaty in late 1986 and early 1987, respectively. The Reagan administration announced in February 1987 that the United States would not sign the protocols. Great Britain also announced that it would not sign the protocols. On October 20, 1987, the U.S. House of Representatives passed a resolution calling on the Reagan administration to reconsider its refusal to sign the protocols. In the 101st Congress, the House passed a resolution on this issue (H.Con.Res. 218) on November 7, 1989.

Palau

The United States maintains responsibility for the defense of the Micronesian state of Palau. U.S. planners reportedly have considered—in the event of a U.S. withdrawal from bases in the Philippines or other circumstances—the option of constructing a base in Palau. In particular, the capacity to service U.S. nuclear-capable warships and aircraft would seem to be important to the effectiveness of such a base. U.S. military access to Palau remains complicated by Palau's 1981 constitution, which does not allow nuclear weapons on Palau's territory.

The U.S. government attempted to deal with the potential problem in negotiating a compact of free association with Palau. Palau, along with the Northern Mariana Islands, the Federated States of Micronesia, and the Marshall Islands, is part of a strategic trust territory in the Pacific in transition to self-rule from U.S. administration. Under a U.N. trusteeship arrangement, U.S. agreements (compacts) with three of the four governments were negotiated in the 1980s and set the terms for self-rule. The fourth, the Northern Mariana Islands, obtained commonwealth status with the United States. In the late 1980s, arrangements with the Marshall Islands and the Federated States of Micronesia were approved by Congress and were being implemented by the United States, although they were yet to be acted on by the U.N. Trusteeship Council and the U.N. Security

Council. In late 1990, U.S. and Soviet officials had reached agreement on the issue, paving the way to U.N. sanction of the new arrangements in December 1990.

The terms of the U.S. compact with Palau would allow U.S. nuclear-capable warships to transit Palau and would allow the use of military facilities there on a contingency basis. The compact was supported by a majority of Palau voters. The impediment of Palau's constitutional prohibition on nuclear weapons has been addressed in several referenda that have received majority support, but less than the 75 percent needed.

Legislation to authorize implementation of the compact was proposed by President Reagan. The U.S. Senate approved authorizing legislation (S.J.Res. 231) on March 28, 1988, and the House approved a separate bill (H.J.Res. 597) on October 6, 1988. A compromise was reached too late to be enacted in the 100th Congress.

On March 8, 1989, legislation (H.J.Res. 175) to authorize implementing the compact with Palau was introduced. H.J.Res. 175 was approved by the House on June 27, 1989. A final version passed the Senate and House on November 21-22 and was signed by President Bush on December 12, 1989. But the impediment of Palau's constitutional prohibition on nuclear weapons remained to be dealt with.

Soviet Influence

During the 1980s, the Soviet Union made some efforts to broaden its presence in the region. The Soviets' diplomatic missions in Oceania were long confined to Australia and New Zealand; their fishing fleet was long confined to a station in New Zealand. In July 1985, however, the Soviet Union and the Micronesian state of Kiribati signed a one-year fishing agreement. Kiribati is a poor but strategically located nation, covering a wide expanse of the central Pacific Ocean. Since the mid-1970s, the Soviets had made overtures to Fiji, Tonga, Solomon Islands, Papua New Guinea, Vanuatu, and others to establish a commercial or diplomatic presence, but without success until the agreement with Kiribati.

In 1986, Soviet officials began negotiating a new agreement with Kiribati. The negotiations were unsuccessful and the fishing rights lapsed in 1986. Moscow announced that it had established diplomatic relations on July 1, 1986, with the left-leaning government of Vanuatu. This move was followed three months later by the announced U.S. intention to establish relations with the South Pacific state. Papua New Guinea said in September 1986 that it would establish relations with the USSR, while Vanuatu and Fiji held talks with Soviet fishing and trade officials. In 1987, Vanuatu signed a one-year fishing agreement that allowed Soviet vessels to use Vanuatu ports. The accord lapsed after one year. A planned Soviet fishing agreement with Papua New Guinea was postponed by New Guinea in August 1989. A fishing agreement was signed in June 1990, a few months after a Soviet diplomatic mission opened in Papua New Guinea.

U.S. Association with France

U.S. relations with Oceanian states have been complicated as a result of U.S. refusal to join them in criticizing French nuclear testing—and from time to time French colonial administration—in Oceania. Although the French government has granted local authorities greater autonomy in recent years, it views French Polynesia as an Overseas Territory of France, maintains its active nuclear testing site at Mururoa Atoll, and stations several thousand troops there. Australia, New Zealand, and other members of the South Pacific Forum have repeatedly condemned the French testing; they have urged the United States to sign the protocols for the Forum-endorsed treaty creating a South Pacific Nuclear Free Zone and to take other steps that condemn the French testing. The administration announced on February 5, 1987, that the United States would not sign the treaty protocols.

At times, the Forum countries have taken a firm stand against French administration in the mineral-rich French Overseas Territory of New Caledonia. At their meeting in August 1986, Forum members urged the U.N. General Assembly to reinscribe the French possession in its list of non-self- governing territories. France lobbied against this move and attempted to enlist the support of the United States. Although the Forum governments were not known to have complained about U.S. refusal to join them in criticizing French policy in New Caledonia, political groups and media comment in the region were critical of the American position on this issue.

From time to time, internal tensions in New Caledonia make it difficult for the United States to maintain its reserved stance. A sometimes violent split has developed in the territory since the late 1970s between proponents of continued French rule and those favoring full independence. The split has tended to follow ethnic lines, with native Melanesians favoring independence and settlers from France favoring continued French rule. The demands of the native Melanesians, led by the Kanak Socialist National Liberation Front, have been supported by Melanesian states and Australia and New Zealand.

The demands of the Kanak Front met a firm response from the French administration of conservative prime minister Jacques Chirac. This response was supported by the many ethnically French settlers who have built comfortable lives working in the mineral-rich territory. (The annual per capita income in New Caledonia is over $8,000, a standard comparable to developed countries.) The Chirac government amended previous plans for self-rule that were seen as favoring the demands of the Melanesians, announced a plebiscite in 1987 on continued French rule, and strongly criticized Australia and other South Pacific Forum countries for their policy regarding the French territory. The plebiscite was held on September 13, 1987; voters strongly supported continued French rule, but the election was boycotted by the Kanak Front.

In late April 1988, Kanak insurgents killed three French gendarmes and kidnapped twenty-two others and a magistrate. French commandos freed the twenty-three hostages after an eight-hour siege on May 5, 1988, in which fifteen of the Kanak insurgents and two commandos were killed.

After French elections in May 1988, the new French government seemed more accommodating to some of the interests of the Kanak Front. A compromise was reached in August 1988, which moved New Caledonia toward a referendum on a new federal system in 1988 and one on possible self-determination for the territory ten years later. It was approved by French voters on November 6, 1988. The compromise helped to improve French relations with South Pacific Forum countries. The Kanak Front negotiator of the August 1988 compromise was assassinated in New Caledonia in May 1989. But elections for provincial posts in New Caledonia were carried out peacefully in June 1989.

U.S. Tuna Fishing; U.S. Farm Export Policy

Many of the small Pacific island states depend heavily on income derived from fishing, claiming rights to the fishing resources in large maritime economic zones—known as exclusive economic zones (EEZs)—around their territory. Most countries recognize such zones. The United States takes the position that the zones, extending 200 miles from the island state's land area, do not apply to tuna, a highly migratory fish species. As a result, American tuna-fishing fleets have been perceived as repeatedly violating the claimed rights of several Pacific island governments, and some governments have seized and fined U.S. tuna boats.

The U.S. government attempted to ease the problem by negotiating a regional fisheries agreement with the Pacific states that would be acceptable to them and the U.S. tuna-fishing interests. Talks began in 1983 and ended in late October 1986 with a five-year, $60 million agreement. The accord, in the form of a treaty, was signed on April 2, 1987. Under its terms, the United States agreed to a $12 million annual financial package, made up of $2 million from the U.S. tuna-fishing industry ($1.75 million in license fees for thirty-five boats in the first year, plus $.25 million in technical assistance). A U.S. government assistance package would be divided between $9 million in aid grants and $1 million in project assistance. The Senate ratified the treaty on November 6, 1987. Thus far, the administration and Congress have followed through with the $10 million in annual aid required under the treaty. President Bush announced in October 1990 that the United States would seek to negotiate to extend the treaty. Meanwhile, Congress took action in July 1986 that prompted the Reagan administration to propose subsidized sales of U.S. wheat and other farm products abroad. This kind of action cuts deeply into Australia's wheat, sugar, and other export markets. The Australian government vehemently criticized the U.S. moves. Australian officials claimed that they reduced Australian popular support for the alliance relationship with the United States; made it more difficult for Prime Minister Hawke to resist the anti-nuclear pressures from the left wing of his party, New Zealand, and much of the rest of the region; and complicated Australian efforts to persuade small South Pacific countries to remain close to the West and steer clear of the self-serving economic expediency of signing lucrative fishing, trade, or other agreements with the Soviet Union.

Political, Economic, and Environmental Issues Affecting Pacific Island Nations

Most of the Pacific Island nations are poor, small in size, have few natural resources, and have difficulty sustaining economic development without outside help. They often face problems of rapid population growth, unplanned urbanization, rising popular aspirations, and political instability. In the late 1980s, political instability was featured in Fiji, Papua New Guinea, and Vanuatu. With little land and few natural resources, Pacific island leaders tend to be very sensitive to perceived environmental dangers to the sea. Thus, they oppose French nuclear testing on these grounds, are in the lead in international efforts to ban drift-net fishing, and are concerned about reported U.S. plans to destroy the U.S. chemical weapons stored on the Pacific territory, Johnston Island.

Options for U.S. Policy

U.S. policymakers in Congress and the administration face a number of decisions that will likely affect U.S. relations with Australia, New Zealand, and the Pacific island countries. In each case, American policymakers face trade-offs between measures that would improve relations with the governments and peoples of Oceania, and measures that would further other interests at the expense of the U.S. position in the Pacific.

South Pacific Nuclear Free Zone

The thirteen members of the Pacific Forum have readied for signing the protocols of the treaty declaring the South Pacific to be a nuclear free zone. The Soviet Union signed two of the protocols on December 15, 1986. China signed two protocols in February 1987. A prompt U.S. decision to sign the protocols would have pleased Australia's Labor government and other South Pacific Forum representatives who were pressing the United States to endorse the treaty. But such action would have antagonized the French government, whose nuclear testing is strongly criticized in the treaty. Moreover, while the Australian government maintains that the treaty does not curb existing U.S. freedom of navigation in the South Pacific, some U.S. observers saw a prompt U.S. endorsement of the treaty as encouraging New Zealand to pass pending legislation banning the visits of U.S. and other nuclear-capable ships, and precluding broader access to the region by U.S. nuclear-capable forces under future circumstances. Perhaps of more importance, endorsing this nuclear free zone might have encouraged anti-nuclear sentiment in other parts of the world more sensitive to U.S. interests. The administration announced on February 5, 1987, that it would not sign the treaty protocols. Great Britain also said it would not sign them.

Destruction of Chemical Weapons and Other Environmental Issues

There are many Pacific island critics of the Bush administration's plan reported in 1990 to destroy chemical weapons stored on Johnston Island—located several hundred miles southwest of Hawaii—and to destroy chemical weapons being shipped to the island from West Germany for that purpose. A South Pacific Forum delegation reportedly visited Washington in September 1990 to press the United States to give a commitment to halt the destruction once the weapons located on the island and those shipped from Germany have been destroyed. The Forum has been concerned particularly about the safety and environmental impact of the U.S. plans to destroy chemical weapons in the Pacific.

Meanwhile, Congress and the administration have taken actions to curb the use of "drift net" fishing in the South Pacific. President Bush on September 25, 1990, transmitted to the Senate for approval the South Pacific environmental convention of 1986. The House had gone on record in favor of ratification by passing H.Res. 398 on September 17, 1990. Many in the South Pacific are extremely concerned with global warming, which will soon cause rising in ocean levels that will inundate low-lying atolls, according to some observers. They favor a more active policy in the Bush administration.

New Caledonia

A trade-off between U.S. interests in Oceania and U.S. relations with France arose as a result of the South Pacific Forum countries' effort to urge the U.N. General Assembly to reinscribe New Caledonia on its list of non-self-governing territories. The action was approved by the General Assembly on December 2, 1986. The United States abstained. Although the 1988 compromise agreement discussed above has eased tension in New Caledonia and reduced international criticism of France's policy, the situation there remains potentially volatile. Some Forum countries may continue to press for U.S. support for independence in opposition to French policy.

U.S. Farm Export Policy

The Australian government has made clear its opposition to American government efforts to promote agricultural sales abroad, similar to the actions in 1986. It has also voiced concern over existing and proposed U.S. measures that it perceived as unfairly limiting Australia's access to the American market in such goods as sugar, lamb, beef, and dairy products. The administration and the Congress face continued pressure from U.S. farmers, concerned about U.S. agricultural surpluses and declining farm exports, who can be expected to argue for U.S. policy steps, similar to the 1986 actions, that are designed to reduce U.S. agricultural problems but will also have the effect of antagonizing countries like Australia.

U.S. Political Attention, Foreign Assistance, Diplomatic Presence

Some U.S. observers and representatives from Oceania argue that the United States could improve its influence in the region through more generous aid programs or greater U.S. diplomatic or political presence. President Bush took the initiative in holding an unprecedented summit meeting with eleven Pacific island leaders on October 27, 1990. U.S. assistance would promote stability, help compensate for the recent cutbacks in Australia's aid effort, and strengthen the resolve of regional governments to resist others' offers of fishing and trade pacts. However, U.S. ability to increase its modest aid programs or to expand its diplomatic presence in Oceania runs up against strong budget constraints that have forced recent substantial cutbacks in foreign assistance programs to other key areas. As a result, any increase in the U.S. programs in Oceania is likely to come at the expense of already hard-pressed programs in other parts of the world.

One option for U.S. policymakers involves encouraging Japan to increase its development assistance to the region. Official Japanese assistance to Oceania in the Japanese fiscal year covering March 1985 to March 1986 amounted to $24.1 million, well above the level provided by the United States. The Japanese foreign minister traveled to the region in January 1987 and declared that Japan would increase aid efforts there. In 1988, Japan provided $57.3 million in assistance. In 1989, the level of Japanese aid was $93.1 million. It remains unclear if the increased Japanese aid efforts are well-received in the region or involve possible trade-offs in Japanese policy affecting U.S. interests in other areas.

U.S. Fisheries Treaty with Pacific Island States

This treaty was submitted for Senate ratification in June 1987. It commits the United States to a $50 million aid program over five years. The Senate approved the treaty on November 6, 1987. Thus far, the administration and Congress have fulfilled the commitments for $10 million a year in U.S. assistance. The United States is seeking to extend the treaty.

New Zealand's Anti-Nuclear Stance

The Labor government followed through with its stated intent to pass legislation supporting the government's anti-nuclear policy, and Prime Minister David Lange on April 25, 1989, threatened to pull New Zealand out of ANZUS. With the passing of time, some U.S. observers argued for a moderate U.S. response that keeps intact the ANZUS alliance framework and allows resumed high-level contacts with New Zealand. But other U.S. observers argued that a more forceful U.S. approach, perhaps involving economic as well as military-political restrictions, was needed to check the spread of anti-nuclear sentiment in the region and elsewhere. Secretary of State Baker's 1990 resumption of U.S. ministerial-level meetings with New Zealand after a hiatus of five years received mixed reviews and some criticism in Congress. By contrast, congressional advocates of improved U.S.–New Zealand relations supported their position by referring to President Bush's acceptance of the call from Prime Minister Jim Bolger congratulating the president on the victory in the Persian Gulf war; New Zealand's sending of medical teams and transport aircraft as part of the allied effort in the Gulf, and Prime Minister Bolger's strong support for a continued U.S.-backed collective security arrangement in the South Pacific.

Notes

1. Some useful studies on U.S. relations with the countries of Oceania are cited in the suggested readings section below. Among useful U.S. government publica-

tions, see, U.S. Congress, House, Committee on Foreign Affairs, "Regional Security Developments in the South Pacific," 101st Congress, 1st Session, House, Report No. 95-630 (Washington, DC: Government Printing Office, 1989); U.S. Congress, House, Committee on Foreign Affairs, Subcommittee on Asian and Pacific Affairs, *U.S. Interests in the South Pacific*, hearing, 101st Congress, 1st Session, July 27, 1989 (Washington, DC: Government Printing Office, 1990); *Problems in Paradise: U.S. Interests in the South Pacific*, report (Washington, DC: Government Printing Office, 1990); U.S. Library of Congress, Congressional Research Service, "Pacific Island Nations: Overview of Trends," Luella Christopher (Washington, DC: July 29, 1990, CRS Report 90-396 F); and "Pacific Island Nations and the United States," Luella Christopher (October 23, 1990, CRS Report 90-541 F).

10

Conclusion: A Framework for Assessing Overall Trends in U.S. Policy Toward East Asia and the Pacific

The numerous issues and variables affecting U.S. policy noted in this book make it difficult for readers to chart the general direction of U.S. policy toward the region. The task is made all the more difficult because the previous framework for U.S. policy toward the region, based on the primacy of security issues and opposition to Soviet expansion, is now obsolete. Imperatives of economic competitiveness, democracy, human rights, and other values have achieved greater prominence in U.S. policymaking. The ability of the executive branch of government to use the argument of U.S. strategic competition with the Soviet Union as a means to keep foreign policymaking power in its hands is also at an end. American policymaking will likely reflect more sharply the pluralistic nature of U.S. society and the various pressure groups and other representative institutions there.

History has shown that this fluidity and competition among priorities is more often than not the norm in American foreign policy. Presidents Wilson and Roosevelt both set forth comprehensive concepts of a well-integrated U.S. foreign policy, but neither framework lasted long. The requirements of the Cold War were much more effective in establishing rigor and order in U.S. foreign policy priorities, but that era is now over. In retrospect, it appears as the aberration rather than the norm in the course of U.S. foreign policy.

One way to make sense out of the fluid situation we face today is to track the success or failure of the programs and preferences advocated by different schools of thought concerned with American foreign policy in the post–Cold War environment. Although contemporary U.S. foreign policy advocates cover a wide range of opinion and issues, one can discern three general schools of thought influencing American policy. By understanding what these schools stand for and observing the actions of U.S. policy in specific areas of Asia and the Pacific, readers can get a better sense as to the general direction of U.S. policy in the region.

At the outset of this book, I argued for a cautious U.S. policy that would emphasize close relations with longstanding friends and allies, centered on Japan. The policy stressed continued strong U.S. involvement with these states; more cautious interchange with the unsettled and preoccupied regimes in Russia, China, and India; and only moderate cutbacks in U.S. military presence in the region.

In a broad sense, this policy is in line with that of the Bush administration and with others whom I would call "realists" in foreign policy. These advocates see a need for U.S. policy toward Asia and the Pacific that calls for the United States to work harder to preserve important interests, but with fewer U.S. resources and less U.S. influence available to do the job. These leaders' review of recent developments causes them to expect further changes in world affairs, sometimes in unexpected ways. They see relatively limited or declining U.S. power and influence to deal with those changes.

They stress in particular several "realities" governing the current U.S. approach to Asia and the Pacific and world affairs in general:

- U.S. attention to Asia and the Pacific has been diverted by developments elsewhere in the world and by the need to focus on pressing U.S. domestic problems.
- U.S. government decision making will remain difficult because of the possibility that the executive branch will remain in control of one U.S. political party, and the Congress in control of another party.
- The U.S. government and the U.S. private sector have only limited financial resources to devote to domestic and foreign policy concerns.
- The priorities in U.S. policy toward the region will remain unclear. Security, economic, and cultural-political issues will vary in receiving top priority in U.S. policy.
- There remains no obvious international framework to deal with regional issues. U.S. policy must use a mix of international, regional, and bilateral efforts to achieve policy goals.

Under these circumstances, the "realists" see a strong need for the United States to work prudently and closely with traditional U.S. allies and associates in the region. The realists' cautious approach argues, for example, that it seems foolish and inconsistent with U.S. goals not to preserve the longstanding U.S. stake in good relations with Japan and with friends and allies along the periphery of Asia and in Oceania. Their

Conclusion

security policies and political-cultural orientations are generally seen as in accord with U.S. interests. Although opinion surveys claim that the American pubic and some U.S. leaders see Japan as an economic competitive "threat" to U.S. well-being, surpassing the military threat posed to the United States by the former Soviet Union, these observers stress a different line of argument. They highlight the fact that few polls of U.S. public opinion or U.S. leaders support the view that it is now in America's interest to focus U.S. energies on the need to confront the Japanese economic threat, in a way that confrontation with the Soviet Union came to dominate U.S. policy during the Cold War.

In the view of the "realists," caution is in order in anticipating future U.S. relations with other major regional actors—the former Soviet Union, China, and India. All three are preoccupied with internal political-development crises. None appears to be seeking to foment tensions or major instability in the region. All seek better ties and closer economic relations with the West and with the advancing economies of the region. U.S. policy would appear well advised, the realists say, to work closely with these governments wherever there is possible common ground on security, economic, or political issues.

In considering U.S. assets available to influence trends in the region, realists call on U.S. leaders to go slow in reducing U.S. military presence in the region. The economic savings of such a cutback would be small; the political costs could be high inasmuch as most countries in Asia have been encouraging the U.S. to remain actively involved in the region to offset the growing power of Japan or the potential ambitions of China or others.

A second major school of thought on U.S. foreign policy emerged in 1991. Basing its arguments on the same "realities" seen by the realists, these proponents have argued for major cutbacks in U.S. international involvement and a renewed focus on solving U.S. domestic problems concerning crime, drugs, lagging economic competitiveness, and educational standards, homelessness, and poverty, decaying cities and transportation infrastructure, and other issues. Variations of this view are seen in the writings of William Hyland, Patrick Buchanan, and other well-known commentators.[1]

Often called an "America First" or "Neoisolationist" school, these advocates argue for sweeping cuts in U.S. military, diplomatic, and foreign assistance spending abroad. They are skeptical of the utility of the international financial institutions, the United Nations, and the international efforts to promote free trade through the GATT and other means. They argue that the U.S. has become overextended in world affairs; has been taken advantage of in the current world security-economic system; and must begin to retreat from international commitments in order to gather together the resources needed to deal with American domestic problems. As to specific recommendations, these proponents tend to favor a complete U.S. pullback from foreign bases; drastic cuts in foreign assistance and foreign technical/information programs; and termination of various international economic talks that help to perpetuate a world trading system, which they see as basically contrary to American economic interests. Many in this school favor stronger government intervention in the domestic U.S. economy and related areas of promoting technology, education, and social welfare. Some favor trade measures that are seen as protectionist by U.S. trading partners.

Meanwhile, on the other side of the realists and the neoisolationists lies a third, somewhat less well articulated school of thought that I will call "idealists." This school of thought generally judges that U.S. policy needs to more strongly and actively promote U.S. views of the world political, military, and economic order; to press those countries that do not conform to the U.S. view of an appropriate world order; and to lead strongly in world affairs, attempting to avoid compromises and accommodations with others that would reduce the impact and strength of U.S. leadership.

This school of thought has always been present in American politics. But it appears far stronger today than at any other time since at least the 1960s for several reasons:

- *Impact of Reagan policies*—After a prolonged period of introspection and doubt following the Vietnam War, the oil shocks, and the Iran hostage crisis, U.S. opinion became much more optimistic about the United States and its future after two terms of Ronald Reagan.[2]
- *Victory in the Cold War*—This represented a great accomplishment for the U.S.-backed system of collective security and for U.S. political and economic values.
- *Persian Gulf war*—U.S. military doctrine, equipment, and performance were strong; U.S. ability to lead in a world crisis also appeared strong.
- *Economic developments*—Although the U.S. is seen facing still serious difficulties, advocates point to analysts who are now more optimistic about U.S. ability to prosper in the increasingly competitive world economic environment.
- *Values-Culture*—The U.S. is seen as better positioned than any other country to exert leadership in all major areas of cultural influences; i.e., ideas and values, political concepts, life-style, and popular culture.

Further considerations giving impetus to this school of thought is the perception of a power vacuum in the world, in which the United States is more free to exert its influence. Thus, proponents of this viewpoint are

Conclusion

not deterred by the seeming decline in economic resources available to U.S. policymakers. In particular, the former Soviet Union, China, and India are likely to remain internally preoccupied for some time. Meanwhile, Japan and Germany are acknowledged to be economically powerful; but politically they have shown themselves to be uncertain as to how to use their new power and culturally they appear to be not nearly as influential as the United States.

In recent years, the idealists have been most vocal in pressing their concern for strong U.S. policy in support of U.S. political values of democracy and human rights. In this regard they have sometimes argued for a more active U.S. foreign policy, leading some recipient countries to view U.S. policy as illegitimate interference in a country's internal affairs. They have also reinforced the strength and determination of the U.S. case in opposition to economic or trading policies seen in the United States as grossly inequitable or predatory; and they have reinforced strongly the U.S. policy against the proliferation of weapons of mass destruction. Other areas where the idealists have entered more influence involve international sanctions against countries that harbor terrorists or promote the drug trade. They have also pushed the U.S. government to be more assertive in promoting humanitarian relief and in recognizing politically the legitimacy of people's right to self-determination.

As Americans and others grapple with the complexity and fluidity of U.S. policy in East Asia and the Pacific, they may find it useful to see where recent trends fit into the broad spectrum of debate on U.S. foreign policy. Do recent events support those who would have America "come home"? Do they substantiate the perceived benefits propounded by realists who are interested in only incremental change in a status quo they see as basically advantageous to the United States? Or do they reflect the more assertive international posture in key areas of foreign policy advocated by those Americans I call idealists?

Notes

1. See, among others, a review article by Don Oberdorfer, *Washington Post*, Outlook Section, October 27, 1991.

2. Interview with Reagan administration pollster, Washington, DC, September, 1989.

Suggested Readings

Listed below are a number of articles, books, and U.S. government publications dealing with a wide range of contemporary issues in U.S. policy toward Asia and the Pacific. The necessarily selective nature of this list means that priority has been given to the most recent publications and those from the U.S. government, especially Congress.

Ahn, Byung-Joon. "Decision-Sharing in Korea-U.S. Relations." *Korea and World Affairs* 13 (Spring 1990).

Alagappa, Muthiah. "U.S.-ASEAN Security Relations: Challenges and Prospects." *Contemporary Southeast Asia* 11 (June 1989).

Armacost, Michael H. "The Asia-Pacific Region: A Forward Look." *Department of State Bulletin* 85 (April 1985).

———. *U.S.-Japan Relations: A Global Partnership for the Future*. Washington, DC: U.S. Department of State, Bureau of Public Affairs, 1986.

Armitage, Richard L. "U.S. Security in the Pacific in the 21st Century." *Strategic Review* 18 (Summer 1990).

Aspen Institute. Indochina Policy Forum. *Recommendations for the New Administration on United States Policy Toward Indochina*. Queenstown, MD: The Institute, 1988.

Assessing America's Options in the Philippines. Prepared by the Congressional Research Service, Foreign Affairs and National Defense Division, Washington, DC: Government Printing Office, 1986.

Atlantic Council of the United States. Pacific Policy Working Group. *Strategic Stability, Economic Performance, and Political Leadership in the Pacific Basin: A Framework for U.S. Policy and Atlantic-Pacific Cooperation in the 1990s*. Washington, DC: Atlantic Council of the United States, 1989.

Bacho, Peter. "U.S.-Philippine Relations in Transition: The Issue of the Bases." *Asian Survey* 28 (June 1988).

Bandow, Doug. "Leaving Korea." *Foreign Policy*, no. 77 (Winter 1989–1990).

Barnett, A. Doak. *China Policy: Old Problems and New Challenges*. Washington, DC: Brookings Institution, 1977.

Bloch, Julia Chang. *A U.S.-Japan Aid Alliance: Prospects for Cooperation in an Era of Conflict*. Cambridge, MA: Program on U.S.-Japan Relations, Harvard University, 1989.

Bobrow, Davis Bernard, and Robert Thomas Kurdle. "U.S. Policy and Japan: Beyond Self-Indulgence." *Comparative Strategy* 9, no. 2 (1990).

Bond, Douglas G. "Anti-Americanism and U.S.-ROK Relations: An Assessment of Korean Students' Views." *Asian Perspective* 12 (Spring-Summer 1988).

Brown, Gary. *The Joint Defense Facilities as Bargaining Chips: Pros and Cons*. Canberra, Australia: Department of the Parliamentary Library, Legislative Research Service, 1986.

Brown, Harold. "Competitiveness, Technology, and U.S.-Japan Relations." *Washington Quarterly* 13 (Summer 1990).

Brown, William A. *Indochinese Refugees and Relations with Thailand*. Washington, DC: U.S. Department of State, 1988.

Bullock, Mary Brown, and Robert E. Litwark, eds. *The United States and the Pacific Basin: Changing Economic and Security Relationships*. Washington, DC: Woodrow Wilson Center Press, 1991.

Burton, Sandra. "Aquino's Philippines: The Center Holds." *Foreign Affairs* 65, no. 3 (1987).

Chang, Jaw-ling Joanne. *United States-China Normalization: An Evaluation of Foreign Policy Decisionmaking*. Denver, CO: Graduate School of International Studies, University of Denver, 1986.

Chappell, David, and Richard J. Kessler, "U.S. Security and the Philippines: An Exchange." *Bulletin of the Atomic Scientist* 41 (May 1985).

Cheney, Richard B. "To Remain in Asia: A Firm U.S. Defense Commitment." *Speaking of Japan* 11 (June 1990).

The China Factor: Sino-American Relations and the Global Scene. New York, NY: American Assembly, Columbia University and Council on Foreign Relations, 1981.

"China In Transition." *Journal of International Affairs* 39 (Winter 1986).

Cleveland, Paul M. "U.S.-New Zealand Relations: Some Parting Observations." *Department of State Bulletin* 89 (June 1989).

Clubb, O. Edmund. "China and America: A Look at a Long and Ambivalent Relationship." *New York Times Magazine* (January 28, 1979).

Cohen, Marc J. "One China or Two: Facing Up to the Taiwan Question." *World Policy Journal* 4 (Fall 1987).

Colbert, Evelyn. "Standing Pat." *Foreign Policy*, no. 54 (Spring 1984).

_____. *The United States and the Philippine Bases*. Washington, DC: Foreign Policy Institute, Johns Hopkins University, 1987.

Conboy, Kenneth J. *U.S. Policy Toward Indochina: Time for a Reassessment*. Washington, DC: Heritage Foundation, 1990.

Congressional Quarterly. *China: U.S. Policy Since 1945*. Washington, DC: 1980.

Dalton, John. "The Solarz Report—New Strategies for U.S. Relations with the South Pacific?" *Asian Defense Journal* (February 1991).

Destler, I. M., and Michael Nacht. "Beyond Mutual Recrimination." *International Security* 15 (Winter 1990-1991).

Dorrance, John C. *The Australian-American Alliance Today: An American Assessment of the Strategic/Security, Political and Economic Dimensions*. Canberra, Australia: Strategic and Defense Studies Centre, 1990.

_____. *Oceania and the United States: An Analysis of U.S. Interests and Policy in the South Pacific*. Washington, DC: National Defense University, Research Directorate, 1980.

Suggested Readings

"East Asia." *Current History* 88 (April 1989).
Economic Cooperation in the Asia-Pacific Region. Edited by John P. Hardt and Young C. Kim. Boulder, CO: Westview Press, 1990.
Fallows, James. "Contain Japan." *Atlantic Monthly* 263 (May 1989).
Gardner, Paul F. "Tuna Poaching and Nuclear Testing in the South Pacific." *Orbis* 32 (Spring 1988).
Gong, Gerrit W. "U.S.-China Relations in the Post-Deng Era." *World & I* 5 (August 1990).
Gordon, Bernard K. *New Directions for American Policy in Asia*. London, New York: Routledge, 1990.
———. "The Third Indochina Conflict." *Foreign Affairs* 65 (Fall 1986).
Harrison, Selig S., and Clyde V. Prestowitz, Jr. "Pacific Agenda: Defense or Economics?" *Foreign Policy*, no. 79 (Summer 1990).
Hitchock, David I., Jr. "The United States in a Changing Pacific Rim: Asian Perceptions and the U.S. Response." *Washington Quarterly* 12 (Autumn 1989).
Ito, Kan. "Trans-Pacific Anger." *Foreign Policy* 78, (Spring 1990).
"Japan." *Current History* 90 (April 1991).
Kessler, Richard J. "Marcos and the Americans." *Foreign Policy*, no. 63 (Summer 1986).
Kreisberg, Paul H. "The U.S. and Asia in 1990" *Asian Survey* 31 (January 1991).
MacFarquhar, Emily. "On the Defensive: As Washington Debates Whether to Get Tough, China Braces Itself." *U.S. News and World Report* 110 (May 27, 1991).
Makin, John H., and Donald C. Hellmann, ed. *Sharing World Leadership? A New Era for America and Japan*. Washington, DC: American Enterprise Institute for Public Policy Research, 1989.
Manning, Robert A. "Reagan's Chance Hit." *Foreign Policy*, no. 54 (Spring 1984).
Mansfield, Mike. "The U.S. and Japan: Sharing Our Destinies." *Foreign Affairs* 68 (Spring 1989).
Mochizuki, Mike M. "Japan After the Cold War." *SAIS Review*, 10 (Summer–Fall 1990).
Morse, Ronald A. "Japan's Drive to Pre-eminence." *Foreign Policy*, no. 69 (Winter 1987–1988).
Okazaki, Hisahiko. "Burdensharing for a Military Balance." *Japan Echo* 15 (Autumn 1988).
Oksenberg, Michel. "A Decade of Sino-American Relations." *Foreign Affairs* 61 (Fall 1982).
Olsen, Edward A. "U.S.-ROK Relations: Common Issues and Uncommon Perceptions." *Korea and World Affairs* 13 (Spring 1989).
Orr, Robert M., Jr. "Collaboration or Conflict? Foreign Aid and U.S.-Japan Relations." *Pacific Affairs* 62 (Winter 1989–1990).
Packard, George R. "The Coming U.S.-Japan Crisis." *Foreign Affairs* 66 (Winter 1987–1988).
Plunk, Daryl M. "U.S.-Korean Relations: An American Perspective." *Korean and World Affairs*, 13 (Spring 1989).
Robinson, Thomas W. "U.S.-Soviet Relations in Asia: Cooperation or Competition?" *American Enterprise* 1 (July–August 1990).

Sadow, Jeffrey D. "America, the South Pacific and Benign Neglect." *Asian Thought and Society* 15 (May 1990).
Scalapino, Robert A. "Asia and the United States: The Challenges Ahead." *Foreign Affairs* 69, no. 1 (1990).
"Southeast Asia." *Current History* 89 (March 1990).
Spencer, Edson W. "Japan as Competitor." *Foreign Policy*, no. 78 (Spring 1990).
Stokes, Bruce. "Kid Korea Grows Up." *National Journal* 21 (July 1, 1989).
_____. "Who's Standing Tall?" *National Journal* 21 (October 21, 1989).
The Summit of the United States and the Pacific Island Nations, October 27, 1990, concluding remarks and background papers. Honolulu, HA: East-West Center, 1990.
"A Survey of Asia in 1990: Part I." *Asian Survey* 31, (January 1991).
Tow, William T. "The Anzus Dispute: Testing U.S. Extended Deterrence in Alliance Politics." *Political Science Quarterly* 104 (Spring 1989).
U.S. Congress. House. Committee on Foreign Affairs. *The Political Situation in China; Report of a Staff Study Mission to Shanghai, Nanjing, Beijing, Chengdu, Guangzhou, Shenzhen, and Hong Kong, December, 1990*. Washington, DC: Government Printing Office, 1991.
_____. *Problems in Paradise: United States Interests in the South Pacific*. Report of a Congressional Delegation to the South Pacific, August 5–16, 1989. Washington, DC: Government Printing Office, 1990.
U.S. Congress. House. Committee on Foreign Affairs. Subcommittee on Asian and Pacific Affairs. *Arms Control in Asia and U.S. Interests in the Region*. Hearings, 101st Congress, 2nd Session. January 31–March 13, 1990. Washington, DC: Government Printing Office, 1990.
_____. *Issues Affecting the Question of United States Relations with Vietnam*. Hearing before the Subcommittees on Asian and Pacific Affairs and on International Economic Policy and Trade of the Committee on Foreign Affairs, House of Representatives, 101st Congress, 1st Session. November 1989. Washington, DC: Government Printing Office, 1990.
_____. *Overview of Recent Events in the East Asian and Pacific Region*. Hearing, 101st Congress, 2nd Session. February 22, 1990. Washington, DC: Government Printing Office, 1990.
_____. *Taiwan: The National Affairs Council and Implications for Democracy*. Hearing, 101st Congress, 2nd Session. October 11, 1990. Washington, DC: Government Printing Office, 1991.
_____. *United States Interests in the South Pacific*. Hearing, 101st Congress, 1st Session. July 27, 1989. Washington, DC: Government Printing Office, 1990.
_____. *United States Policy Toward Cambodia: Prospects for a Negotiated Settlement*. Hearing, 101st Congress, 2nd Session. September 12, 1990. Washington, DC: Government Printing Office, 1991.
_____. *United States Political and Economic Policy Toward China*. Hearing before the Subcommittees on Asian and Pacific Affairs and International Economic Policy and Trade of the Committee on Foreign Affairs, House of Representatives, 101st Congress, 1st Session. December 13, 1989. Washington, DC: Government Printing Office, 1990.

Suggested Readings

U.S. Congress. House. Committee on Ways and Means. Subcommittee on Trade. *United States–People's Republic of China (PRC) Trade Relations, Including Most Favored-Nation Trade Status for the PRC.* Hearing, 101st Congress, 2nd Session. June 19–21, 1990.

U.S. Congress. Senate. Committee on Energy and Natural Resources. *Palau Compact of Free Association Implementation Act: Report to Accompany H.J.Res. 175.* Washington, DC: Government Printing Office, 1989.

U.S. Congress. Senate. Committee on Foreign Relations. *Major Issues of U.S. Policy in East Asia; A Staff Report.* Washington, Government Printing Office, 1989.

———. *U.S. Policy Toward China.* Hearing, 101st Congress, 2nd Session. February 7, 1990. Washington, DC: Government Printing Office, 1990.

U.S. Congress. Senate. Committee on Foreign Relations. Subcommittee on East Asian and Pacific Affairs. Sino-Soviet Relations After the Summit. Workshop Sponsored by the Senate Foreign Relations Committee and the Congressional Research Service, May 15, 1989. Washington, DC: Government Printing Office, 1990.

U.S. General Accounting Office. *U.S.-Japan Burdensharing: Japan Has Increased Its Contributions But Could Do More; Report to the Chairman.* Committee on Armed Services, House of Representatives. August 15, 1989, Washington, DC: Government Printing Office, 1989.

Wanner, Barbara. *Domestic and International Factors Challenge Kaifu Administration.* Washington, DC: Japan Economic Institute, 1990.

Wolferen, Karel Van. *The Enigma of Japanese Power: People and Politics in a Stateless Nation.* New York: Alfred A. Knopf, 1989.

Woon, Eden Y. "Chinese Arms Sales and U.S.-China Military Relations." *Asian Survey* 29 (June 1989).

Index

Afghanistan, 24, 53
   Soviet invasion of, 21, 23
Agency for International Development (AID), 74
Agricultural products
   Japanese imports, 41, 42
   U.S. exports, 86, 93. *See also* Farm export policy; Farm products
Aid
   Japanese, 30, 38–39, 43
   by Japan to North Korea, 91–92
   by Japan to Oceania, 153
   to South Pacific countries, 142
   by the Soviets to the Vietnamese in Cambodia, 120
   by the U.S. to Cambodia, 109–110, 111, 113, 116
   by the U.S. to Israel, 135
   by the U.S. to Oceania, 152
   by the U.S. to the Philippines, 127, 128–129, 133, 135–136, 138, 139
   by the U.S. to South Pacific countries, 149–150, 153
   by the U.S. to South Korea, 93
   by the U.S. to Vietnam, 114–115, 119, 121, 122, 123
   See also Foreign aid; Foreign assistance; Military aid
Aircraft
   U.S., 141, 144
   U.S. nuclear-capable, 146
   See also Fighter aircraft
Algeria, nuclear reactor in, 67
America. *See* United States
American Institute in Taiwan (AIT), 73
American Samoa, 142
Antarctica, 143
Aquino, Corazon, 130, 133, 137
Aquino government
   attempted coup against, 127, 130, 138

   efforts to spur economic growth, 131
   and U.S. withdrawal from Subic Bay, 134
Arms, supplied to Taiwan by U.S., 72. *See also* Arms sales; Defense technology; Military equipment; Weapons
Arms control, 12, 66
Arms limitation, in the Persian Gulf, 1
Arms race, in Asia, 10
Arms reductions, 139
Arms sales
   Chinese, 68
   to Taiwan, 22, 24, 74, 75, 77, 84, 89
   See also Arms; Military equipment; Military sales; Weapons
Asia
   Chinese foreign relations in, 56
   Russian military presence in, 31
   U.S. military forces in, 72
   U.S. policy in, 1–13
   U.S.-Soviet collaboration in, 53
   U.S. travel to, 2
Asian Development Bank (ADB)
   programs in China, 65
   and Taiwan, 75, 77, 83, 84
Asian-Pacific basin, and the U.S., 141–159
Asian Pacific Economic Council (APEC), 126
Assassinations, of Americans in the Philippines, 134, 139
Association of Southeast Asian Nations (ASEAN), 6, 11, 105, 106, 107, 108, 112, 113, 116, 118, 119–120, 122
Australia
   aid to South Pacific countries, 142
   anti-nuclear faction in, 143, 150
   and French nuclear testing, 148
   and New Caledonia, 148
   U.S.-Australia relations, 144–145, 150
   U.S. defense alliance with, 4, 19
   and U.S. farm export policy, 152

U.S. military access to facilities in, 136, 137
Australia-New Zealand-U.S. (ANZUS) alliance, 142–143, 144, 153

Baker, James, 12, 45, 65, 117, 143, 153
Bank of China, 87
Bank of Korea, 93
Banks, and the Philippines, 138, 139
Belize, 78
Bolger, Jim, 153
Bolivia, 75
Brunei, 137
Brzezinski, Zbigniew, 21
Buchanan, Patrick, 157
Budget deficit
    Japanese, 41
    U.S., 1, 7, 25, 29, 30
Bulgaria, 101
Bumpers, Dale, 97
Burma, 10
    Chinese arms sales to, 68
    democratization movement in, 7, 27
Bush, Barbara, 61, 64
Bush, George, 143, 151, 153
    and U.S.-Chinese relations, 7, 50, 58–59, 60, 61–65, 66, 68, 69
Bush administration
    and Cambodia, 106, 109, 110, 112–113, 121
    and chemical weapons stored on Johnston Island, 151
    and China, 58, 66
    and foreign aid to the Philippines, 135, 136
    and South Korea, 101, 103
    and Taiwan, 83
    and U.S.-Japanese relations, 30, 34, 35, 38, 39, 40
    and U.S. military bases in the Philippines, 126, 127, 131, 132, 136, 137–138
    and U.S. policy in Asia and the Pacific, 156
    and Vietnam, 114, 116–117, 121
Business, and political risk in the Philippines, 138–139, 140
Business executives, in Hong Kong, 86, 88

Cairo conference, 19
Cambodia, 10, 53, 65
    conflict in, 56
    peace process regarding, 66
    peace settlement in, 105–113, 118, 120–121, 122
    pressures against Vietnamese occupation of, 119–120
    Soviet support for Vietnam's military occupation of, 24
    U.N. agreement on, 67–68
    U.S. aid to, 111, 116
    U.S.-backed regimes in, 20
    Vietnamese military occupation of, 105, 108, 109, 119, 123
    Vietnamese troop withdrawal from, 105, 109, 112, 114, 116, 117, 120, 121, 122
Camp David accords, 21
Camp John Hay, 129
Capitalist ideas, in Hong Kong, 87
Carter, Jimmy
    and Soviet invasion of Afghanistan, 21, 23
    and Taiwan, 73
    and U.S. armed forces in Asia, 6
Carter administration
    and the Soviets, 21
    and U.S. policy in Asia, 21–23
    and Vietnam, 115–116
Central African Republic, 78
Central America, 135
Chemical weapons, 150, 151
Cheney, Richard, 38, 97, 137
Chiang Ching-kuo, 71, 79, 80
Chiang Kai-shek, 71, 72, 79
China
    aid programs to, 65
    Americanization of, 17
    anti-Soviet basis of Sino-American policy in Asia, 53
    arms sales by, 68
    Boxer uprising in, 16
    and Bush administration, 58, 66
    and Cambodia, 67–68
    and Cambodian conflict, 105, 108, 116, 119, 120
    and Cambodian peace settlement, 106
    and changes in Soviet bloc, 51
    and Congress, 60, 66, 67–69
    debate in Congress over, 58, 69
    democratization movement in, 7, 27
    denied recognition and trade, 4, 19
    dissidents in, 55, 64
    downturn in U.S.-Chinese relations, 107, 112
    economic reforms in, 56

Index

economic retrenchment in, 51
exports to U.S. markets, 60
family planning in, 68
foreign policy of, 53–54
goal of reunification with Taiwan, 86
and heroin traffic, 68
and Hong Kong, 68, 85–89
human rights in, 60, 62, 64, 65, 66, 67, 68, 69
invasion of northern Vietnam, 119
Japanese economic aid to, 38
and Korea, 91
leaders of, 51, 53–54, 55, 56, 57, 58, 59, 61, 62, 65, 66
loans for, 50, 57
military sales to, 58
missile and nuclear proliferation by, 67, 68, 69
modernization in, 15–16
and most-favored-nation status, 51, 60, 62, 65, 67, 68–69
and most-favored-nation tariffs, 50, 60
and the Pacific, 131
and Persian Gulf war, 1, 55, 56–57, 66–67
political repression in, 53, 54
potential ambitions of, 12, 157
and President Bush, 7, 50, 58–59, 60, 61–65, 66, 68, 69
prison labor in, 68
and Reagan administration, 24
reformers in, 16–17
in Roosevelt's vision of U.S. policy in Asia, 19
and the Sino-British agreement on Hong Kong, 85
social and cultural changes in, 19
South Korean relations with, 101
and South Pacific Nuclear Free Zone Treaty protocols, 146, 151
Soviet jet fighter sold to, 76
and the Soviets, 24, 64
students in U.S. from, 55, 57, 58
and Taiwan, 71, 75–76, 78, 81, 83, 84, 85
and Tibet, 67
trade with Japan, 20
and U.S., 5, 6, 9, 10, 16
U.S. China policy and Taiwan, 76–77
U.S. cooperation with, 119
U.S. diplomatic relations with, 21, 22–23, 72, 73
U.S. measures against, 57–58, 62, 65
and U.S. policy concerning Taiwan, 71, 72

U.S.-PRC rapprochement, 20
U.S.-PRC-Taiwan relations, 73–75, 83–84
U.S. relations with, 12, 49–69, 89, 156, 157
U.S. technology transfer to, 49
U.S. trade deficit with, 65, 67
U.S. trade with, 49, 69
U.S. views of, 7–8
and Vietnam, 122
and world politics, 52. *See also* People's Republic of China; Republic of China; Sino-Soviet relations; Sino-Soviet summit; Taiwan
Chinese Nationalists, in Taiwan, 71, 72, 75, 79–81, 82, 83, 84, 89
Chinese students, in the U.S., 27, 55, 57, 58
Chirac, Jacques, 148
Chirac government, in New Caledonia, 148, 149
Chun Doo Hwan, 23, 93
Clark Air Force Base, 126, 127, 128, 129, 130, 132, 133, 136, 137
Cold War, 8
and American–East Asian relations, 19
and U.S. foreign policy, 11, 59
U.S. strategy in, 4–5
victory in, 158
Combined Forces Command, in South Korea, 98, 103
Communication routes, in Southeast Asia, 118–119
Communications technology, 27
Communism, failure of, 7. *See also* Communists
Communist Party of the Philippines (CPP), 133–134, 139
Communists
  in Afghanistan, 21
  Cambodian, 106
  in the Philippines, 127, 130, 134, 138
  neighbors of South Korea, 101
  See also Communism
Computer sales, to China, 69
Congress, U.S.
  and aid to the Philippines, 135
  approval of compacts with South Pacific countries, 146, 147
  and Cambodia, 106, 110, 111, 116
  and China, 86
  control of, 11, 156
  criticism of Aquino government in, 137
  debate over China policy, 58, 69

and drift-net fishing in the South Pacific, 151
and fisheries treaty with South Pacific countries, 150, 153
and foreign investors, 35
and the FSX jet fighter in Japan, 40
and the FX-Korean fighter aircraft program, 98–99
and Hong Kong, 86, 88
and human rights, 21
and the "Koreagate" scandal, 22
measures against China, 57–58, 62, 65
omnibus trade legislation, 26
pressure from U.S. farmers in, 152
and South Korea, 94, 100
and the South Pacific Nuclear Free Zone Treaty protocols, 146
and technology policy issues with Japan, 36–37
and Tibet, 67
and unfair trading of foreign competitors, 94
and U.S. Asia policy, 23
and U.S.-Chinese relations, 60, 66, 67–69
and U.S. forces in the Western Pacific, 127, 134
and U.S. military forces in Japan, 38
and U.S. military forces in South Korea, 96, 97–98
and U.S. recognition of the PRC, 23
and U.S. relations with Japan, 33
and Vietnam, 115, 121
Coordinating Committee for Multilateral Export Controls (CoCom), 57
Coordination Council for North American Affairs (CCNAA), 73
Copyrights, 94
China's infringement on U.S., 67
and Taiwan, 79
Crow Valley training range, 130
Cubi Point Naval Air Station, 129
Cultural influence, U.S., 27, 158, 159
Cultural issues, and U.S. policy in Asia and the Pacific, 156
Cultural relations, U.S.-Asian, 15–16, 17, 66, 73
Currency
Korean, 95
Taiwanese, 78, 79
U.S. and Japanese, 30. *See also* Dollar; Yen

Dalai Lama, 67, 68

Debt
Latin American, 25
Philippine, 135, 136, 138
Third World, 94
Defense
allied burden of, 125
of Asia, 5, 20
Australia's spending on, 145
burden-sharing, 135, 143
issues in U.S.-Korea relations, 102
Japanese, 5, 41, 43, 45, 46
Japanese spending on, 24, 37–38
of Palau, 146
South Korean spending on, 97–98
of Taiwan, 75–76
in the Western Pacific, 131
Defense Advanced Research Projects Agency (DARPA), 36
Defense alliances, U.S.-Asian, 4. *See also* Mutual Defense Treaty
Defense appropriations bill, 97, 98, 99
Defense authorization bill, 97, 98
Defense Department. *See* Department of Defense
Defense policy
Australian, 145
Japanese, 20, 139
Defense technology
sold to Taiwan by U.S., 73
U.S. transfer of, 96
Democracy, 17, 18
in Asia, 15
in the Philippines, 132, 133, 138
in South Korea, 94, 101
and U.S. foreign policy, 159
U.S. interests in, 5
and U.S. policy in Asia, 3–4
See also Democratization
Democratic Liberal Party (DLP), 100
Democratic political development
in the Pacific, 131
in the Philippines, 127, 130
Democratic Progressive Party (DPP), in Taiwan, 81, 82
Democratization, in South Korea, 100. *See also* Democracy
Demonstrations
South Korean antigovernment, 100
Deng Xiaoping, 55, 63, 88
Department of Commerce, and Japanese language scientific information, 36

Index

Department of Defense
  and cooperative research agreements with Japan, 36
  leases of land on Tinian and Saipan, 137
  report on U.S. strategy in the Pacific, 131
  surplus commodities, 111
  and U.S. military bases in the Philippines, 132
Detente, 20
  U.S.-Soviet, 5, 20
Diego Garcia military base, 130, 137
Diplomacy
  secret, 7, 59
Dissidents
  in China, 55, 64, 88
  in Taiwan, 82
Dixon, Alan, 98, 99
Dollar
  Hong Kong, 85
  U.S., 7, 25, 26, 44, 78, 95
  See also Currency
Domestic factors
  in U.S.-Chinese relations, 50
  in U.S.-Japanese relations, 31–32
Domestic opinion, and U.S. foreign policy, 59
Domestic problems, U.S., 11, 156, 157, 158
Drug trade, 159. *See also* Heroin traffic

Eagleburger, Lawrence, 62
East Asia, U.S. policy in, 155–159
Eastern Europe
  changes in, 51, 52, 53, 55, 59
  collapse of communism in, 7, 112
  instability in, 2
  and Japanese aid, 38
  radical change in, 107
  U.S. aid recipient, 135
  U.S. foreign policy focused on, 10
Economic aid. *See* Aid
Economic crisis, world, 4, 18
Economic decline, U.S., 25, 27
Economic development, 9
  in Asia, 3, 5
  in Oceania, 141, 142, 150
  South Korean, 94
  Taiwanese, 72
  See also Economic growth; Economic progress
Economic embargo, against Vietnam, 107, 114, 121, 122
Economic environment, international, 9

Economic factors, in U.S.-Japanese relations, 30–31
Economic groupings, Pacific Rim, 126
Economic growth
  of Asia, 7
  of Japan, 5, 19–20
  South Korean, 93
  in Taiwan, 78–79
  U.S., 5
  U.S. ability to promote, 6, 25
  See also Economic development; Economic progress
Economic interdependence, of U.S. and Asia, 6, 25
Economic interests, U.S., 11, 15
Economic issues
  in U.S.-Japanese relations, 33–35, 41, 45
  and U.S. policy in Asia and the Pacific, 156
  in U.S. relations with ASEAN, 125–126
  in U.S.-South Korean relations, 94–96, 102
Economic power, U.S., 2, 4
Economic progress, in Asia, 25. *See also* Economic development; Economic growth
Economic reforms, in China, 56
Economic relations, of the U.S. with Vietnam, 114
Economic retrenchment, in China, 51, 53, 54
Economic sanctions. *See* Sanctions
Economic threat, to U.S. by Japan, 11, 157
Economic ties, between the U.S. and Japan, 16
Economy
  Hong Kong, 87, 88
  in the Philippines, 138
  U.S., 7, 25, 158
Educational reform, in China, 16–17
Egypt
  Taiwanese assistance to, 83
  U.S. aid to, 135
Elections
  in Cambodia, 105–106, 109, 113
  in Taiwan, 81
Emergency Chinese Immigration Relief Act, 58, 60
Emigration, from Vietnam, 118
Environmental dangers, to the sea, 150
Environmental impact, of nuclear testing in French Polynesia, 144

Environmental issues
 in the South Pacific, 151
 in U.S.-Japanese relations, 43
Estanislao, Jesus, 133
Exclusive economic zones (EEZs), in the Pacific, 142, 149
Executive branch, and U.S. foreign policy, 8, 59, 155
Export controls, on technology for China, 57–58
Export-Import Bank, 58
 financing in China, 65
 financing in Taiwan, 74
Export licenses, for U.S. satellites, 57, 58
Export markets, Taiwanese, 79
Exports
 of ASEAN to the U.S., 125
 of Chinese goods to U.S. markets, 60
 countries that restrict U.S., 95
 of other countries to the U.S., 6
 Taiwanese, 78
 U.S., 25
 U.S. farm export policy, 152
 of the U.S. to Hong Kong, 86
 U.S.-Japanese, 29
 to the U.S. market, 25
 to the U.S. by South Korea, 93
 to Vietnam from the U.S. banned, 114. See also Export controls

Family planning, in China, 68
Fang Lizhi, 55, 58, 63, 64, 65
Farm export policy, U.S., 152. See also Agricultural products; Farm products, U.S. exports
Farm products, U.S. exports, 150. See also Agricultural products; Farm export policy
Federated States of Micronesia, 146
Fighter aircraft
 Chinese F-8, 58
 FSX, 40
 sale of to China, 58
 sale of Soviet, to China, 76
 South Korean, 98–99, 102
 Taiwanese development of a new, 77
 use of U.S., during attempted coup in the Philippines, 127, 130
Fiji, 10
 political instability in, 150
 and the Soviets, 147

Financial institutions, international, 49, 50, 51, 56, 57, 66, 107, 157
First Convention of Peking treaty, 85
Fisheries treaty, with South Pacific states, 149–150, 153
Fishing
 drift-net, 150, 151
 by the Soviets in the South Pacific, 147–148
Ford, Gerald, and Vietnam, 114–115
Foreign aid
 by Australia to South Pacific countries, 145
 Japanese, 45, 46
 U.S., 6, 11, 25
 by the U.S. to the Philippines, 133, 135
 See also Aid; Foreign assistance
Foreign assistance
 cuts in U.S., 157, 158
 by the U.S. in Asia, 2
 by the U.S. to Oceania, 152
 See also Aid; Foreign aid
Foreign exchange income, in Hong Kong, 87
Foreign exchange markets, and the Reagan administration, 26
Foreign Military Sales (FMS), to South Korea, 93
Foundation for Exchanges Across the Taiwan Straits, 78
France, 26
 and New Caledonia, 148–149, 152
 and Oceania, 148–149
French nuclear testing, 150, 151
French Polynesia, nuclear testing in, 144, 146, 148
Fulbright professors, in China, 58

General Accounting Office (GAO), 99, 111
General Agreements on Tariffs and Trade (GATT), 5, 11, 20, 103, 157
 and the People's Republic of China (PRC), 78
 and Taiwan, 83, 84
General Dynamics, 99
Generalized System of Preferences (GSP) program, 74, 79
Germany, 26, 159
Gorbachev, Mikhail, 6, 52
 outreach to the West, 107–108
 President Roh met with, 103
 and Soviet foreign policy in Asia, 24

Index

and Vietnam, 120
visit to Beijing, 63
Great Britain, 26, 76, 142
  in Roosevelt's vision of U.S. policy in Asia, 19
  and the South Pacific Nuclear Free Zone Treaty protocols, 146, 151
Great Depression, 4, 18
Grenada, 78
Gross domestic product (GDP), Australian, 145
Gross national product (GNP)
  Japanese, 20, 24, 38
  South Korean, 97
  Taiwanese, 78
  U.S.-Japanese combined, 29
Group of Five, 26
Guam, military bases on, 137, 142
Guinea-Bissau, 78
Gulf crisis
  Japan's reaction to, 11
  U.S. leadership in, 1
  See also Iraq-Kuwait crisis; Persian Gulf war

Hau Pei-tsun, 80
Hawaii, 137
Hawke, Bob, 143, 144, 150
Hawke government, in Australia, 144, 145
Heinz, John, 98
Heroin traffic, in China, 68. *See also* Drug trade
Hong Kong, 6, 10
  and China, 68, 85–89
  Chinese settlement with the British over, 76
  U.S. policy concerns in, 85–89
Human rights, 17, 18, 19, 21
  in Asia, 15
  in China, 60, 62, 64, 65, 66, 67, 68, 69, 77
  North Korean, 92
  and President Carter, 22, 23
  in South Korea, 100
  and U.S. foreign policy, 62, 159
  U.S. interest in, 5
  U.S. moral sensibilities on, 61
  and U.S. policy in Asia, 3, 4
  in Vietnam, 119
Hungary, 101
Hussein, Saddam, 69
Hyland, William, 157

Immigrants
  from Asia in the U.S., 1, 27
  to the U.S. from Vietnam, 118
Imports
  Chinese restrictions on, 65
  Japanese, 32
  Japanese restrictions on, 35
  restrictions on Korean, 94, 95
  U.S., 25
  of U.S. farm products into Japan, 41
  U.S. restrictions on Korean, 96
India, 159
  U.S. relations with, 12, 156, 157
Indian Ocean
  buildup of American forces in, 137
  Diego Garcia military base in, 130
  U.S. military power in, 139
Indochina
  protracted U.S. conflict in, 2
  U.S. policy in, 105–123
  U.S. withdrawal from, 5
Indonesia, 125
Industrial sector, in China, 56
Insurance, Korean market for, 95
Intellectual property, 126
  and South Korea, 94, 95
  and Taiwan, 79
  U.S., 68
Interest rates, 26
International Monetary Fund (IMF), 5, 11, 18, 20
  Japan in, 30
International Security Assistance Act, 23
Investments
  by Asia in the U.S. 24–25
  by China in Hong Kong, 87
  Japanese, 30
  in Korea, 95
  by the U.S. in Asia, 3, 15
  by the U.S. in Hong Kong, 86
  in the U.S. by Japan, 35
  Vietnamese inability to attract, 120
Iran hostage crisis, 21, 158
Iraq
  economic sanctions against, 83
  invasion of Kuwait, 1, 9, 50, 65, 96
  war with, 130
Iraq-Kuwait crisis
  and South Korea, 99
  and U.S.-Japanese relations, 29, 39–40
  See also Gulf crisis; Persian Gulf war
Isolationist posture, U.S., 4, 18

Israel, 135
Ivory, 43

Jackson-Vanik Amendment, of the Trade Act, 60
Japan, 6, 9, 26, 93, 159
  accomplishments of, 54
  aid to Eastern Europe by, 38–39
  aid program in China, 65
  aid to South Pacific countries, 142
  and allied defense burden, 125
  Americanization of, 17, 27
  assistance to Indochina by, 107
  assistance to Oceania by, 153
  assistance to Vietnam by, 123
  and the ASEAN countries, 126
  attitudes of Asian countries toward, 10
  budget deficits of, 41
  and the Bush administration, 30, 34, 35, 38, 39, 40
  and a Cambodian peace settlement, 106
  and changes in the Soviet bloc, 51
  and Congress, 33, 36–37, 38
  defense budget, 37–38
  defense capabilities, 43
  defense efforts, 41
  destructive policies of, 18
  economic factors in U.S. relations with, 30–31
  economic growth of, 5, 19–20
  economic issues in U.S.-Japanese relations, 33–35, 41, 45
  economic threat to U.S. by, 11, 157
  encouraged to rearm, 4
  environmental issues in U.S.-Japanese relations, 43
  foreign aid by, 46
  and the FSX jet fighter aircraft, 40
  growing power of, 12, 157
  and Hong Kong, 88
  investment in the U.S. by, 1, 30, 35
  leadership difficulties in, 42
  loan programs for China, 50
  military in, 17–18, 20
  modernization in, 15–16
  in the 1930s, 4
  and the Pacific, 131
  and the Persian Gulf war, 1, 33, 39, 42
  political issues in U.S.-Japanese relations, 40–42
  security issues in U.S.-Japanese relations, 37–40, 45
  technology policy issues in U.S.-Japanese relations, 36–37
  and the U.S., 5, 6, 10
  U.S. cooperation with, 119
  U.S. economic disputes with, 24
  U.S. economic ties with, 16
  U.S.-Japanese security ties, 31
  U.S. military forces in, 37, 38, 44, 46
  U.S. relations with, 11–12, 29–46, 156
  U.S. reliance on bases in, 137
  and U.S. retreat from Asia, 22
  U.S. trade deficit with, 30, 33, 34, 36, 41, 44, 45, 46, 72
  U.S. trade with, 33–35, 41
  U.S. war with, 16
  and the Vietnamese economy, 122
  wartime antagonism with the U.S., 17
  and the yen, 44
Japanese Technical Literature Act, 36
Jet fighter aircraft. See Fighter aircraft
Johnston Island, 150, 151
Jordan, 83

Kaifu, Toshiki, 39, 42
Kanak Socialist National Liberation Front, 148, 149
Khmer Rouge
  in Cambodia, 105–122 passim
  China's support for, 68
Kim Dae Jung, 23, 94, 100
Kim Il Sung, 92
Kim Jong Pil, 100
Kimmett, Robert, 68
Kim Young Sam, 100
Kiribati, 147
Kissinger, Henry, 62
Korea, 10, 53
  and arms proliferation, 12
  defense issues in U.S.-Korea relations, 102
  Korean unification, 103
  modernization in, 15–16
  political liberalization in, 7
  security issues in U.S.-Korean relations, 96–99, 102
  social and cultural changes in, 19
  U.S.-Korean relations, 91–103
  See also North Korea; Republic of Korea; South Korea
"Koreagate" scandal, 22
Korean Foreign Trade Act, 94
Korean War, 19, 93

Index

Kuwait
  Iraq invasion of, 1, 9, 50, 65, 96
  Iraq-Kuwait crisis and South Korea, 99
  Taiwan and crisis in, 83
Kwajalein, 142

Labor party
  in Australia, 143, 144, 151
  in New Zealand, 142, 143, 146, 153
Labor strife, in South Korea, 101
Lange, David, 153
Leaders
  Chinese, 53–54, 55, 57, 58, 59, 61, 62, 65, 66, 88, 89
  U.S., 3
  Vietnamese, 120, 122
Leadership
  Chinese, 51, 54, 55, 56, 86, 88
  North Korean, 92
  in Taiwan, 79–80
  by the U.S. in world affairs, 158
Lee Huan, 80
Lee Teng-hui, 77, 78, 80, 81, 82
Lending policies, U.S. influence on, 107
Lesotho, 78
Levin, Carl, 97
Liberal Democratic Party (LDP), in Japan, 42, 45
Liberia, 78
Lilley, James, 61
Loans, for China, 57
Logging, Japanese, 43

Mainland Affairs Council, in Taiwan, 78
Malaysia, 125
Mao Zedong, 53, 54
Marcos, Ferdinand, 80
Marcos government, 130
Maritime transportation, Korean market for, 95
Marshall Islands
  missile test site in, 142
  U.S. compact with, 146
Martial law
  in Beijing, 58
  in Taiwan, 80, 81
McCollum Amendment, 111
McDonnell Douglas Corporation, 99
Media coverage, of U.S.-Japanese relations, 32. *See also* Press coverage
Melanesians, in New Caledonia, 148, 149
Micronesia, U.S. spending programs in, 142

Middle East
  arms control, 66
  instability in, 2
  sale of missiles to, 59, 67
  U.S. foreign policy focused on, 10
Military
  Chinese, 55–56
  in Japan, 17–18, 20, 31
  of the U.S. in Asia, 2, 12, 16
  and U.S. foreign policy, 17
  of the U.S. in the Pacific, 157
  See also Armed forces; Military forces
Military aid, by the U.S. to the Philippines, 128–129, 136, 138. *See also* Aid; Military support
Military bases
  in Asia, 4
  U.S., in the Pacific, 142
  U.S., in the Philippines, 125–138
  U.S. pullback from foreign, 158
  in Vietnam, 118–119, 122
  See also Military facilities
Military construction appropriations bill, 98
Military equipment
  and Taiwan, 73, 75
  of the U.S. to the Philippines, 135–136
  See also Arms
Military facilities
  in Palau, 147
  U.S.-Australia joint, 144
  See also Military bases
Military forces
  of Japan and the Iraq-Kuwait crisis, 39
  North Korean, 22, 91
  South Korean, 93
  of the U.S. in Asia, 6, 72
  of the U.S. in Japan, 37, 38, 44, 46
  of the U.S. in South Korea, 93, 96, 97–98, 102
  See also Armed forces; Military
Military leaders, Chinese, 57
Military officers, Chinese, 58
Military sales, to China, 58, 77. *See also* Arms sales
Military support, against the Vietnamese occupiers in Cambodia, 108. *See also* Military aid
Military threat, by former Soviet Union, 11, 31, 157
Missile Technology Control Regime (MTCR), 67

Missiles
  Chinese marketing of, 67, 68, 69
  to Middle East countries, 59
  of North Korea, 91
  purchased from the People's Republic of China (PRC) by Saudi Arabia, 76
Missing in action (MIAs), from the Vietnam War, 107, 113–123 passim
Missionaries, from U.S. in Asia, 4, 15, 16
Mitchell, George, 68, 69
Miyazawa, Kiichi, 42
Money issues, in U.S.-Philippine negotiations on base rights, 135–136
Mongolia, political liberalization in, 7
Morality, in U.S. foreign policy, 59
Most-favored-nation (MFN) status
  and China, 51, 60, 62, 65, 67, 68–69
  of Taiwan, 74
Most-favored-nation (MFN) tariff, and Chinese imports, 50, 60
Multilateral Assistance Initiative, for the Philippines, 129, 135, 138
Mururoa Atoll, 148
Mutual Defense Treaty
  U.S.-Philippine, 128, 130
  U.S.-South Korean, 93
  U.S.-Taiwanese, 73

Nakasone, Yasuhiro, 6, 41
National Security Council, 61
National Trade Estimate Report on Foreign Barriers, 95
National Unification Council, in Taiwan, 77
Naval disarmament agreements, in the Pacific, 17
Nazi Germany, 4, 18
"Neoisolationist," 157
Netherlands, weapons sales to Taiwan, 75
Neutron bomb, 21
New Caledonia, 148–149, 152
New Democratic Union Party, in South Korea, 100
Newly industrializing countries (NICs), 5, 125
New Zealand
  anti-nuclear stance by, 142, 153
  and ANZUS alliance, 142–143, 144, 153
  and French nuclear testing, 148
  legislation banning nuclear-capable ships, 151, 153
  and New Caledonia, 148
  U.S. defense alliance with, 4, 19

U.S.-New Zealand relations, 142–143, 153
  and U.S. nuclear-capable warships, 142, 143
Nixon, Richard, 53
  and China, 72
  resignation of, 20
"Nordpolitik," President Roh's, 101, 103
North Korea, 20
  development experiences in, 54
  forward deployed force posture of, 97
  leadership of, 92
  military force of, 91
  nuclear program in, 91, 92
  threat from, 101, 102
  and the U.S., 10, 92
  U.S. troops deterring, 22
Northeast Asia
  military balance in, 43, 96
  stability in, 92, 93
Northern Mariana Islands, 137, 142, 146
Nuclear cooperation, with China, 57
Nuclear free zones, 146
Nuclear program, in North Korea, 91, 92
Nuclear proliferation, Chinese, 67, 68, 69
Nuclear reactor, in Algeria, 67
Nuclear safety cooperation program, and China, 65
Nuclear testing
  French, 150, 151
  in French Polynesia, 144, 146, 148
Nuclear weapons
  and New Zealand, 142, 143, 146
  nuclear weapons–free Zone of Peace, Freedom and Neutrality, 125
  Oceania opposition to, 141, 142–145
  and Palau, 137, 146, 147
  proliferation of technology for, 61
  removed from South Korea, 92
  U.S., 127
Oceania
  and France, 148–149
  Japanese aid to, 153
  Soviet influence in 141–142, 147–148
  and the U.S., 11, 141–159
Oil prices, and Taiwan, 78
Oil shocks, 5, 158
Orderly Departure Program, 118
Organization for Economic Cooperation and Development (OECD), 11
Overseas Private Investment Corporation (OPIC)
  and China, 65

Index

and Taiwan, 74

Pacific
  economic forums proposed for, 103
  U.S. policy in, 1–13, 15–27, 155–159
  U.S. strategy in, 131
Pakistan
  Chinese efforts to sell missiles to, 67
  Japanese economic aid to, 38
Palau, 137
  U.S.-Palau relations, 146–147
Panama Canal treaty, 21
Papua New Guinea, 10
  political instability in, 150
  and the Soviets, 147, 148
Paris peace agreement, on Vietnam, 114–115
Party for Peace and Democracy, 100
Patents, 94, 126
  Chinese infringement on U.S., 67
  Japanese, 35
Peace Corps, in China, 58
People's Republic of China (PRC). See China
People's Republic of Kampuchea (PRK), 108, 112
Persian Gulf
  and China, 56
  U.S. forces in, 37, 130, 131, 137, 139
Persian Gulf war, 12, 143, 153, 158
  approval for President Bush after, 66
  and the Chinese, 55, 56–57, 66–67
  and Japan, 33, 42
  U.S. aid to Israel after, 135
  See also Gulf crisis; Iraq-Kuwait crisis
Philippine National Defense College, 130
Philippines, 10
  alternative to U.S. bases in, 142
  democratization movement in, 27
  Filipino attitudes toward U.S. bases in, 127, 132–134
  Japan's economic aid to, 38
  political liberalization in, 7
  political prospects in, 10
  U.S. aid to, 127, 128–129, 133, 135–136, 138, 139
  U.S. military bases in, 125–138
  U.S.-Philippines relations, 137–138
  war in, 16
Pinatubo, Mt., 126, 127
Pol Pot, 109
Poland, 101

Political instability
  in Pacific Island nations, 150
  in the Philippines, 138, 139
Political interests, in U.S. policy, 11
Political issues
  in U.S.-Japanese relations, 40–42
  in U.S.-Korean relations, 100–101, 102
  and U.S. policy in Asia and the Pacific, 156
Political liberalization
  in South Korea, 96
  in Taiwan, 72, 84–85
Political prisoners, in South Korea, 94, 100
Political reforms, in Asian states, 7
Political repression, Chinese, 53, 54
Politics
  in Taiwan, 79–82
  and U.S.-Chinese relations, 60
Potsdam conference, 19
Press coverage, of President Bush's visit to China, 63, 64. See also Media coverage
Prison camps, Vietnamese, 118
Prisoners of war (POWs), from the Vietnam War, 107, 113–123 passim
Prison labor, in China, 68
Progressive movement, 16
Protectionism, 7
  international, 78
  and U.S. trade, 25, 26

Qian Qichen, 65, 66

Racial equality, 4, 18
Ramos, Fidel, 138
Reagan, Ronald, 36
  and U.S. armed forces in Asia, 6
  on U.S. arms sales to Taiwan, 74
  and U.S. Asia policy, 23
  and U.S. compact with Palau, 147
Reagan administration
  and Cambodia, 112
  foreign trade and monetary policies of, 25–26
  and the South Pacific Nuclear Free Zone Treaty protocols, 146
  and subsidized farm product sales abroad, 150
  and U.S. Asia policy, 23–25
  and U.S.-Japanese relations, 41
  and Vietnam, 116, 117, 118
Reagan policies, impact of, 158
Red Cross Society, 77

Reform Armed Forces Movement (RAM), 134, 138, 139
Refugees
　from Asia in the U.S., 27
　from Indochina, 116, 118
Republic of China, 83, 84
　U.S. diplomatic relations with, 22
　See also Taiwan
Republic of Korea (ROK)
　and President Carter, 22
　See also Korea; South Korea
Rice, Japan's restrictions on imports of, 35
Roh Tae Woo, 100–101
Roosevelt, Franklin, 4, 18, 155
Russia
　and a Cambodian peace settlement, 106
　Japanese war with, 16
　U.S. relations with, 12, 156
　See also Soviet Union

Saipan, 137
Sales tax, Japanese, 41
Sanctions
　against China, 9, 57, 60, 65
　against Iraq, 83
　international, 159
　by the U.S. involving Hong Kong, 89
San Miguel Naval Communications Center, 129
Satellites
　export licenses for U.S., 57, 58
　launched on Chinese rockets, 65, 69
Saudi Arabia
　breaking of ties with Taiwan, 75
　purchase of PRC missiles, 76
Schifter, Richard, 66
Scowcroft, Brent, 53, 58, 62
Second Convention of Peking treaty, 85
Security
　in East Asia, 2
　in the Pacific, 5, 17
　U.S.-Japanese, 31
Security interests
　of the U.S. in Taiwan, 72
　and U.S. policy in Asia, 8, 9, 11
Security issues
　in U.S.-Japanese relations, 37–40, 45
　in U.S.-Korean relations, 96–99, 102
　and U.S. policy in Asia and the Pacific, 156
Security policies, in Asia and Oceania, 156–157

Self-rule
　in New Caledonia, 148, 149
　in the Pacific, 146
SEMATECH, 36, 37
Semiconductor market, in Japan, 34
Senate Foreign Relations Committee, 111
Seventh Fleet, U.S., 129, 130
Shanghai, 87–88
Shevardnadze, Eduard, 12
Ships, nuclear-powered, 146. See also Warships
Sihanouk, Norodom, 105, 106, 108, 109, 112, 117
Singapore, 6
　U.S. military access to facilities in, 136–137
Sino-Soviet relations, 24, 63, 76. See also China; Soviet Union
Sino-Soviet summit, 120. See also China; Soviet Union
Sino-Soviet tensions, 49. See also China; Soviet Union
Socialist Party, Japanese, 42
Solomon, Richard, 66
Solomon Islands, and the Soviets, 147
Son Sann, 105, 106, 108, 109, 112
South Korea, 6, 20
　defense spending, 97–98
　democratization movement in, 27
　economic issues in U.S.–South Korean relations, 94–96, 102
　and the Iraq-Kuwait crisis, 99
　Japanese economic aid to, 38
　jet fighters in, 102
　political opposition in, 80
　and President Carter, 22
　trade with the PRC by, 75–76
　U.S. interests in, 93–94, 102
　U.S. military profile in, 98
　U.S. policy approaches to, 101–103
　U.S.–South Korean relations, 92–93
　See also Korea; Republic of Korea
South Pacific, Australia's leadership in, 144
South Pacific Forum, 11, 145, 148, 149, 151, 152
South Pacific Nuclear Free Zone Treaty, 144, 145, 148, 151
Southeast Asia
　buildup of American forces in, 137
　U.S. policy options in, 121–123
Southeast Asia Collective Defense Treaty, 128

Index

South Vietnam, U.S.-backed regimes in, 20
Soviet bloc
 changes in, 54
 domestic U.S. opinion regarding, 8
 See also Soviet Union
Soviet empire, collapse of, 31
Soviet missile tests, 144
Soviet naval movements, 129
Soviet power, and U.S.-Chinese relations, 64
Soviet Union
 breakup of, 9–10
 and the Cambodian conflict, 105
 and the Carter administration, 21
 changes in, 51, 52, 53, 55, 59
 collapse of, 2, 7
 decline in threat by, 8, 2, 131, 137
 foreign policy in Asia, 6, 24
 improvement in U.S.-Soviet relations, 135
 influence in Asia, 24
 influence in Oceania, 141–142, 147–148
 influence in Southeast Asia, 118–119
 instability in, 107
 intentions in Asia and the Pacific, 9
 and Korea, 91
 lucrative agreements with, 150
 military confrontation with the U.S., 4, 19
 military threat by, 11, 31, 157
 reform in, 8, 9
 in Roosevelt's vision of U.S. policy in Asia, 19
 South Korean relations with, 101
 and the South Pacific Nuclear Free Zone Treaty protocols, 146, 151
 support for Vietnam's occupation of Cambodia, 24, 108, 120
 U.S. foreign policy focused on, 10
 U.S.-Soviet collaboration in Asia, 53
 U.S.-Soviet relations, 8, 12, 59, 157
 U.S.-Soviet rivalry in China's worldview, 52
 and Vietnam, 115, 120, 122
 See also Russia; Sino-Soviet relations; Sino-Soviet summit; Sino-Soviet tensions; Soviet bloc
Spanish American War, 3, 16
Spending deficit, U.S., 102
State Department, report on Cambodia, 111
State of Cambodia (SOC), 108, 109, 110, 111, 112
Status-of-Forces Agreement (SOFA), U.S.-South Korean, 98
Steel imports, U.S., 96
Stock exchange, Hong Kong, 87
Structural Impediments Initiative (SII), 34, 44
Students
 from Asian countries in the U.S., 1–2, 27
 in the U.S. from China, 55, 57, 58
Subic Bay Naval Base, 126, 127, 129, 130, 132, 133, 134, 136, 137
Submarines, sale of to Taiwan's navy, 75. *See also* Arms sales; Military equipment
Super 301 provisions, 102
 of the 1988 Trade Act, 34, 44, 95, 126
Supreme National Council
 in Cambodia, 109
Syria
 Chinese efforts to sell missiles to, 67

Taiwan, 6
 Carter's policy toward, 23
 China's goal of reunification with, 86
 economic growth in, 78–79
 and Hong Kong, 86, 87, 88, 89
 isolation and defense of, 75–76
 political liberalization in, 7, 84–85
 politics in, 79–82
 and the Reagan administration, 24
 trade with mainland China, 76
 travel to and contacts with mainland China, 77–78
 and the U.S., 6
 U.S. arms sales to, 22, 24, 74, 75, 77, 84, 89
 and U.S. China policy, 76–77
 U.S. policy concerning, 71–89
 U.S.-PRC-Taiwan relations, 73–75, 83–84
 U.S. trade deficit with, 71, 72, 79
 See also Republic of China
Taiwan Relations Act (TRA), 72, 73, 74, 77
Takeshita, Noboru, 36, 41, 42
Tariff sanctions, U.S., 35
Technology
 export controls on, 57–58
 and U.S.-Japanese relations, 36–37
Technology transfer
 to China, 49
 in the Persian Gulf, 1
 to South Korea, 99
 U.S. controls on, 65
Telecommunications, Korean market for, 95
Television broadcasting, by U.S. armed forces in South Korea, 98

Terrorism, 93, 134, 159
Textiles
  illegal export of, 67
  imports into the U.S., 96
Thailand, 125
  and the Cambodian conflict, 108, 112, 116, 122
  economic nationalism in, 126
  Japanese economic aid to, 38
  and a peace settlement in Cambodia, 118
  U.S. ally, 107
Tiananmen Square, 7–8, 27
Tiananmen Square massacre, 49–66 passim
  and demonstrations in Hong Kong, 86, 88
Tibet, 67
Tinian, 137
Tonga, 147
Tourism
  Japanese in U.S., 27
  U.S. in China, 66
  U.S. in East Asia, 4
Trade
  Hong Kong–Chinese, 87
  with Japan, 33–35, 41
  Japanese, 30, 43
  Japanese–Chinese, 5, 20
  measures seen as protectionist, 158
  Sino-U.S., 65
  by South Korea with Iraq, 99
  by Taiwan with mainland China, 76
  Taiwanese international, 76
  U.S.-ASEAN, 119, 125–126
  U.S.-Asian, 3, 6, 15, 24
  U.S.-China, 49, 69
  U.S. foreign, 7
  by the U.S. in Hong Kong, 86
  U.S.-Oceania, 142
  U.S.-Philippines, 135
  U.S.-South Korea, 93–96, 102–103
  U.S.-Vietnam, 115
  Vietnamese inability to attract, 120
  See also Exports; Imports
Trade Act
  Jackson-Vanik Amendment to, 60
  of 1988, 33, 35, 36, 94
  Section 301 of the 1988, 34, 44, 68, 95, 126
Trade bills, and U.S. trade imbalance, 79
Trade deficit
  U.S., 7, 25–26, 84
  of the U.S. with China, 67
  of the U.S. with Japan, 30, 33, 34, 36, 41, 44, 45, 46, 67, 72
  of the U.S. with South Korea, 94, 103
  of the U.S. with Taiwan, 71, 72, 79
Trade Development Program, and China, 65
Trade issues, U.S.-Taiwan, 79, 84
Trade legislation, U.S., 26
Trade policies, protectionist, 88
Trade restrictions, against China, 9
Trading partners, of the U.S., 1, 94
Trading systems, world, 158
Training facilities, in the Philippines, 130, 137
Treaty of Nanking, 85
Tuna fishing, 142
  by the U.S. in the South Pacific, 149–150
Turkey
  Japanese economic aid to, 38
  Taiwanese assistance to, 83

United Nations, 11, 157
  both Koreas joined, 91
  and Cambodia, 105–107, 109, 111, 116, 119, 120
  and Hong Kong, 85
  trusteeship scheme under, 19
  Vietnamese application for membership in, 115
United Nations General Assembly, and New Caledonia, 148, 152
United Nations High Commissioner for Refugees, 118
United Nations Security Council, 1, 50, 146–147
  and Cambodia, 109, 112, 113
  and China, 56, 61, 65, 66
  and economic sanctions against Iraq, 83
  PRC support for resolutions in, 9
  U.S. member of, 107
  and Vietnamese U.N. membership, 115
United Nations Trusteeship Council, 146
United States
  "America first," 157
  and ANZUS alliance, 142–143, 144, 153
  defense issues in U.S.-Korea relations, 102
  downturn in U.S.-Chinese relations, 107
  Filipino attitudes toward, 132–134
  foreign investment in, 35
  foreign policy in Asia, 15–27

Index

foreign policy in East Asia and the Pacific, 155–159
investment in Japan by, 1
and Japan, 5, 6
and Japanese economic growth, 19–20
largest debtor nation, 25, 30
leverage in Cambodia, 107
and New Caledonia, 148, 152
and Oceania, 141–159
policy in Asia and the Pacific, 1–13
policy in Cambodia, 106–107, 108
policy concerns in Hong Kong, 85–89
policy in Indochina, 105–123
in Roosevelt's vision of U.S. policy in Asia, 19
security issues in U.S.-Korean relations, 96–99, 102
and the South Pacific Nuclear Free Zone, 145–146
and the South Pacific Nuclear Free Zone Treaty protocols, 146, 148, 151
and Taiwanese economy, 78–79
U.S.-Chinese relations, 49–69
U.S.-Japanese relations, 29–46
U.S.-Korean relations, 91–103
U.S.-Palau relations, 146–147
U.S.-Philippines relations, 137–138
U.S.-PRC-Taiwan relations, 73–75, 83–84
U.S.-South Korean relations, 92–93
U.S.-Soviet relations, 8, 52
U.S.-Vietnam relations, 114–118, 121–123
wartime antagonism with Japan, 17
Uno, Sosuke, 42
Uruguay, 75
U.S.-ROC Security Treaty, 22
U.S.-ROK Security Treaty, 22
USSR. *See* Soviet Union

Vance, Cyrus, 21
Vanuatu, 10
  political instability in, 150
  and the Soviets, 147
Vessey, John, 116, 117, 118
Vietnam
  and the Carter administration, 115–116
  development experiences in, 54
  economic embargo against, 107
  invasion of Cambodia, 115
  military occupation of Cambodia by, 105, 108, 109, 119, 123
  political prospects in, 10
  pressures against its occupation of Cambodia, 119–120
  SOC backed by, 110
  social and cultural changes in, 19
  troop withdrawal from Cambodia, 105, 109, 112, 114, 116, 117, 120, 121, 122
  U.S. aid to, 114–115, 119, 121, 122, 123
  U.S. diplomatic relations with, 22
  U.S. policy options in, 121–123
  U.S. policy toward, 112, 113
  U.S. relations with, 106, 107, 112, 113, 114–118, 121–123
Vietnamese boat people, 125
Vietnam War, 158
  origins and consequences of, 19
  U.S. experience in, 112–113
  use of Clark Air Force Base during, 128, 130
Violence, in the Philippines, 138, 139
Voice of America (VOA), broadcasts in China, 58

War Powers Resolution, 21
Warships
  nuclear-capable, 144, 146, 147
  of the U.S. and Australian facilities, 144
  of the U.S. denied access to New Zealand ports, 142
  U.S., 141
Washington Conference, of 1921–1922, 17
Watergate scandal, 20
Weapons
  to the Khmer Rouge, 106
  of mass destruction, 159
  of North Korea, 91
  supplied by the U.S. to Taiwan, 83
  U.S. suspension of exports of, 57
  See also Arms; Arms sales; Defense technology
Western Europe, assistance to Vietnam, 123
Western Pacific, U.S. military access to facilities in, 136–137
West Germany, chemical weapons from, 151
Whaling, Japanese, 43
Wheat, U.S. sales abroad, 150
Wilson, Woodrow, 155
  and U.S. foreign policy, 3–4, 17
Wilsonianism, 18
Woodcock, Leonard, 115

World affairs
  U.S. leadership in, 158
  U.S. overextended in, 157
World Bank, 11, 18
  loan program for China, 50
  programs in China, 65

Yalta conference, 19

Yen, Japanese, 44. *See also* Currency
Young Officers Union (YOU), 134, 138, 139
Yugoslavia, 101

Zhao Ziyang, 55
Zone of Peace, Freedom and Neutrality (ZOPFAN), 125